Breaking Records

Breaking Records

100 Years of Hits

William Ruhlmann

Routledge
Taylor & Francis Group

NEW YORK AND LONDON

Published in 2004 by
Routledge
29 W 35th Street
New York, NY 10001
www.routledge-ny.com

Published in Great Britain by
RoutledgeFalmer
11 New Fetter Lane
London EC4P 4EE
www.routledge.co.uk

RoutledgeFalmer is an imprint of the Taylor & Francis Group.
Printed in the United States of America on acid-free paper.

10 9 8 7 6 5 4 3 2 1

Cataloging-in-Publication Data is available from the Library of Congress.

ISBN 0-415-94305-1

For my parents, William Edwin and Margaret Mary Neagle Ruhlmann, as meager recompense for their love, wisdom, and patience.

CONTENTS

INTRODUCTION

In the early years of the twenty-first century, the American record business considered itself to be in big trouble. For the year 2000, sales of albums increased 4 percent, from just under 754 million copies in 1999 to just over 785 million, but due to the precipitous decline in the sales of singles (which the major record labels were trying to eliminate), total sales of albums and singles combined actually declined slightly. In 2001 album sales were down 2.85 percent, the first drop since 1991, and total sales were down 5.25 percent. And in 2002 album sales fell another 10.7 percent, with combined sales down 12.7 percent. Significantly, sales of CDs were down 8.8 percent, the first time the format had seen a decline since it was introduced in the United States in 1983. This pattern continued through the first quarter of 2003, with album sales down 10 percent and total sales down 10.9 percent.

At the Billboard Music & Money Symposium, sponsored by music industry trade journal *Billboard* and held at the St. Regis Hotel in New York City on March 6, 2003, Michael Nathanson, European media analyst at Sanford C. Bernstein & Co., "voiced a view that the current music industry downturn is structural rather than cyclical, and he was pessimistic about the progress made thus far to develop a workable new business model, according to an article published on the front page of *Billboard*'s March 22 issue." Others at the symposium felt that the downturn was cyclical, but all agreed that the industry had problems.

And what were those problems? From the industry viewpoint, they were, as usual, all due to external forces. The rise of the Internet in the 1990s had made it possible for music fans to easily download and trade copyrighted music among themselves without ever visiting record stores. The industry had taken aim at Napster, one of the main Internet companies facilitating these efforts, and brought it to grief, but there were many more services developing all the time. It also was possible, with newly available copying equipment, to "burn" CD copies easily, so that one commercially obtained album could serve as the source for an untold number of exact digital replicas. And if all that weren't enough, a general economic downturn in the early years of the George W. Bush administration could be combined with consumer reluctance due to the uncertainties of terrorism and war, along with increasing competition for the consumer's leisure spending, to explain the music industry malaise.

If such an analysis was correct, then the downturn might well be cyclical. The industry might prevail in its attempts to police the Internet and seek restrictive legislation; it might find a technical way to prevent the copying of its CDs; and it might develop an effective and profitable way of selling its recordings directly to consumers as downloads over the Internet. As for the rest, economies recover, wars end, and competing consumer fads fade.

But suppose the problems the industry identified were not the correct ones. To anyone with a sense of the history of the music industry, the attacks on the Internet and CD burning were eerily familiar. They echoed the same industry's complaints about radio in the 1920s and blank cassettes in the 1970s. It was ironic, as it had been for over a hundred years, that the recorded music industry, itself born out of advances in technology, always viewed subsequent advances in other forms of technology with skepticism often spilling over into outright hostility, before some accommodation was reached and it was realized that the increase in the dissemination of music ultimately would lead to *higher* record sales. "The coming of the phonograph," wrote Sigmund Spaeth in *A History of Popular Music in America*, "caused a gradual decline in the sale of sheet-music, but made up for it in providing a new source of revenue and a far quicker and more effective method of musical promotion." Something similar could be said about the coming of movies, radio, television, videos, and the Internet, if the music industry could only see it.

Suppose that the problems were in fact structural rather than cyclical. From this point of view, the record industry was actually a mature industry—one in which constant growth simply was not possible because it was already reaching its audience as fully as possible. By this argument, the industry might have matured during the last downturn in the late 1970s, only to be set back temporarily upon a growth pattern due to the introduction of the CD (which, ironically, the industry initially resisted). The growth in the 1980s and '90s might have been built on the steeply increased prices for the new medium and the reissue of older music, and the end of that growth at the start of the new century simply might have meant that everyone who wanted to replace their collections of LPs with CDs had done so.

If that was the case, the industry had a solution. CDs may have saved business models twenty years before, so why not a new recording format? As of 2001, several formats, including DVD-Audio, Super Audio CD (SACD), and Dataplay, were on the horizon or already being test-marketed. In an article in the October 20, 2001, issue of *Billboard* entitled "Strong Staying Power Seen for CDs Despite New Music Formats," reporter Ed Christman wrote that "some industry executives wonder if the CD format will eventually follow the cassette in its almost-complete journey toward technological oblivion—a fate that befell vinyl a decade ago. Other retail and label executives tell *Billboard* that the CD definitely has a strong short-term future of at least five years—and that it might even have a long-term future measuring 10–20 years." Unspoken but implied was the inevitability that a new format would replace the CD eventually (and perhaps sooner rather than later), and that, just as the industry benefited from the format change from LPs and cassettes to CDs, it might be able to resell its catalog yet again. That might be what a historian would see as a temporary solution, but in a business in which "a long-term future" was defined as "10–20 years," it might be enough to get the current crop of executives to their retirements.

And there was another indication that the sales downturn of the twenty-first century might be cyclical rather than structural, might in fact mirror previous downturns such as the one in the early 1950s and the one in the late 1970s from which the industry recovered. Again, the evidence came from the pages of *Billboard*, which reported on the 2001 sales drop in its issue of January 12, 2002, in an article by Michael Ellis headlined "U.S. Albums Sales Drop Year-to-Year." "The biggest factor in the poor showing is that the top-selling albums of 2001 sold far fewer units than 2000's biggest titles," wrote Ellis, who detailed the differences between years in which, for example, teen-pop group 'N Sync sold 9.9 million copies of their album *No Strings Attached* (2000) and then only 4.42 million copies of its follow-up, *Celebrity* (2001). "The combined sales of the 10 biggest sellers thus dropped a steep 20 million, or 33 percent, from 2000 to 2001," Ellis concluded. "This drop almost completely accounts for the overall year-to-year decline of 22 million." It wasn't just that the teen-pop trend that had arrived in the second half of the 1990s was now diminishing, however. It was that American consumers didn't like the most heavily promoted music that the major record companies were releasing in 2001 as much as they had in 2000. Just as in 1953, when the novelty sounds of songs like "[How much is] The Doggie in the Window" were about to give way to rock 'n' roll, and in 1979, when the "Disco Sucks" backlash began, America was telling the record industry that it wanted to hear something other than what the industry was selling. If the industry found a way to respond to that complaint, the cycle might turn again.

To understand what is happening now, it is necessary to know what happened before. This book is intended as a survey history of the American record business as it developed during its first full century. It already existed, just barely, when the century began, and by the start of the twenty-first century, whatever its troubles, it had become a very big business: 785 million albums in 2000 might not have represented much of an increase over the previous year, but it was still a lot of records. The story of the industry's development is a financial and commercial one, concerning sales, competition, and economic forces, and it is also a musical one, concerning musicians and songwriters. The history of a country's music is, to an extent, the history of the country itself, and much more could be said—indeed, much more has been said—about that than can be attempted here. But it is hoped that with this overview the reader will gain a certain perspective on that history and the way that the creation of an art form interacts with the machinery of its distribution—or has, thus far, anyway.

SHINE ON, HARVEST MOON

SONG
BY
NORA BAYES and
JACK NORWORTH

NORA BAYES

"The Fo

1

THE 1900s

THE BIRTH OF THE
RECORDING INDUSTRY

When we discuss the worth of an artist or works of art, we often cite
the "test of time" as a measure, usually prematurely. But in looking
back one hundred years to the first decade of the twentieth century,
the test of time is a good way to begin to examine the history of
recorded music. Consider a list of the music and the musicians of the
1900s, and there are people and songs that remain familiar a century
later. Among the musical figures, several names (Irving Berlin,
George M. Cohan, Scott Joplin, and John Philip Sousa) remain generally well known, and a few others (Enrico Caruso, Victor Herbert,
and Jerome Kern) are recognizable to many music fans. When it
comes to songs, however, a greater number remain immediately hum-
mable, among them "Bill Bailey, Won't You Please Come Home?,"
"By the Light of the Silvery Moon," "Casey Jones," "The Enter-
tainer," "Give My Regards to Broadway," "In the Good Old Summertime," "Sweet Adeline," "Meet Me in St. Louis, Louis," "Shine On,
Harvest Moon," "Take Me Out to the Ball Game," "Toyland," "Wait
till the Sun Shines, Nellie," "The Yankee Doodle Boy," and "You're a
Grand Old Flag."

These lists in themselves tell us a great deal about the state of
recorded music between 1900 and 1909. Of the seven musical figures
cited, six (excepting Kern) made recordings at one time or
another—if you include Joplin's piano rolls—but only one, Caruso,
was a popular recording star. The others were all composers, although
Cohan, Joplin, and Sousa also performed. And if the songs remain
well known, the recording artists who were most closely associated

with them at the time now are unjustly forgotten: figures like the American Quartet, Arthur Collins, Byron G. Harlan, the Haydn Quartet, Ada Jones, Harry MacDonough, Corrine Morgan, Billy Murray, J.W. Myers, Elise Stevenson, and Harry Tally. Collins, Harlan, the Haydn Quartet, Jones, MacDonough, Murray, and Myers were, along with Frank Stanley and Henry Burr, among the top recording artists of the decade, according to chart researcher Joel Whitburn. That none is remembered today and that the musicians' names we *do* remember were not primarily recording artists are indications of the size and significance of the recording industry during the decade: it was small, and it was not very important within the music business as a whole. But over the course of the period, it grew tremendously. In 1900, 3.75 million records were manufactured; by 1909, that figure stood at 27.5 million, an increase of more than 700 percent.

A technological entity, the record business was subject to technological development, and during the 1900s, as it would be later in its history, it was bedeviled by a format war. Thomas Edison had first demonstrated a machine that could record sound in 1877, then largely abandoned the invention as he moved on to the electric lightbulb. He didn't return to developing his phonograph until 1887, using a solid wax cylinder to record on, by which time Emile Berliner, the inventor of the microphone, had come up with the gramophone, which played flat discs. Edison founded the North American Phonograph Company in 1888; on January 1, 1889, the Columbia Phonograph Company was launched as its mid-Atlantic licensee. By the following year, when it issued its first catalog, Columbia had emerged as a major rival to Edison; one hundred years and several changes of ownership later, Columbia was still releasing records. Berliner founded the Berliner Gramophone Company in 1895, and at the turn of the century Berliner, Columbia, and Edison were the nation's major record labels.

Former Berliner employee Eldridge Johnson launched the Consolidated Talking Machine Company in May 1900; it issued flat discs on the Gram-o-Phone label. Shortly after, Berliner went out of business, but in October 1901 he and Johnson would be back together with a new firm, the Victor Talking Machine Company, which like Columbia would go through many changes but still exist at the next turn of the century.

By 1900, the recording industry was no longer in its infancy, because commercial recordings had been sold for nearly a decade, but it was still very much a toddler. For one thing, at the turn of the century, to create enough copies, it was still necessary for recording artists to record the same song over and over rather than just once. As Tim Gracyk, a biographer of those artists, writes, "Masters were used in the 1890s but they wore out after a few dozen duplicates were made." What Gracyk calls the "permanent master," from which a virtually unlimited number of copies could be made, was not developed for use by the major labels until 1902. And the industry did not get much help from the more established areas of entertainment. Because the record companies were not required to pay royalties to song publishers until a copyright revision that was enacted in 1909, the publishers, who dominated the music business at the time, had a limited incentive to assist the fledgling record business. They did have *some* incentive, in the sense that a hit recording of a song might have a positive impact on sales of sheet music for that song. (There doesn't seem to have been much fear that someone might buy a record of a song *instead of* the sheet music.) But the publishing business was far more invested in the use of live performances in vaudeville and on the legitimate stage to promote its wares.

Similarly, vaudeville and musical theater had limited incentive to help out, and here competition was perceived. Popular singing stars only rarely became recording artists, for a variety of reasons. One was technical, as the primitive and demanding conditions of the "acoustic era" of recording (the electrical microphone was not introduced until the mid-1920s) contrasted greatly with the way singers performed onstage. To make a record, an artist had to perform in front of a large horn and, as noted above, this performance had to be repeated many times to create numerous masters. Another was scheduling, because stage performers often had to perform several times a day, they had limited time to travel to recording studios, and their voices might not be rested when they did. Finally, stage producers, not perceiving a promotional advantage to having stars record songs from their shows and thinking instead that purchase of a record might lead a potential ticket buyer to stay home, discouraged their singers from recording.

As a result, the record industry turned to a group of singers whose voices recorded well and who were available to record frequently. And the industry did not cultivate them as stars. That list of the decade's top recording artists may be utterly unfamiliar a century later, but it was not all that familiar even at the time. "Although a few became household names, professional recording artists were not famous in the way stage or opera celebrities were," writes Gracyk. "Billy Murray, Arthur Collins, Ada Jones, and Henry Burr could walk down a busy street and go unrecognized." Not surprisingly, they didn't become rich from their efforts, either. Royalties were no more commonly paid to performers than they were to publishers, although performers at least got a recording fee. "Some artists in the first decades of the twentieth century earned a living by making records, but it took extraordinary commitment," writes Gracyk, although he adds that, had they been paid royalties, "several would have earned fortunes."

That said, it is extremely difficult to obtain accurate sales information on individual records from the 1900s. In an industry rampant with exaggeration, one early on encounters claims for "million sellers" (a standard of achievement cited throughout the century and beyond), but such claims are difficult to verify. As is true of other areas of history, there is a divide among music historians that is worth exploring briefly here. Responding to the human tendency to rank things, and in parallel with the record charts that came to dominate the business from the 1950s onward, some historians have gone back and—using the information that is available, including (for the 1900s) the magazine *Talking Machine World*, publications issued by the record labels, and sheet music sales—retroactively constructed charts that resemble the charts published later in the century. The primary book of this sort is Whitburn's *Pop Memories, 1890–1954: The History of American Popular Music*, an alphabetical listing of recording artists providing dates, peak positions, and weeks charted for records, similar to the chart books Whitburn has published for later eras. Another is Edward Foote Gardner's *Popular Songs of the Twentieth*

Century: Volume I—Chart Detail & Encyclopedia, 1900–1949, which contains monthly popularity charts for records and extensive details about individual songs. These books have come to be commonly cited in periodicals, liner notes, and press releases, almost always without the caveats about the lack of solid data that the books themselves contain.

With or without the caveats, these reconstructions enrage other historians and discographers, who scorn any attempt to make the vagaries of available sources conform to current statistical analysis. Gracyk, in a section of the introduction to his book *Popular American Recording Pioneers, 1895–1925* (written with Frank Hoffmann) pointedly entitled "Record Sales—Not Known Today," disputes many of the claims for massive sales of individual titles in the acoustic era, flatly stating, "We do not know what record was first to sell a million copies or two million." And he specifically disparages retroactive chart-making. "At no time in the acoustic era," he writes of the period up to 1925, "was enough information compiled or made available about sales for anyone to create accurate charts or rank best-sellers, and the further back in time we go, the more difficulty we have in identifying hits." Further, even if such information *were* available, it would refer to relatively small sales figures and would be limited by the lack of national distribution. In order for a record to accurately reflect the kind of chart arc of a rising, peaking, and falling sales pattern that most records exhibited in the second half of the century (which is mirrored in the chart reconstructions), it would have to have been available for sale simultaneously around the country, which simply wasn't possible in the 1900s. "All chart positions concerning records of the acoustic era are fictitious," Gracyk concludes, "and since they mislead novice collectors, they do much harm."

All of which is fair enough. But if one is not a novice and is mindful of the hedges against complete accuracy, the chart books can be useful. Granted, the specific reconstructed statistics must be taken with a grain of salt. For example, Whitburn lists Henry Burr's Edison recording of "In the Shade of the Old Apple Tree" (music by Egbert Van Alsystne, lyrics by Harry Williams) as spending seven weeks at number one, starting on April 22, 1905, and not only is that not verifiable, it is not even really possible in contemporary terms. But that is not to say that the record, by available indications, was not successful; on the contrary, the indications are that it was, and the overly specific ranking is one way of saying so. Also, it is worth noting that if such claims about records of the acoustic era must be viewed with a certain skepticism, so should later claims made of actually published charts. The march toward legitimacy in measuring success in the record business is a long and gradual one that does not suddenly end in 1935, when the *Your Hit Parade* radio series went on the air with its weekly countdown, or in 1940, when *Billboard* inaugurated its "Best Selling Retail Records" chart. Well into the 1990s, complaints were registered about the accuracy of charts and the ways in which they might be skewed for someone's benefit. There is an equally suspect history having to do with "gold records" and "million sellers" not entirely dispelled by the establishment of a certification system by the Record Industry Association of America (RIAA) in 1958. So, it would be fair to say that, whether viewing reconstructed charts or actual ones, one must proceed with suspicion. That said, this book will employ the terminology of chart hits as determined by Whitburn and Gardner, now that the reader has been warned to view them as generally, but not specifically, correct.

According to Whitburn, the number-one record on January 1, 1900, was Arthur Collins's "I'd Leave My Happy Home for You" on Edison. As was typical of the time, Collins also recorded the song for Berliner; recording artists tended not to be signed to exclusive recording contracts, or to disregard them if they were. The thirty-five-year-old Collins was a baritone who had begun as a vaudeville performer doing minstrel and comedy material, but he really came into his own when he began recording for Edison. "I'd Leave My Happy Home for You" had been composed by probably the most successful songwriter of the 1900s, Harry von Tilzer, with lyrics by Will A. Heelan, and introduced by vaudeville singer Blanche Ring at Tony Pastor's Music Hall in New York before being picked up by Collins. The confluence of these names is typical of the music business of the decade. Three years later, von Tilzer probably coined the term that described his part of the music business: Tin Pan Alley. (It was first used in a newspaper article in the *New York Herald* by Monroe Rosenfeld after an inter-view with von Tilzer at his office on 28th Street, where all the major music publishing companies were then located.) Ring was a develop-ing vaudeville performer who would cross over to the legitimate musi-cal stage and introduce many popular songs, but record relatively few of them. Tony Pastor was, in 1881, the first person to present a variety show in New York and adopt the French word *vaudeville* to describe it. In 1900 and for the rest of the decade, vaudeville and the music publishing companies soon to be known as Tin Pan Alley were the major elements of the music business, and the record industry was rel-atively small potatoes in comparison.

As the twentieth century began, march king John Philip Sousa was considered the most popular musician in the world (so says Paul Bierly, his biographer), and the hottest new trend in popular music was ragtime, which was emerging out of the Midwest. The term was first popularized by a newspaperman in Chicago in 1897, and Scott Joplin's first major composition, "Maple Leaf Rag," was published in St. Louis in September 1899. (His best-known one, "The Enter-tainer," followed in 1902.) Sigmund Spaeth traces ragtime's origins to the South, "where the Negroes had been using it for years." Spaeth notes the 1897 publication by the Witmarks (a major Tin Pan Alley publisher of the era) of Ben Harney's book *Rag-Time Instructor*, and although he criticizes "the double-talk with which Harney tried to explain the new art," adds, "The one thing that Harney made clear was that rag-time was not a *kind* of music but simply a *way of playing*. In other words, any melody could easily be subjected to a rag-time treatment by merely syncopating the time, bringing the accent on the off-beat." Three-quarters of a century later, when ragtime enjoyed a brief revival due to the use of Joplin's rags in the movie *The Sting*, a movie that was set, oddly enough, in the 1930s, "ragtime" was taken to refer exclusively to the involved instrumental compositions of Jop-lin; in the 1890s and 1900s, it was, as Spaeth says, more a matter of rhythmic arrangement than a full-fledged musical genre, and all the more pervasive for that.

But ragtime was not the most broadly popular style of music in its time. The most influential, and perhaps the most successful, song of

1900 was composer Harry von Tilzer and lyricist Arthur J. Lamb's "A Bird in a Gilded Cage," a sentimental tearjerker that von Tilzer described as "the key that opened the door of wealth and fame" for him, and that certainly opened the floodgates for ballads. "Although ragtime and the [Cakewalk] dance caught the headlines, the real sellers from 1900 to 1914 were the *big ballads*," writes historian Ian Whitcomb. Surprisingly, no particular performer is credited with introducing "A Bird in a Gilded Cage" (von Tilzer himself tried it out in a brothel, and it brought the prostitutes to tears), but it sold 2 million copies of sheet music, and there were two best-selling records, Jere Mahoney's for Edison and Steve Porter's for Columbia.

The greatest competition for 1900 song of the year (on records) came from the 1898 copyright "When You Were Sweet Sixteen," which attracted hit recordings by George J. Gaskin for Columbia and Jere Mahoney for Edison (plus 1901 versions by J.W. Myers and by Harry MacDonough, both for Victor) and has gone on to become a barbershop quartet standard; the comic number "Ma Tiger Lily," introduced in the musical *Aunt Hannah* and recorded by Arthur Collins for Berliner and Len Spencer for Columbia; and 1899's "Mandy Lee," recorded by Collins for Edison, Albert Campbell for Edison, and Harry MacDonough for Berliner, another eventual barbershop quartet favorite.

If big ballads were the biggest hits of the era, however, they weren't always sad and sentimental. Indeed, "A Bird in a Gilded Cage" can be thought of as a throwback to the big hit of the 1890s, that tale of lost love, Charles K. Harris's "After the Ball." In the new century, the ballads tended to become happier. "During the ragtime age," writes historian David A. Jasen, "the tear-jerker gave way to the pleasant love song." And as the decade went on, an important source for such songs, in competition with Tin Pan Alley, was the Broadway stage.

On September 6, 1900, the revue *Fiddle-dee-dee* opened at the Weber and Fields Music Hall in New York. Joseph Weber and Lew Fields were the top comedy team of the day, and the show was a big hit. The hit song from it was "Ma Blushin' Rosie," which was introduced by Faye Templeton, a major vaudeville star who was crossing over to the legitimate stage. Typically, Templeton did not record the song, which instead was cut by Albert Campbell for Gram-o-Phone and was in the charts by the end of the year, going on to become one of the two biggest hit records of 1901, with a competing version by S.H. Dudley, also for Gram-o-Phone. *Fiddle-dee-dee*, meanwhile, despite an unusually long run of 262 performances, was not the longest-running Broadway show of the 1900–1901 season. That honor belonged to a sleeper called *Floradora*.

Floradora was a British import, having opened in London on November 11, 1899. When it got to New York, a year and a day later, the critics were skeptical (just as they would be of British musicals that arrived later in the century), and early business was poor. Then, one of the songs took off. It was "Tell Me, Pretty Maiden" (music by Leslie Stuart, lyrics by Ernest Boyd-Jones and Paul Rubens), and it was sung in the show by a double sextet of six men and six women. (The women, naturally, became known as the Floradora Girls.) The first hit recording, which topped the charts in May 1901, was a duet by Harry MacDonough and Grace Spencer on Edison. But it was succeeded by a longer-running number-one version on Columbia by Byron Harlan, Frank Stanley, Joe Belmont, and the Floradora Girls that equaled the run of "Ma Blushin' Rosie" and made "Tell Me, Pretty Maiden" the most successful song on records of 1901. Sparked by this success, *Floradora* became the longest-running show in Broadway history up to its time, lasting 505 performances.

The year 1901 also marked the Broadway debut of perhaps the best-remembered songwriter of the decade, George M. Cohan. "Born on the Fourth of July," 1878 (even if his birth certificate said July 3), Cohan had toured in vaudeville with his parents and sister ever since. On February 25, 1901, he brought *The Governor's Son*, a vaudeville skit he had expanded into a musical, into the Savoy Theater in New York, where it played for only thirty-two performances before going out on the road for two years. But Cohan would be back. More successful in his first Broadway outing was producer Florenz Ziegfeld, who brought *The Little Duchess*, a show built around his wife, Anna Held, into the Casino Theater on October 14, 1901, and saw it run a healthy 136 performances. Broadway would see more of Ziegfeld, too.

The trend toward stage-derived ballads did not eliminate a style of music that had been popular before 1900 and continued, though decreasingly, after: comic minstrel songs (in their most vulgar form, "coon" songs). The biggest hit record of 1902 was a revival of the comic 1850s tune "Arkansaw Traveler" (a.k.a. "The Arkansas Traveler") by Len Spencer on Victor; the second biggest was Arthur Collins's Columbia recording of "Bill Bailey, Won't You Please Come Home?" (music and lyrics by Hughie Cannon), also a comic minstrel number (the wayward Bailey is clearly intended to be black), although it has lost that connotation over the years. (There were competing versions by Dan Quinn and by Silas Leachman, both on Victor.)

Bert Williams emerged with a series of hits for Victor in 1902, two solo ("Good Morning, Carrie" and "The Fortune Telling Man"), and two with his vaudeville partner, George Walker ("I Don't Like That Face You Wear" and their joint composition "When It's All Going Out and Nothing Coming In"). Williams was one of the most successful recording artists of the decade and one of the most unusual. Unlike most of his peers, he was primarily a stage performer, having made his Broadway debut on September 21, 1896, in *The Gold Bug* and subsequently appeared in *In Gotham* (September 19, 1898), *The Policy Players* (October 16, 1899), and *Sons of Ham* (October 15, 1900). Most unusual was that, unlike the many white performers who blacked up to perform minstrel songs, Williams actually was black, born in New Providence, Nassau, the Bahamas, on November 12, 1874. Although some of his early recorded material did fall into the minstrel category, he was able to reduce or subvert it, writing his own songs (notably his signature tune, "Nobody," with lyrics by Alex Rogers, a major hit in 1906) and becoming the first black performer to achieve stardom on Broadway when he began appearing in the *Ziegfeld Follies*.

The third-biggest hit of 1902 (which went on to be the biggest hit of 1903) was another ballad, "In the Good Old Summertime," which was introduced by Blanche Ring in the Broadway musical *The Defender* on July 3, 1902. (Actually, it had already been sung in vaudeville and was interpolated into the show.) It made Ring famous, but was taken over by others for recordings. J.W. Myers cut it for Columbia, William Redmond for Edison, and the Haydn Quartet (probably consisting of John Bieling, S.H. Dudley, William F. Hooley, and Fred Rycroft at this time), Sousa's Band (featuring Harry MacDonough and S.H. Dudley), and Harry MacDonough solo, all for Victor.

Almost as popular in 1903 was "Come Down, Ma Evenin' Star," which Lillian Russell introduced in Weber and Fields's show *Twirly Whirly* on September 11, 1902. Mina Hickman and Henry Burr (both on Columbia) each topped the charts with it for several weeks; it was Burr's first big hit, launching his career as a ballad singer. Henry Burr was born Harry Haley McClaskey on January 15, 1882, in St. Stephen, New Brunswick, Canada. His tenor won him local acclaim, and he moved to New York early in the new century. By 1903 he was recording for Columbia, eventually becoming perhaps the most recorded singer of the acoustic era and certainly one of the most popular; Whitburn ranks him seventh among recording artists of the 1900s and the top recording artist of the 1910s.

Another major hit of the year 1903 was the drinking song "Down Where the Wurzburger Flows" (music by Harry von Tilzer, lyrics by Vincent P. Bryan). Wurzburger was a brand of beer, although a London *Times* critic once incorrectly identified it as a "western American stream." The song was written for a 1902 musical called *The Wild Rose*, but it wasn't used, and Nora Bayes introduced it at the Orpheum Theatre in New York with von Tilzer at the piano. Bayes, a Broadway star, later would make many recordings, but in 1903 it became one of the first big successes for the team of baritone Arthur Collins and tenor Byron G. Harlan on Edison. Both had a long string of hits to their credit already, but they became even more successful together. Their other big hit of 1903 was "Hurrah for Baffin's Bay" (subtitled "Nautical Nonsense"), a Gilbert & Sullivan–styled comedy song fashioned for the comedy team of Montgomery and Stone to be interpolated into a stage musical adaptation of *The Wizard of Oz* that opened January 20, 1903. (The famous 1939 movie version, of course, had an entirely different song score.)

Billy Murray also broke into the charts in 1903. In contrast to Burr, Murray, another tenor, was a singer of primarily comic and up-tempo material. He was "arguably the most popular recording artist of the acoustic era," according to Gracyk, and "the first singing star to achieve his stardom solely *by making records*, and not by performing on the musical stage or vaudeville touring circuit," notes historian Allen Lowe. Murray was born William Thomas Murray in Philadelphia on May 25, 1877. His family moved to Denver when he was a child, allowing Victor Records to bill him later as "The Denver Nightingale." By 1893 he was touring in vaudeville, later working in minstrel shows. He appears to have made his first recordings in San Francisco in 1897, though they have not survived. By 1903 he was in New York, where he recorded for Edison, Victor, and Columbia, beginning a record career that earns him, by Whitburn's estimate, the status of the top recording artist of the 1900s.

In 1904 Murray began topping the charts, and his biggest hit of the year was "Meet Me in St. Louis, Louis," inspired by the Louisiana Purchase Exposition, held in that city that year. But the most successful song of the year, and a trendsetter, too, was "Sweet Adeline," introduced by the Quaker City Four at the Victoria Theater in New York, and given best-selling recordings by the Haydn Quartet on Victor and the Columbia Male Quartet, which was what the Peerless Quartet was called initially when it recorded for Columbia. In this period, the group consisted of Henry Burr, Albert Campbell, Steve Porter, and Tom Daniels.

But the record companies weren't only interested in ballads, minstrel songs, and barbershop quartets; they aspired to culture. And that was why, in 1904, Victor Records signed Italian opera singer Enrico Caruso to an exclusive recording contract when he arrived in New York to join the Metropolitan Opera. Caruso got the first superstar contract; he was paid $4,000 for his first ten sides, with royalties of 40 cents per disc, and was given a $10,000 advance. It is estimated that he earned between $2 million and $5 million on records during his lifetime. He began to pay off that expense immediately with his first recording of the aria "Vesti la guibba" from the 1892 opera *Pagliacci*, a major hit in 1904 that became an even bigger hit in a re-recording in 1907.

Two major composers made their first important appearances on Broadway in the fall of 1904, though both had been there before.

Jerome Kern had had his first songs in a Broadway show the previous January ("To the End of the World Together" and "Wine, Wine," both with lyrics by Edgar Smith, in *An English Daisy*), but the opening of *Mr. Wix of Wickham* on September 19 marked the first time he had written most of the score for a show. No hits emerged, but Kern was on his way. Seven weeks later, on November 7, George M. Cohan returned to Broadway with *Little Johnny Jones*, in which he sang both "The Yankee Doodle Boy" and "Give My Regards to Broadway," his own compositions. Cohan didn't record the songs; instead, Billy Murray became his voice on records. Murray's recordings of both songs for Columbia topped the charts in 1905.

Murray dominated record sales in 1905, placing four songs at number one for a combined total of twenty-four out of the fifty-two weeks in the year, by Whitburn's reckoning: "Yankee Doodle Boy," eight weeks, and "Give My Regards to Broadway," five weeks, both on Columbia, and "In My Merry Oldsmobile," seven weeks, and "Come Take a Trip in My Air-Ship," four weeks, both on Victor. But the biggest hit of the year, said to be the best-selling record of the first two decades of the twentieth century, was Arthur Collins's rendition of the comic novelty song "The Preacher and the Bear" for Edison. It is thought to have sold 2 million copies, and may have been the first record ever to sell a million. The next most popular song of the year on records probably was "In the Shade of the Old Apple Tree," which benefited from hit recordings by Henry Burr (under the name "Irving Gillette") for Edison, Albert Campbell for Columbia, and the Haydn Quartet for Victor.

Jerome Kern finally scored his first major hit with "How'd You Like to Spoon with Me?" (lyrics by Edward Laska), which was interpolated into the musical *The Earl and the Girl* on November 4, 1905, and sung by Georgia Caine and Victor Morley. Corrine Morgan and the Haydn Quartet recorded it for Victor, and it topped the charts in January 1906. That same month, George M. Cohan was back with another hit show, *Forty-Five Minutes from Broadway*. Again it was Corrine Morgan who made a number-one record, out of "So Long, Mary," from the score. It was succeeded at number one by another Cohan song from another Cohan show that opened in February, *George Washington, Jr.* Cohan had heard a Civil War veteran nostalgically referring to the American flag as "the grand old rag," and he wrote another of his patriotic march songs with that title. Billy Murray (who had just enjoyed a hit with Cohan's title song from *Forty-Five Minutes from Broadway*) recorded it, and it became the biggest hit of Victor's first decade of existence. But critics forced Cohan to change the title, and it became "The Grand Old Flag." (Arthur Pryor scored an instrumental hit with a version under the revised name.) Other notable record hits of 1906 included "Wait till the Sun Shines, Nellie," recorded in best-selling versions by Byron G. Harlan and by Harry Tally, both for Victor; and "Love Me and the World Is Mine," recorded by Henry Burr for Columbia and Albert Campbell for Victor.

Byron G. Harlan had the two longest-running hits of 1907, Will D. Cobb and Gus Edwards's "School Days (When We Were a Couple of Kids)" and "My Gal Sal," but the year was also notable on the charts for Caruso's supposedly million-selling remake of "Vesti la giubba" and Billy Murray's hit with George M. Cohan's "Harrigan" from the musical *Fifty Miles from Boston*. The year also marked the start of Murray's long-term teaming with Ada Jones. Jones, born in June 1873 in Lancashire, England, became the most popular female singer on records of the first two decades of the twentieth century in the United States. Her family had moved to Philadelphia by 1879, and she was appearing onstage before the age of ten. She recorded for Edison, possibly as early as 1893, but then stayed away from the recording studios for more than a decade as sound engineers struggled to capture the timbre of the female voice. She returned to recording in 1904 and proved remarkably versatile, handling a variety of accents and styles. "I Just Can't Make My Eyes Behave" from the musical *A Parisian Model* was a big hit for her in 1907 on Columbia, and her pairing with Murray, who matched her sense of humor, was ideal. Their version of "Let's Take an Old-Fashioned Walk," recorded for both Columbia and Zon-o-Phone, was their first major hit.

There were also two major developments in the theater in 1907: On July 8, Ziegfeld unveiled his *Follies of 1907*, the first of a long-running series; in the cast was Nora Bayes. And on October 21, Franz Lehár's *The Merry Widow* opened in New York, ushering in a ten-year fashion for Viennese operetta on Broadway. Also in 1907 Columbia Records stopped making cylinders, leaving Edison alone with the format and destining it to fail. (The following year, Columbia introduced the two-sided record.) And a singing waiter who had just renamed himself Irving Berlin published his first song, "Marie from Sunny Italy."

Harry von Tilzer's brother Albert composed the biggest hit record of 1908, "Take Me Out to the Ball Game" (lyrics by Jack Norworth), which was recorded by Billy Murray and the Haydn Quartet for Victor. The song became a perennial, sung at baseball games ever after. Murray again dominated the year, figuring, by Whitburn's estimation, in twelve of the forty most successful records of 1908, including his solo performances of "Under Any Old Flag at All" (by George M. Cohan, from the 1907 musical *The Talk of New York*), two songs by lyricist Harry Williams and composer Egbert Van Alstyne, "I'm Afraid to Come Home in the Dark" and "It Looks Like a Big Night To-Night," for Victor. Murray was also successful in a number of duets with Ada Jones, including "Cuddle up a Little Closer, Lovey Mine" (an early hit for lyricist Otto Hauerbach [later Harbach], with music by Karl Hoschna, from the musical *The Three Twins*) and "Wouldn't You Like to Have Me for a Sweetheart?" (from the 1907 musical *A Yankee Tourist*) on Victor, and "When We Are M-A-Dou-ble-R-I-E-D" (by George M. Cohan, from *The Talk of New York*) on Edison. The other major song hit for the year was "The Glow-Worm" (from the 1907 musical *The Girl Behind the Counter*), which generated best-selling records for Lucy Isabelle Marsh on Columbia and an instrumental by the Victor Orchestra on Victor, and which would return to the hit parade with new lyrics nearly half a century later.

The final year of the 1900s found the Haydn Quartet on top again with "Put On Your Old Gray Bonnet" on Victor, although second-place finisher "Shine On, Harvest Moon" (introduced by Nora Bayes in the Ziegfeld *Follies of 1908*; Bayes took joint credit for the music along with her husband, lyricist Jack Norworth), recorded by Harry MacDonough and "Miss Walton" (probably Elise Stevenson), also for Victor, remains more memorable. Ada Jones and Billy Murray also had a hit version for Edison, as did Frank Stanley and Henry Burr for

Indestructible Records. The other major hit song on records for the year was "I've Got Rings on My Fingers" (introduced by Blanche Ring in the musical *The Midnight Sons*), recorded by Ada Jones for Columbia and, surprisingly, by Broadway star Ring herself on Victor. Just before the end of the year, the decade's last major recording artist to emerge was young tenor Walter Van Brunt (a.k.a. Walter Scanlan), who scored on Victor with "When I Dream in the Gloaming of You."

As the decade closed, other technological innovations were affecting the field of entertainment. In 1906 the Biograph 14th Street film studio had opened in New York to make silent films; by 1908 film production had begun to shift to the West Coast. By March 1908 there were four hundred movie houses in New York City. The year 1906 also saw the invention of the jukebox, and on December 24, R.A. Fessenden conducted the first radio broadcast. The first radio station went on the air on January 16, 1908. At the end of the 1900s, Tin Pan Alley still ruled the music business: while only two or three individual records seem to have sold a million copies each, if that many, historian David Ewen estimates that "Between 1900 and 1910 there were nearly a hundred songs that sold in excess of a million copies [of sheet music] each." All that would change as the decades continued, but as we shall see, the progression was anything but smooth.

2

THE 1910S

STAGE, SHEET MUSIC, AND DISC: A NEW SYNERGY

Dividing time up by decades is an arbitrary convenience that often does not reflect reality. Nothing magical happens at the stroke of midnight on a New Year's Day marking the change of a decade, but setting off history in ten-year segments allows us to examine change from one point to another. In a sense, there was not much difference in the record business from the 1900s to the 1910s; several important characteristics carried over into the new decade. Although record sales had increased enormously during the 1900s, the record industry was still only a small part of the popular music business, which continued to be dominated by the music publishers of Tin Pan Alley. Estimates of the size of that business vary greatly. The reliable historian Russell Sanjek puts aggregate sales of sheet music in 1910 at 30 million copies with higher figures to come, but other sources claim 2 *billion* copies of sheet music were sold in what they say was the business's peak year. In any case, music publishing, not records, drove the business, and, as was true of the 1900s, today we recall the most popular songs of the 1910s ("Alexander's Ragtime Band," "Over There," "Let Me Call You Sweetheart," "Moonlight Bay," "Rock-A-Bye Your Baby with a Dixie Melody," to name only a few) and some of the major songwriters of the day (Irving Berlin, Jerome Kern, Victor Herbert, George M. Cohan) but not most of the major recording artists. According to Joel Whitburn, five of the decade's ten top recording artists had also ranked in the top ten of the 1900s—Henry Burr, Arthur Collins, Byron Harlan, Billy Murray, and Ada Jones—all names virtually lost to history.

And yet, things *were* changing, and an important change in 1909 would profoundly affect the development of the record industry in the twentieth century's second decade. That year, Congress enacted a new copyright law that, on its surface, appeared to hinder the industry: the law provided that recording companies, which had hitherto recorded whatever songs they wanted without charge, now had to pay the music publishers two cents per disc or cylinder for the "mechanical reproduction" of their songs, what came to be known as "mechanical royalties." But the law ended up helping the record industry instead of hurting it. Before 1909 music publishers would try to get their songs performed by vaudeville singers who toured the country, but the publishers had little reason to work with record companies, which tended to record songs that had already become popular; now, the music publishers had an incentive to try to use records to help popularize their products, since they stood to gain directly. As a result, it gradually became more typical for a song to be recorded at about the same time it was being published and sung onstage; sometimes songs were even introduced on records, a practice previously unheard of. This was one reason record sales continued to climb throughout the decade.

A good example of the change occurred before the end of 1910. Victor Herbert, arguably the most prolific and successful Broadway composer of the 1900s—with fourteen musicals during the decade, including *Babes in Toyland*, *Mlle. Modiste*, and *The Red Mill*—continued the same pattern in the 1910s, during which he had fifteen shows produced. The first of these was *Naughty Marietta* ("the greatest success of his career," writes Sigmund Spaeth), which began out-of-town tryouts in Syracuse, New York, on October 24 and came to Broadway on November 7. But even before the tryout performances had started, the popular recording artists Frank Stanley and Byron Harlan had recorded a song from the score, "Tramp! Tramp! Tramp!," for Victor Records, and it was on sale. The record hit number one within a week of *Naughty Marietta*'s New York opening, no doubt helping the show to a successful run of 136 performances, in addition to the pennies it put directly into Herbert's pocket.

Nothing exactly like that had happened before, although Harry MacDonough and Lucy Isabelle Marsh had come close, recording composer Karl Hoschna and lyricist Otto Hauerbach's "Every Little Movement" for Victor that summer, prior to the August 30 opening of the musical *Madame Sherry*, in which it was featured; their version topped the charts in October. The pattern didn't become a regular occurrence for a while. Typically, as we will see, emerging media are viewed as competition by existing media before they all learn to promote each other. A similar pattern also to be repeated is that established stars in one medium are reluctant to try their hands at another, which is one reason why, in the 1900s, the vaudeville and Broadway stars who introduced songs rarely recorded them, leaving that to the new crop of recording artists.

This too began to change in the 1910s, as early, in fact, as the first week of the decade. On January 6, 1910, Nora Bayes opened in a new musical, *The Jolly Bachelors*, which featured among its songs "Has Anybody Here Seen Kelly?" Toward the end of the show's eighty-four-performance run on March 7, Bayes, a twenty-nine-year-old stage veteran who had made her debut nine years before and was now one of Broadway's leading figures (and, as previously mentioned, the songwriter, with her husband Jack Norworth, of the 1909 hit "Shine On, Harvest Moon"), went into a Victor studio and recorded "Has Anybody Here Seen Kelly?"; it was her first recording session. *The Jolly Bachelors* closed, yet Bayes's recording hit number two, and she continued to record regularly until her death in 1928.

The first performer to exploit fully the growing power of records to complement a successful stage career was Al Jolson, who was an emerging star, not yet an established one, in the early 1910s. According to Whitburn, Jolson ranks as the ninth biggest recording artist of the decade, but he is the only one of the top ten who also was a Broadway star (in fact, eventually the biggest Broadway star of his time), and he was the only one who continued to rank in the top ten for the 1920s. Jolson was the most successful overall entertainer of the two decades, and records were a big part of that success. Born in what is now Lithuania sometime in the mid-1880s, he immigrated to the United States in 1894 and began a performing career in his youth. After years of playing in vaudeville and in minstrel shows, Jolson made his Broadway debut on March 20, 1911, in *La Belle Parée*, a show that helped open the Winter Garden (one of the few "Broadway" theaters actually located on the street named Broadway), for the next fifteen years his professional home. The show ran 104 performances, and he was back on November 20 with *Vera Violetta*, which ran 112 performances. On December 22 he made his recording debut with Victor singing songs from his second show, among them George M. Cohan's "That Haunting Melody," which became his first number-one hit in May 1912, followed by eight more chart toppers during the decade.

But the merging of the interests of records, publishing, and the stage, as well as the emergence of a new brand of performers who gave as much attention to records as to live performing, were gradual processes. The two biggest songs on records in 1910, both among the five most successful records of the decade, had achieved prominence through sheet music sales the year before. Significantly, both were recorded by the same soloist with two different vocal groups, marking the ascension of the barbershop quartet to prominence on records. "By the Light of the Silvery Moon" had been introduced by Georgie Price in one of songwriter-producer-director-performer Gus Edwards's vaudeville revues, then interpolated into the Ziegfeld *Follies of 1909* the previous summer. But it wasn't until April 1910 that Billy Murray and the Haydn Quartet topped the charts with it, recording for Victor. The Haydn Quartet had been scoring hits since 1898, and they were the only really popular quartet of the 1900s. Murray had also formed the American Quartet in 1909 when he signed one of the first exclusive recording contracts with Victor (for discs, while continuing to make cylinders for Edison), and with them in July he scored the biggest hit of the decade, "Casey Jones," also on Victor. This recording, sometimes cited as a million seller, exploited the popularity of the 1909 composition that may stand as the most popular train song of all time, and a true story to boot. There was a real Casey Jones, actually named John Luther Jones and nicknamed for his hometown of Cayce, Tennessee, and he was indeed a railroad engineer. His heroic efforts in a head-on collision, resulting in his death, occurred on Sunday night, April 29, 1900, near Vaughn, Mississippi, and were accurately described by lyricist T. Lawrence Seibert.

Quartets—consisting of lead, tenor, baritone, and bass, now known as the classic barbershop lineup—were the most popular vocal groups on early recordings. Although the lead singer might be named on a disc, the other members were more or less anonymous. Often a quartet would take a different name when working for a different label—i.e., the Columbia Male Quartet, which was the nom de disc for the Peerless Quartet when it worked for that label. Because the record labels were only beginning to promote individual performers as "stars," names given to performers on records—particularly house bands and vocal groups that often had floating memberships—were somewhat loosely applied.

The American Quartet consisted of Murray, John Bieling, and William F. Hooley (who were also members of the Haydn Quartet), and Steve Porter (who had been a member of the Peerless Quartet). When recording for Edison, and later for other labels, the group was known as the Premier Quartet. As the American Quartet, it went on to become one of the most successful recording acts of the 1910s, exceeded only by ballad singer Henry Burr and comic singer Arthur Collins, both of whom were members of the Peerless Quartet (a.k.a. the Columbia Male Quartet), a group that had existed since 1904 with varying personnel, but really became a force in 1911 singing the number-two hit "I Want a Girl Just Like the Girl that Married Dear Old Dad" and the second-biggest hit of that year, "Let Me Call You Sweetheart," both on Columbia. "Sweetheart" was also recorded in another popular version by Arthur Clough on Edison. The song is estimated to have sold an amazing 6 million copies of sheet music.

The biggest hit of 1911 was the career-making song of the most successful songwriter of the twentieth century. Irving Berlin had been publishing songs since 1907, but "Alexander's Ragtime Band," which he wrote for himself to sing at the Friars Club then gave to vaudeville star Emma Carus before publishing it on March 18, 1911, was the song that turned him into a big success. Arthur Collins and Byron Harlan recorded it for Victor, and their version went to number one upon release in September. Tim Gracyk notes that the song had a slow start, not catching on initially in its stage renditions, and that the Victor single placed it on the B-side, with Eddie Morton's recording of "Oceana Roll" as the A-side. (It was not unusual at that time for records to be issued with different performers on each side.) The song's popularity marked the peak of ragtime as a popular musical style and, some have said, its demise. "Alexander's Ragtime Band," in fact, was not really a ragtime song; it was only a song about a ragtime band with occasional syncopated sections. Scott Joplin might not have approved, but his more complicated music was already on the wane; when he died in April 1917, ragtime died with him, only to be reborn as an archival music form many decades later.

Irish tenor John McCormack scored his first giant hits, "I'm Falling in Love with Someone" (from Victor Herbert's *Naughty Marietta*) and "Mother Machree" (from the musical *Barry of Ballymore*) for Victor in 1911. Like Caruso's, McCormack's background was in opera, and he did not perform popular music, at least at first. Born in Athlone, Ireland, in June 1884, the son of Scottish parents, he left a career in the civil service when his singing attracted the attention of the choirmaster at Dublin Cathedral. By 1903 he was winning awards; he began recording in 1904; and he made his opera debut in 1906. In 1909 he made his American opera debut, and he was a member of the Boston Opera (1910–11) and the Chicago Opera (1912–14). But when Victor purchased his contract from the British Odeon label, he was recorded singing both popular and classical music, and by the middle of the decade he had largely abandoned opera to become a concert artist singing music in a variety of styles.

A couple of veterans teamed up in 1911 to form one of the most popular duos of the era. Henry Burr was an established tenor, and Albert Campbell, also a tenor, had found success both as a solo performer and as a member of the Peerless Quartet with Burr. On December 12, 1910, Frank C. Stanley, who had been Burr's duet partner, died, and soon after, Burr and Campbell began recording together as a pair for Columbia, scoring their first success with "On Mobile Bay" that spring. In a recorded partnership that would last for the next fourteen years, they would score another forty-seven hits, according to Whitburn.

Having exploited ragtime with "Alexander's Ragtime Band," Irving Berlin went on to promote another musical trend, this time an emerging one, with the song Collins and Harlan used to follow up "Alexander's Ragtime Band," the number-two hit "Everybody's Doing It Now" on Victor in 1912. "It," in this case, was the turkey trot, one of a series of "animal dances" such as the bunny hug and, especially, the fox trot that initiated a dance craze in the 1910s. The leading figures of this craze were not musicians, but dancers, naturally enough. They were English-born Vernon Castle and his American wife Irene, who first gained attention dancing in Paris, then returned to the United States, where they appeared in two Broadway shows, *The Lady of the Slipper* (October 28, 1912) and *The Sunshine Girl* (February 13, 1913), dancing the fox trot and the tango. Thereafter, they had their own dance pavilion in New York City, Castles-in-the-Air, and a summer one in Long Beach, Long Island, Castles-by-the-Sea. Irene Castle became a fashion leader, her slender figure and bobbed hair drastically changing women's styles. (Appropriately, Fred Astaire and Ginger Rogers starred in the couple's film biography, *The Story of Vernon and Irene Castle*, in 1939.) The American Quartet may have had the best-selling record of 1912 with the ballad "Moonlight Bay," but by the end of the year they were also topping the charts with the dance song "Everybody Two-Step" Both discs appeared on Victor.

Irving Berlin continued to score number-one hits throughout the decade, including: "When the Midnight Choo Choo Leaves for Alabam'," another success for Collins and Harlan on Columbia in 1913; "When I Lost You," the sad ballad written after the death of his first wife and recorded by Henry Burr for Victor, also in 1913; and "My Bird of Paradise," cut by the Peerless Quartet for Victor in 1915. Berlin rapidly crossed over from Tin Pan Alley to the Broadway stage, writing his first complete score with *Watch Your Step* (December 8, 1914), another show featuring Vernon and Irene Castle, and following it with *Stop! Look! Listen!* (December 25, 1915), a show that spawned two number-one hits: "I Love a Piano" for Billy Murray and "The Girl on the Magazine Cover" for Harry MacDonough, both on Victor.

In addition to "Everybody's Doing It Now," "Moonlight Bay," and "Everybody Two-Step," 1912 spawned hit recordings of many songs that went on to become standards and help define the decade. The 1910 copyright "Down by the Old Mill Stream" (music and lyrics by Tell Taylor), a reported 6-million-seller in sheet music, was a hit in late 1911 for Arthur Clough and the Brunswick Quartet on Columbia, but this version was eclipsed by Harry MacDonough's version for Victor, which dominated sales in early 1912. "Waiting for the Robert E. Lee" was a ragtime minstrel song that effectively evoked the Mississippi riverboats. It was introduced by Al Jolson at one of the concerts he gave at the Winter Garden in addition to his regular stage musicals, performed by Sophie Tucker on tour, and also featured by Ruth Roye in vaudeville, but none of them had a record hit with it. That was left to the Heidelberg Quintet (which was actually the American Quartet of Billy Murray, John Bieling, Steve Porter, and William F. Hooley, with the addition of countertenor Will Oakland) on Victor, although there were competing recordings by Arthur Collins and Byron Harlan for Edison and by Dolly Connolly for Columbia. The team of Ada Jones and Billy Murray scored their biggest hit of the year with the humorous and charming "Be My Little Baby Bumble Bee" on Victor, originally introduced by the Dolly Sisters in the musical *A Winsome Widow* (a Ziegfeld production that opened April 11, 1912). Al Jolson's other chart topper of the year, in addition to "That Haunting Melody," was "Ragging the Baby to Sleep" on Victor, a disc cited by historian Joseph Murrells as the only one of the year to sell a million copies. Henry Burr's biggest hit of the year came as part of his duo with Albert Campbell on "When I Was Twenty-One and You Were Sweet Sixteen," recorded for Columbia, with a competing version by Harry MacDonough and the American Quartet on Victor. And "Oh, You Beautiful Doll," which Billy Murray and the American Quartet recorded for Victor, remains a familiar tune.

Irving Berlin wasn't the only major songwriter to emerge in the decade and succeed on Broadway. Jerome Kern had been writing theater songs since 1904, but it wasn't until *The Red Petticoat* (November 13, 1912) that his first complete score was heard on Broadway. He followed it with fifteen more musicals before the decade was out, among them the famous series of Princess Theatre shows written with lyricists/librettists Guy Bolton and P.G. Wodehouse that were among the major theatrical achievements of the 1910s. His hit songs in the period included "They Didn't Believe Me" (lyrics by Michael E. Rourke) from *The Girl from Utah* (August 24, 1914), which topped the charts for Harry MacDonough and Olive Kline (under the pseudonym Alice Green) on Victor in 1915, and "Till the Clouds Roll By" (lyrics by Wodehouse) from the Princess Theatre show *Oh, Boy!* (February 20, 1917), a number-one record for Anna Wheaton (who had helped introduced it onstage) and James Harrod on Columbia.

The decade also saw the rise of operetta composers to challenge Victor Herbert and the many European composers who had dominated the field. Rudolf Friml had his first Broadway score with *The Firefly* (December 2, 1912), to be followed by nine more during the 1910s; it spawned the number-one hit "Sympathy" (lyrics by Otto Hauerbach), recorded by Walter Van Brunt and Helen Clark on Victor in 1913. Sigmund Romberg wrote twenty-six Broadway scores in the 1910s, but most of them were rudimentary efforts done for hire; it wasn't until his seventeenth show, *Maytime* (August 15, 1917), the longest-running musical of the 1917–18 season, and its hit "Will You Remember?" (lyrics by Rida Johnson Young), recorded by Olive Kline and Lambert Murphy (as Alice Green and Raymond Dixon on Victor), that he gained recognition.

Other legends in the making had their first efforts heard during the decade. Cole Porter wrote his first two Broadway scores, *See America First* (March 28, 1916) and *Hitchy-Koo of 1919* (October 6, 1919), although both shows were flops. And in 1919 George Gershwin enjoyed his first major song hit when Al Jolson began singing "Swanee" (lyrics by Irving Caesar) in his show *Sinbad* (although Jolson didn't have a record hit with it until 1920). Gershwin wrote his first full score for Broadway with *La, La, Lucille* (May 26, 1919).

Another important, if less-well-remembered, stage composer of the era, who was also a stage performer and a recording artist, was Chauncey Olcott. Born Chancellor John Olcott in Buffalo, New York, in July 1857, he began his performing career as a blackface minstrel, and made his Broadway acting debut in *Pepita or, The Girl with the Glass Eyes* on March 16, 1886, the first of twenty-eight musical productions in which he would appear in New York. By 1890, with *The Seven Suabians*, he was starring in those productions, his specialty being portrayals of Irishmen so convincing that it was largely forgotten he was in reality an American. As of *The Irish Artist*, which opened October 1, 1894, Olcott was both writing and performing all the songs. On January 9, 1899, he introduced his composition "My Wild Irish Rose" in his latest show, *A Romance of Athlone*. It became the biggest song hit of his career, attracting successful recordings at the time by George J. Gaskin (on Columbia) and Albert Campbell (on Berliner and Edison), and later by Harry MacDonough (1900, on Gram-o-Phone), the Haydn Quartet with MacDonough on lead vocals (1907, on Victor), the composer himself (1913, on Columbia), John McCormack (1915, on Victor), and, in the swing era, Jan Garber and His Orchestra with vocals by Tony Allen (1937, on Brunswick). Olcott's next hits came with two songs he introduced in *Barry of Ballymore* (January 30, 1911): "I Love the Name of Mary," which became a best-selling record for Will Oakland on Columbia, and, even more popular, "Mother Machree," recorded, as noted, by McCormack and also by Oakland for Edison and later Columbia.

Two years later, on January 27, 1913, Olcott opened in *The Isle o' Dreams*, in which he reprised "Mother Machree" and added two more songs that would become hits, the title song and "When Irish Eyes Are Smiling." On February 25–27, 1913, he recorded eight songs for Columbia, among them "When Irish Eyes Are Smiling," "My Wild Irish Rose," "Mother Machree," and "I Love the Name of Mary." His recording of "When Irish Eyes Are Smiling" went on to become the biggest hit of 1913, according to Whitburn. (Harry MacDonough also had a successful rendition on Victor.) On July 30, 1913, Olcott returned to Columbia's studio and recorded a song he had not written, "Too-Ra-Loo-Ra-Loo-Ral (That's an Irish Lullaby)," which earned him another number-one hit. He continued to appear on Broadway through 1918 and had a couple more recording sessions through 1920 before retiring and dying at age seventy-four in March 1932. In 1947 Dennis Morgan starred in a film biography of him, naturally called *My Wild Irish Rose*.

The major new recording artist to emerge in 1913 was Charles Harrison, a tenor who made his debut at age twenty-one on Columbia with a version of "I'm Falling in Love with Someone" in 1912. His first big hit came on Victor in late 1913 with "Peg o' My Heart," which had been introduced by José Collins in the *Ziegfeld Follies of 1913* when it opened at the New Amsterdam Theatre on Broadway on June 16. (Henry Burr also had a successful version on Columbia.) Harrison continued to record well into the 1920s.

Arguably the most commercially successful records of 1913 were two by Al Jolson, the first for Victor and the second as part of his new exclusive contract with Columbia. The comic song "The Spaniard that Blighted My Life," written by British performer Billy Merson, who first performed it, was introduced to American audiences by Jolson in his show *The Honeymoon Express*, which opened at the Winter Garden on February 6, 1913. Jolson recorded it a month later, and by the end of May, according to Whitburn, it was at the top of the charts. According to Murrells, it was also a million seller. Whitburn accords million-seller status as well to Jolson's recording of "You Made Me Love You, I Didn't Want to Do It," a song that Spaeth calls "plaintive ... combining ragtime with the good old motif of self-pity." Jolson added the song to *The Honeymoon Express* when he unveiled a revamped "second edition" of the show on April 28, 1913. He then recorded it at his first Columbia session on June 4, and it was the country's best-selling record by October, after which it went on to become a much-recorded standard.

If anyone could compete with Jolson for the title of top recording artist of 1913, it would be Henry Burr, whose name appeared on six of the forty top discs of the year, including three of the top ten: the previously mentioned "When I Lost You," "Last Night Was the End of the World" on Victor, and, in a duet with Albert Campbell, "The Trail of the Lonesome Pine" on Columbia. Harry Carroll and Ballard MacDonald, authors of that last song, also wrote another song that found success on records in 1913, "There's a Girl in the Heart of Maryland (With a Heart that Belongs to Me)," recorded by Harry MacDonough for Victor.

Burr again had his name on six of the forty top records of 1914, including the year's top hit, "The Song that Stole My Heart Away" on Columbia. He also teamed with Albert Campbell and Will Oakland on "I'm on My Way to Mandalay" (from the musical *The Gay Modiste*, which closed before reaching Broadway) for Victor, the year's fourth-biggest hit. Perhaps the most successful song of the year, with two recordings that hit number one, was "By the Beautiful Sea," recorded by the Heidelberg Quintet for Victor and by Ada Jones and Billy Watkins for Columbia. Some sources assign million-seller status to the spoken-word comedy number "Cohen on the Telephone," recorded by American-born British comedian Joe Hayman for Columbia. And the team of Arthur Collins and Byron Harlan placed two comic songs among the year's ten best-selling records with "I Love the Ladies" on Columbia and "The Aba Daba Honeymoon" on Victor.

However long it may have been developing beneath popular notice, the musical style called "the blues" finally made its appearance nationally in 1914 with the hit recording of W.C. Handy's "Memphis Blues" by Prince's Orchestra. Handy, a trained musician dubbed the "Father of the Blues," acknowledged adapting music he had heard others play, but also added his own parts to it. He wrote what became "Memphis Blues" as a campaign song for a Memphis politician in 1912, but nonpolitical lyrics were writtten for it by George A. Norton in 1913. In 1914 Handy wrote "St. Louis Blues," recorded by Prince's Orchestra in 1916, which went on to become the best-known blues song of all time. From these beginnings, the blues became a major force in twentieth-century music and one of the building blocks of jazz and rock 'n' roll.

Of course, the major historical event of the 1910s was World War I, which broke out in Europe in July 1914. Although the United States did not enter the war until April 1917, the conflict had a tremendous impact on popular music. Tin Pan Alley recognized the potential for war-related songs when the 1912 British copyright "It's a Long, Long Way to Tipperary," which the troops sang on their way to France, became a massive U.S. hit. By the fall, it was being sung in several Broadway shows, and from December through March 1915, records of it by the American Quartet and John McCormack (both on Victor) spent a combined fifteen weeks at number one. That did not, however, indicate that the United States was ready to jump into the war on the side of Britain; the song's popularity, no doubt, was aided by its not referring specifically to the war, which it predated. Initial American reluctance to enter the fray was explicitly revealed by the ascension to number one of "I Didn't Raise My Boy to Be a Soldier" in April 1915 for the first of seven total weeks, in recordings by Morton Harvey (for Victor) and the Peerless Quartet (for Columbia). (The group followed it up with a number-two hit, the similarly themed "Don't Take My Darling Boy Away," for Victor.) Nevertheless, the subject of the war continued to engage songwriters because it interested the public, and sentiment began to swing decisively after May 7, 1915, when a German submarine sank the British luxury liner the *Lusitania* (which was technically unarmed, but carrying ammunition for the war effort), resulting in the loss of 128 U.S. citizens.

Still, Americans, perhaps prodded by other elements of Tin Pan Alley, were able to disengage from the growing war threat with sentimental and novelty songs in 1915. Many of the most popular had a geographic theme. The year's *Ziegfeld Follies*, which opened June 21, produced a number-one hit in "Hello, Frisco!," introduced onstage by Ina Claire and recorded for Victor by Olive Kline and Reginald Werrenrath under the pseudonyms Alice Green and Edward Hamilton. The taste for Irish fare demonstrated by Chauncey Olcott was confirmed by the success of "A Little Bit of Heaven ('Shure, They Call It Ireland')," introduced by Olcott in the "Irish drama" *The Heart of Paddy Whack* at the Grand Opera House in New York on November 23, 1914, and recorded for a number-one hit by George MacFarlane on Victor. (Charles Harrison also had a hit version on Victor.) Another stage hit successfully transferred to record was "Chinatown, My Chinatown," actually written in 1906 and heard later in the revue *Up and Down Broadway*, which opened July 18, 1910. Five years later, the American Quartet made it a number-one record on Victor, beating out a popular version by Grace Kerns and John Barnes Wells on Columbia. But that revival was nothing compared to another one that occurred in 1915. The year's sole million seller was the 1878 composition "Carry Me Back to Old Virginny," written by African-American expatriate James Bland, who performed in minstrel shows in Great Britain. It was revived by former Metropolitan Opera singer Alma Gluck on Victor in a recording that hit number one in April 1915. (Also successful was Elida Morris and Sam Ash's recording on Columbia.) In 1940 it became the official state song of Virginia. With travels to San Francisco, Ireland, Chinatown, and Virginia, it was perhaps appropriate that the oldest song to be revived for a major record hit was "Home, Sweet Home" (music by Sir Henry Bishop, lyrics by John Howard Payne), originally written for the 1823 opera *Clari or, The Maid of Milan* and revived in 1915 by another former Metropolitan Opera star, Alice Nielsen, on Columbia.

One might suggest that this concentration on any location but Europe, where war was raging, was suggestive of America's desire for isolation and neutrality. But by the start of 1916, the war was clearly back on the country's mind. The British war song "Keep the Home Fires Burning (Till the Boys Come Home)," hit number one in a recording by James F. Harrison (recording under the pseudonym Frederick J. Wheeler) on Victor in January 1916, followed by Harrison and James Reed's Victor recording of "There's a Long, Long Trail." Like "It's a Long, Long Way to Tipperary," "There's a Long, Long Trail" was written prior to the war and did not refer to it directly, but it was associated with the British troops. The lyric had won Stoddard King a literary prize at Yale, after which there was a contest to see who could write the best tune. Yale undergraduate Zo Elliott won, and when he later attended graduate school at Oxford, the song (first published in England in 1913) was taken up by fellow students who shortly after became soldiers.

For much of 1916, the country hewed to the kind of music that had appealed to it before the war started and the kind of escapism that had appealed since. The two biggest record hits were both sentimental ballads recorded by Henry Burr for Victor: "M-O-T-H-E-R (A Word that Means the World to Me)" and "Good-Bye, Good Luck, God Bless You (Is All that I Can Say)." Billy Murray reached number one with his Victor recordings of the up-tempo numbers "I Love a Piano," previously mentioned, and "Pretty Baby." Al Jolson kept record buyers laughing with "I Sent My Wife to the Thousand Isles" on Columbia. The Irish craze continued with "If I Knock the 'L' out of Kelly (It Would Still Be Kelly to Me)," from the musical *Step This Way*, recorded by Marguerite Farrell for Victor, and "Ireland Must Be Heaven, for My Mother Came from There," recorded by Charles Harrison for Victor. And there was a new geographic fad for Hawaii. (Maybe it was as far away from Europe as people—or Tin Pan Alley songwriters—could imagine.) Prince's Orchestra scored a number-one hit on Columbia with "Hello, Hawaii, How Are You?" (Billy Murray had the vocal version on Victor); Arthur Collins and Byron Harlan joked their way through the tongue-twisting "Oh How She Could Yacki Hacki Wicki Wachi Woo (That's Love in Honolulu)" on Victor; and Al Jolson's comic contribution was "Yaaka Hula Hickey Dula," which he introduced in *Robinson Crusoe, Jr.* and recorded for Columbia.

Still, the war was inescapable, and its stirring of American patriotism was reflected (as it would be in later conflicts) by the renewed popularity of perennial standards. Prince's Orchestra had a best-selling Columbia record in August with an instrumental treatment of the 1814 song (and as of March 3, 1931, the American national anthem) "The Star-Spangled Banner," and the Columbia Mixed Double Quartet followed it at number one with its revival of the 1831 song "America," also on Columbia, in September. A lull over the winter allowed for the success of such songs as "Poor Butterfly" from the musical *The Big Show*, recorded as an instrumental by the Victor Military Band, in February and March 1917. (Prince's Orchestra had a competing version on Columbia.) But on April 6, the United States entered the war, and there was another outpouring of war-related hits. In May, the British song "Pack up Your Troubles in Your Old Kit Bag (And Smile, Smile, Smile)" hit number one for James F. Harrison and the Knickerbocker Quartet on Columbia. John McCormack's version of "The Star-Spangled Banner" on Victor was a best-seller in June; the American Quartet's recording of "Good-Bye Broadway, Hello France" (from *The Passing Show of 1917*) scored on Victor in October; and George M. Cohan's "Over There," the most famous American song of the war, was number one for three different artists over a period of fourteen weeks from October 1917 to January 1918. First, there was the American Quartet's version on Victor, then the Peerless Quartet's on Columbia, and next Nora Bayes's on Victor. Meanwhile, "Oh, Johnny, Oh Johnny, Oh!," which was recorded for a number-one hit in June by the American Quartet on Victor, had started out as a war song of sorts, the female narrator marveling, "How you can fight"—but the lyric was quickly changed to "How you can love."

During 1918 almost every top hit seemed to refer to the war in one way or another: "Send Me Away with a Smile," recorded by John McCormack for Victor; "I Don't Know Where I'm Going but I'm on My Way," recorded by the Peerless Quartet for Victor; a revival of the 1862 Civil War anthem "The Battle Hymn of the Republic," recorded by the Columbia Stellar Quartet for Columbia; "Hail! Hail! The Gang's All Here," recorded by Irving Kaufman and the Columbia Quartet for Columbia; "Just a Baby's Prayer at Midnight (For Her Daddy Over There)," recorded by Henry Burr for Victor and reportedly a million seller; "Hello Central, Give Me No Man's Land," introduced by Al Jolson and recorded by him for Columbia; "Over There" again in a recording by Enrico Caruso for Victor; and, two weeks after the November 11 armistice, Irving Berlin's "Oh, How I Hate to Get Up in the Morning" from the musical *Yip, Yip, Yaphank*, recorded by Arthur Fields for Victor. Slightly further down the hit parade were more upbeat and outright comic songs of conflict: "If He Can Fight Like He Can Love (Goodnight, Germany)," recorded by the Farber Sisters for Columbia; two recordings by Billy Murray for Victor, Irving Berlin's "They Were All Out of Step But Jim" and "K-K-K-Katy (Stammering Song)"; and "Just Like Washington Crossed the Delaware, General Pershing Will Cross the Rhine," recorded by the Peerless Quartet for Victor.

The most successful nonwar-related recording of the year was another Jolson offering, "Rock-A-Bye Your Baby with a Dixie Melody," a song he introduced in the musical *Sinbad* and recorded for Columbia. It reportedly sold a million copies, and it became one of his signature numbers. Other memorable nonwar hits of the year included

"I'm Always Chasing Rainbows," recorded by Charles Harrison for Victor, and Shelton Brooks's "Dark Town Strutters Ball," recorded by Arthur Collins and Byron Harlan for Columbia.

Enormous historical importance attaches to one other hit of 1918, the instrumental "Tiger Rag," recorded by the Original Dixieland Jazz Band for Victor, which, according to Whitburn, ascended to number one the day after the armistice. It was the first hit record in the new style of music known as jazz. The origins of the improvisatory approach reach back before the turn of the century, of course, but it took time for national recognition. According to Tim Gracyk, the first performers to use the term on record were Collins and Harlan, who recorded a song called "That Funny Jas Band from Dixieland" on December 1, 1916, for Edison; it was released in April 1917. On January 17, 1917, the Original Dixieland Jazz Band, or ODJB as it came to be called, began playing at Reisenweber's Restaurant in New York. They recorded for Columbia at the end of the month, then in February cut the instrumental "Livery Stable Blues" for Victor, which was their first release in the spring and gained them considerable recognition, with their version of "Darktown Strutter's Ball" (as their version was called) on Columbia, released in September, becoming a real hit, followed by the success of "Tiger Rag" (recorded March 25, 1918). The ODJB was a quintet of white men generally thought to be adapters of a style developed by African Americans (although the band's cornetist Nick LaRocca claimed otherwise). But their significance to this history is that they first popularized jazz on records, leading it to the status it eventually achieved.

Although the war was over by the start of 1919, the country's songwriters and recording artists were not quite through with it. The most successful song on records for the year was what David Ewen calls "the leading ballad of World War I," "Till We Meet Again" (music by Richard A. Whiting, lyrics by Raymond B. Egan), recorded for number-one hits by Henry Burr and Albert Campbell for Columbia, Charles Hart and Lewis James (the latter one of the year's major newcomers) for Victor, and Nicholas Orlando's Orchestra, with vocals by Harry MacDonough and Charles Hart, also for Victor. Other war and postwar sentiments could be heard in "How Ya Gonna Keep 'Em

Down on the Farm (After They've Seen Paree)," recorded by Nora Bayes for Columbia, and "Tell That to the Marines," recorded by Al Jolson, also for Columbia. Almost as successful was what Spaeth calls "possibly the best song of 1918, and certainly its biggest seller through the years, ... that haunting waltz" "Beautiful Ohio," recorded by Henry Burr for Columbia, and as an instrumental by the Waldorf-Astoria Dance Orchestra for Victor (on the same record, 18526, as the Orlando Orchestra version of "Till We Meet Again") and by Prince's Orchestra for Columbia. And the third major hit of the year, perhaps indicative of the country's new postwar mood, was "I'm Forever Blowing Bubbles," recorded in a vocal version by Henry Burr and Albert Campbell for Columbia and by another major newcomer, Ben Selvin and His Orchestra, in an instrumental version for Victor.

It was another big year for Henry Burr, whose name was on seven of the forty top discs, including the top three. Al Jolson remained a big seller, scoring a number-one hit with "I'll Say She Does" on Columbia. And Bert Williams had two best-sellers, "It's Nobody's Business but My Own" (from the *Ziegfeld Follies of 1919*) and the comic "O Death, Where Is Thy Sting?," both on Columbia. In addition to Lewis James and Ben Selvin, the biggest name to emerge in the year was Marion Harris, who scored a number-one version of the vengeful "After You've Gone" (music by Turner Layton, lyrics by Harry Creamer) on Victor. She was born Mary Ellen Harrison, perhaps in 1896, probably in Henderson, Kentucky. There are various accounts of her entry into show business, but by the mid-1910s she seems to have been in New York, apparently appearing in Ziegfeld's *Midnight Frolic* show of 1916. By the end of the year, her first single had been released on Victor, and 1917's "They Go Wild, Simply Wild, Over Me" was a hit. But "After You've Gone" was her first best-seller, and she went on to many more through 1930.

The emergence of blues and jazz during the 1910s indicated the beginnings of a broadening of popular taste beyond the Tin Pan Alley and Broadway styles still dominating pop music. Among the major labels, Victor Records was the most reliable producer of hits, with Columbia a steady second and Edison a fading third. One reason for this was that Victor and Columbia had in December 1903 come to a cross-licensing agreement by which they shared their patents for laterally cut discs. (Edison still made cylinders, although it eventually introduced vertically cut discs that needed their own player.) But the patents began to expire in 1914, and many new companies were founded, gradually lessening the power of the big three and leading to the recording of different kinds of music. Among them were OKeh, founded in 1915, and Brunswick, launched in 1916.

Meanwhile, the more established purveyors of pop music took a step to consolidate their power with the founding of the American Society of Composers, Authors and Publishers (ASCAP) on February 13, 1914. An unenforced law long on the books required songwriters and publishers to be recompensed when their songs were performed, and ASCAP set out to get it enforced and arrange a system by which the payments could be made. A test case launched by ASCAP cofounder Victor Herbert began making its way through the courts, and on January 22, 1917, the Supreme Court confirmed, that ASCAP could collect fees for live performances of music. Songwriters gained compensation for their work, but the growth of ASCAP also tended to restrict the diversity of popular music by limiting access to publishing, recording, and dissemination of songs to its membership.

If we had opted to divide chapters by historical events, it might have been logical to consider the period up to the end of World War I as the first one, with the postwar era to follow. The "acoustic era" of recording, which came to an end in the mid-1920s, might have made another good dividing line. But in fact, there is another signpost that occurs right at the decade divide between the 1910s and the 1920s. On January 29, 1919, an amendment to the U.S. Constitution prohibiting alcoholic beverages achieved passage; it came into effect on January 16, 1920. As much as anything, Prohibition made for a neat dividing line between the war-dominated decade of the 1910s and what is still recalled as the Roaring Twenties.

SONNY BOY
by AL JOLSON
B. G. DESYLVA
LEW BROWN
and RAY HENDERSON
THEME SONG OF
WARNER BROS.'
PRODUCTION
AL JOLSON
IN
"THE SINGING FOOL"
AS SHOWN AT THE
WINTER GARDEN
NEW YORK
A WARNER BROS. VITAPHONE PICTURE

3

THE 1920s

THE JAZZ AGE

F. Scott Fitzgerald, who dubbed the 1920s "the Jazz Age," wrote to his editor, Maxwell Perkins, in 1931 that "it extended from the suppression of the riots of May Day 1919 to the crash of the stock market in 1929—almost exactly a decade." (For the earlier date, he refers to an incident that took place in New York, also depicted in his 1920 short story "May Day," not to the better known "Palmer raids" against suspected Communists instituted by U.S. Attorney General A. Mitchell Palmer in 1919–20.) But a better date for the start of the Jazz Age would be the institution of the Prohibition Enforcement, or Volstead Act, sponsored by Minnesota Congressman Andrew John Volstead. Although intended to prevent Americans from drinking alcohol, the 18th Amendment probably led them to drink more. And while they were drinking they often were listening to music and dancing.

The record industry grew gradually in the first two decades of the century, but by the start of the 1920s it was ready to take its place beside the music publishing industry as a major means of dissemination of popular music. Previously, songs had started with publishers, who persuaded vaudeville performers to sing them; recordings usually were made only after the songs had become big sheet-music sellers. Now things had changed sufficiently that, according to David Ewen, "Beginning in 1920, and increasingly so from then on, a hit song began to be measured more by the number of records it sold than by copies of sheet music." One reason for this was that the record player had begun to replace the piano as the primary source of music in the home, but another was that, due to the increasing popularity of the still-silent movies, vaudeville was already starting to decline. This was hastened by another technological innovation: radio. Although there had been amateur broadcasts earlier, at the turn of the decade radio rapidly came to the fore. General Electric had formed the Radio Corporation of America (RCA) in October 1919 to manufacture radios. The first radio station with scheduled programs, Pittsburgh's KDKA, went on the air November 2, 1920, broadcasting the election returns that made Warren G. Harding the new president. Detroit's WWJ soon followed, and by 1922 there were five hundred radio stations in the country providing the kind of entertainment in the parlor that people used to have to go to a vaudeville theater to hear. In 1926 the first radio network, NBC, was launched, followed a year later by CBS.

Radio truly hurt vaudeville, but it was also perceived to hurt record sales, a notion that seems absurd today, when radio is viewed as the chief means of promoting recorded music. At the time, however, the record industry's fear was that if people could hear music over the air for free, they wouldn't buy it (a fear the industry would invoke again with the rise of cassette recording in the 1970s and of computer downloading in the 1990s). That, for example, Irving Berlin's "All Alone" became the second-biggest record hit of 1925 after having been introduced by John McCormack over a network of eight radio stations on New Year's Day made no impression on the record labels, which viewed radio as an enemy for decades to come.

The record industry was thriving in 1920, however, and the start of the decade marked the popular emergence of several forms of popular music. The 1900s and '10s had been largely an era of sentimental ballads and comic songs sung by individuals or quartets. The first indication that things were changing came dramatically with the emergence of "Dardanella," which was recorded as an instrumental by Ben Selvin's Novelty Orchestra for Victor and went to number one at the end of January, remaining the top seller for thirteen weeks. That was enough to make it the biggest hit of the year and the second biggest of the decade; it may have sold as many as 5 million copies. "Dardanella" ushered in a whole new style in popular music, that of the dance bands. Joel Whitburn's list of the top ten recording artists of the 1920s contains no less than six orchestras, led by Paul

Whiteman (number one), Isham Jones (number four), Selvin (five), Ted Lewis (six), George Olsen (seven), and Fred Waring (nine). For the most part, these bands recorded instrumentals played at quick tempos for dancing.

Although purists cringe to hear it today, much of the music made by the dance bands of the 1920s was known at the time as "jazz." "In the twenties," writes Ewen, " 'jazz' became a generic term covering virtually all forms of popular music, including the songs of Tin Pan Alley and Broadway, as well as concert music then being written utilizing jazz techniques and idioms." Historian Charles Hamm notes, "The music accepted by jazz historians today as 'true' jazz was almost unknown in New York in the 1910s and '20s. ... The term *jazz* ... referred to the ragtime songs of Irving Berlin and other New York composers, and to the syncopated dance music played by such white bands as those of Paul Whiteman, Isham Jones, and Ben Selvin."

Among these, by far the most popular was Whiteman. Born in March 1890, he was given classical training and played in classical orchestras as a violist before leading a navy band during World War I. After the war, he organized a band that played on the West Coast until it was hired to play at the Ambassador Hotel in Atlantic City, New Jersey, in the spring of 1920. There, it was heard by Victor Records executives who were attending a company convention, and Whiteman was signed to the label. In August he recorded his second single, pairing instrumental treatments of "Whispering" and "The Japanese Sandman." Released in September, the disc topped the charts for eleven weeks and reportedly sold 2 million copies, establishing Whiteman as a star.

That was only the beginning. Whiteman went on to score 159 chart entries during the decade, by Whitburn's count, among them sixteen chart toppers, all instrumentals, between 1921 and 1925, with five in 1921 alone, including "Wang Wang Blues," a million seller that January. A part of Whiteman's recording success came from borrowing songs from the Broadway stage, including its key composers like George Gershwin. Whiteman's relationship with Gershwin was enhanced when he commissioned Gershwin to write a piece of serious music for a concert he was planning at the Aeolian Hall in New

York on February 12, 1924. The result was "Rhapsody in Blue," the most celebrated musical work of the day; Whiteman and Gershwin recorded it on a 12-inch single that became a major hit.

Although dance music dominated the early 1920s, individual singers also succeeded, none more than Al Jolson. Jolson began the decade touring the country in *Sinbad*, adding songs to it at will, among them "Swanee," which became a million-selling number-one hit, and "Avalon." Jolson finally closed the tour of *Sinbad* on June 25, 1921, two months after hitting number one again with "O-HI-O (O-My! O!)" He reopened on Broadway in *Bombo* that fall, in which he introduced "April Showers," which topped the charts in January and became the biggest hit of 1922. By May he was back at number one with "Angel Child." At that time, he was in Philadelphia with *Bombo* following the Broadway run, but he took the summer off before launching its national tour in September 1922, interpolating "Toot Toot Tootsie (Goo'bye)," which hit number one in January 1923. When he opened a second year's tour of the show in the fall of 1923, he introduced "California, Here I Come!," which topped the charts in May 1924. Jolson had recorded the song in January as part of his first session for Brunswick Records, following a decade with Columbia. While preparing his next show, *Big Boy*, he returned to number one in November 1924 with "I Wonder What's Become of Sally?" *Big Boy*, which tried out in five cities before it opened on Broadway in January 1925, didn't throw off as many big hits, but the singer continued to score with his recordings of chart-topping independent songs like "All Alone," "I'm Sitting on Top of the World," and "When the Red, Red Robin Comes Bob-Bob-Bobbin' Along."

Whiteman and Jolson were the two top recording artists of the decade, but they weren't the only success stories. Just below 1920's three reported million sellers—Selvin's "Dardanella," Whiteman's "Whispering," and Jolson's "Swanee"—was the first number-one hit by the Ted Lewis Jazz Band, "When My Baby Smiles at Me" on Columbia. Lewis, born Theodore Leopold Friedman, probably in June 1890, in Circleville, Ohio, was a clarinet-playing vaudevillian who had crossed over to the legitimate stage with his appearance in *The Greenwich Village Follies* in July 1919. With his battered top hat (which he had won in a crap game) and his tag line "Is everybody happy?," he was a comic figure who half-spoke his songs with an air of affected nonchalance that was just right for the times. Billed as the "Jazz King" (as opposed to Whiteman, who was billed as the "King of Jazz"), Lewis had a four-song showcase in *The Greenwich Village Follies* that included "When My Baby Smiles at Me." By the time the show closed in January 1920, he was scoring record hits. As with Whiteman, most of them were instrumentals, with his first hit a notable exception.

Lewis exemplified the increasing willingness of stage performers to undertake concurrent recording careers. The same year as his emergence on records, he was joined by another vaudevillian who crossed over to the legitimate stage, Frank Crumit. Crumit, born in September 1889 in Jackson, Ohio, turned to vaudeville with a ukulele after graduating from the University of Ohio. His Broadway debut came on May 4, 1920, at the Casino Theatre in *Betty, Be Good*, but he really made his mark in *The Greenwich Village Follies of 1920*, which opened on August 30. By then, he had already scored the first two of the thirty-one chart hits ascribed to him by Whitburn, appearing on both sides of Columbia 2935, "Oh! By Jingo! By Gee" and "So Long, Oo-Long (How Long You Gonna Be Gone)." Crumit turned away from the stage and from record-making to host radio shows with his wife, Julia Sanderson, in the 1930s and early '40s.

The last important recording artist to emerge in 1920 was tenor saxophonist, songwriter, and bandleader Isham Jones. Born around 1893, Jones formed his first band to play in a church in Arkansas, launching his first professional unit when he was twenty. He eventually based his orchestra in Chicago and signed to Brunswick Records, which issued his first chart record, an instrumental performance of "A Young Man's Fancy" (from the musical *What's in a Name?*) in 1920. Seventy-two more chart entries followed through 1938, with Jones's name on many as a songwriter. His first really big hit came at the end of 1921 with "Wabash Blues," reportedly a million seller.

Nineteen-twenty is also notable for the hits "The Love Nest," introduced in the musical *Mary* and recorded in number-one renditions by vocalist John Steel for Victor and, in an instrumental treatment, Art Hickman for Columbia; "I'll Be with You in Apple Blossom Time," recorded most successfully in this, its first blush of popularity, by Charles Harrison for Victor; Irving Berlin's "I'll See You in C-U-B-A," an early comment on Prohibition (which did not extend to the nearby island of Cuba, then a popular American tourist spot), recorded by Billy Murray for Victor and other labels, and in an instrumental version by Ted Lewis; and the racy "You'd Be Surprised," interpolated into the *Ziegfeld Follies of 1919* by Eddie Cantor, for whom it was a star-making performance, and recorded by him on Emerson.

By 1921, the stylistic turnover to instrumental, danceable "jazz" as the country's dominant popular music was complete. Of the ten most popular records for the year, seven, including the top six, were instrumentals by Whiteman, Jones, and Lewis. The major new recording artist to emerge was another bandleader (as would be most of the important debut artists of the rest of the decade), Leo Reisman. Reisman, born in 1897, started out as a classical violinist, playing with the Baltimore Symphony by the age of seventeen, but saw there was more money in pop music. He got his start as an orchestra leader at the Brunswick Hotel in Boston, where he first displayed his preference for slow tempos. Reisman was spotted by Jerome Kern, who got him a job with his next musical, *Good Morning, Dearie*, in 1921. But even before that, he was contracted by Columbia, scoring his first chart record with an instrumental treatment of "Bright Eyes." His career on records didn't really take off until later in the decade, however.

One of the few big vocal hits of 1921 helped set the style by which the decade was remembered. The comedy team of Gus Van and Joe Schenck had been performing in vaudeville and on Broadway for years, even enjoying a number-one hit with "For Me and My Gal" on Victor in 1917. But their version of "Ain't We Got Fun?," which gave them their second chart-topper on Columbia in September 1921, typified the frivolity of the new decade. It would be followed by even sillier fare. One of these was perhaps the most popular song of 1922, with two number-one renditions, "Mr. Gallagher and Mr. Shean," essentially a comedy routine with music, written and introduced by *Ziegfeld Follies* performers Ed Gallagher and Al Shean and recorded by them for Victor; the team of Billy Jones and Ernest Hare scored with a competing version on OKeh.

Outside of that distraction, the top of the charts for the year was owned by Jolson and Whiteman, plus Isham Jones with an instrumental treatment of "On the Alamo," and two unusually somber efforts, Fanny Brice's "My Man (Mon Homme)" and Henry Burr's "My Buddy." Brice, another *Ziegfeld Follies* star, reached number one in March on Victor with "My Man (Mon Homme)," a classic ballad of male domination and female victimization whose popularity was stimulated by the public knowledge of her difficult marriage to imprisoned gambler Nick Arnstein. (Brice also hit in 1921 with the far cheerier "Second Hand Rose"; Barbra Streisand revived both songs when she played Brice in the biographical musical and film *Funny Girl* in the 1960s.) Like many of the other prominent recording figures of the 1900s and '10s, Henry Burr had struggled in the early 1920s. But he returned to the number-one spot a final time in December 1922 with the maudlin "My Buddy."

Bandleader Vincent Lopez was the most notable musical figure to debut in the charts in 1922, with an instrumental treatment of the tune that became his theme song, the 1916 composition "Nola," on OKeh. A pianist, Lopez was born in Brooklyn in 1895. By 1916, he was leading the band at the Pekin Restaurant on Times Square. In 1921 he was hired as the conductor of the band at the Pennsylvania Hotel, and from that base he became the first bandleader to perform a live "remote" on radio. ("Remote" broadcasts gained their name because they originated outside of the station's studios.) "Nola" was the first of his twenty-nine chart hits through 1939.

The year 1923 had the usual contingent of instrumental dance hits, led by Whiteman's "Parade of the Wooden Soldiers" (from the French musical *Chauve Souris*) and Isham Jones's "Swingin' Down the Lane" (also recorded for his first top-ten hit by Ben Bernie and His Orchestra on Vocalion). But several of the year's most popular songs were upbeat and even novelty numbers. In addition to Jolson's "Toot Toot Tootsie (Goodbye)," there was the perennial "Carolina in the Morning," recorded by Van and Schenck for Columbia; "That Old Gang of Mine" (a.k.a. "Wedding bells are breaking up that old gang of mine"), recorded by Billy Murray and Ed Smalle for Victor, with a competing version by Benny Krueger on Brunswick; and, goofiest of all, "Yes, We Have No Bananas." The story goes that the songwriters heard the title phrase's broken English spoken by a Greek fruit peddler to one of his customers. Eddie Cantor picked it up and made it one of his signature songs, but the biggest hit recordings were by Billy Jones (for Edison) and Ben Selvin's orchestra (with Irving Kaufman on vocals; for Vocalion). Cantor had to be content with a number-three entry for a follow-up, "I've Got the Yes! We Have No Bananas Blues," on Columbia.

Amid all this tomfoolery, 1923 produced two reported million sellers, both in different moods. Violinist and bandleader Art Landry scored the biggest hit of his career with the appropriately named "Dreamy Melody," notable as the first published song by Ted Koehler (sharing the credits with Frank Magine and C. Naset), who would go on to write memorable lyrics to songs by Harold Arlen. The other title said to be a gold record had its roots in an earlier recording. On August 10, 1920, Ralph Peer of OKeh Records had recorded Mamie Smith singing "Crazy Blues," a song she had been performing in an all-black musical called *Maid of Harlem* under the name "Harlem Blues." "Crazy Blues" stunned the record industry when it sold more than 100,000 copies, and labels began catering specifically to the African-American customer, especially by signing black female blues singers. Peer dubbed these discs "race" records, a term that later came to be seen as demeaning, although the idea of marketing specifically to black audiences continued through the rest of the century. In July 1923 Bessie Smith hit number one with "Down Hearted Blues," the year's second million seller. Bessie Smith's sales helped rescue Columbia Records, which had gone into receivership that year but reemerged in 1924.

In addition to Ben Bernie, who originated the catch phrase "Yowsah, yow-sah," 1923's notable new recording artists included two more bandleaders: Jan Garber, whose instrumental "Haunting Blues" on Columbia was the first of his sixty-six chart records through 1951, and, at the end of 1923, Fred Waring, leader of a band called the Pennsylvanians. Waring's theme song, "Sleep," featuring vocals by him and his brother Tom, topped the charts for Victor at the start of 1924, beginning a run of fifty-three chart entries through 1954. Born in June 1900 in Tyrone, Pennsylvania, Waring began playing the banjo and leading a quartet in 1916. He formed the Pennsylvanians while attending Pennsylvania State University and continued to lead the group into the 1980s.

Just as he had pioneered the recording of "race" music on OKeh, Ralph Peer, having moved to Victor, pioneered the recording of another form he dubbed "hillbilly" music. The emergence of hillbilly music can probably be put down to the spread of radio; as stations began to broadcast in the South, the region's own music started to turn up on the air, with Atlanta's WSB being the first major station to program it in 1922. The same year, Victor recorded the hillbilly fiddlers Eck Robertson and Henry Gilliland, and in 1923 Peer went to Atlanta and recorded Fiddlin' John Carson, who scored million sellers with 1924's "You Will Never Miss Your Mother until She Is Gone" and "Fare You Well, Old Joe Clark." An indication of the music's popularity was Tin Pan Alley's rush to copy it. In November 1923 Victor released Wendell Hall's "It Ain't Gonna Rain No Mo," written by the performer. Hall was an early radio star, not a hillbilly, but his song was a comic adaptation of a mountain tune, and it sold over 2 million copies. Even more successful was light-opera singer Vernon Dalhart's "The Prisoner's Song" (music and lyrics by Guy Massey), released on Victor in October 1924. Dalhart was another musical carpetbagger, but his record was reported to have sold over 7 million copies, which, if accurate, makes it the best-selling record until the release of Bing Crosby's "White Christmas" (music and lyrics by Irving Berlin) in 1942.

Ralph Peer continued to search for the genuine article, however, and on August 1, 1927, in Bristol, Virginia, at an open audition, he found both Jimmie Rodgers, whose "Blue Yodel" became a million seller the following year, and the Carter Family, whose 1928 million seller was "Wildwood Flower." These two acts formed the basis of modern country music. Russell Sanjek estimates that by 1930 hillbilly music may have accounted for as much as 25 percent of all record sales of popular music. Yet the record labels, which had tried to foist classical music on consumers in their early days, consistently underestimated the sales potential of this musical style and, when the Depression hit, cut back recording of it severely.

In 1924, the charts continued to be dominated by Al Jolson, Paul Whiteman, and Isham Jones, each of whom scored multiple number-one hits. Jones had two, "Spain" and the standard "It Had to Be You," and for both he provided the music to Gus Kahn's lyrics. Jones's recordings for Brunswick were instrumentals, of course, but Marion Harris also had a hit vocal version of "It Had to Be You" on Brunswick. Another popular version, this one on Pathé, was one of the first chart records by Cliff Edwards, a.k.a. "Ukelele Ike." Edwards, born in Hannibal, Missouri, in June 1895, took up the ukulele to entertain customers when he was a newsboy. He began working in vaudeville by the late 1910s and crossed over to the legitimate theater in the musical *The Mimic World of 1921*, which opened on Broadway in August 1921. Edwards headlined at the Palace Theatre, marking the greatest possible success for a vaudevillian, in April 1924. That same year he began recording, and he was one of the featured performers in the Gershwin musical *Lady, Be Good!* when it opened in December, introducing the standard "Fascinating Rhythm."

Among the 1924 newcomers who were the most successful over the long term is bandleader Ted Weems, who enjoyed a million seller with his instrumental Columbia recording of "Somebody Stole My Gal." Born in Pitcairn, Pennsylvania, around 1901, Weems attended the University of Pennsylvania and formed his first band soon after leaving school. By 1922 he was recording for Columbia, and his band eventually employed a young Perry Como while scoring thirty-six hits through 1948.

Toward the end of 1924 orchestra leader Nat Shilkret made his debut on records under his own name. Actually, he had been making recordings much earlier. Starting out as a clarinetist with the New York Philharmonic and later playing in John Philip Sousa's band, Shilkret became director of light music for Victor Records in 1915 and conducted for many of the label's artists. But in November 1924 he reached the charts himself for the first two of fifty-four times with

Victor 19416, "Tell Me You Forgive Me" and "Charley, My Boy," the latter featuring Billy Murray on vocals.

There is a neat dividing line in the middle of the 1920s in which a technological innovation accompanies a stylistic shift. After five years of dance-tempo instrumentals from Whiteman and the other popular bandleaders, and bravura, stage-derived novelties and ballads from Jolson and other comic singers, the public taste began to shift to more sedate fare. That shift was accompanied by the introduction of the electrical condenser microphone, which vastly improved the sound of records. Rather than playing or singing into a large horn, artists could now "work the microphone"; the sound quality of instrumental recordings was vastly improved, and vocalists were freed from the earlier shouting style to employ a more intimate, "crooning" sound. In July 1925 Columbia Records electrically recorded the Associated Glee Clubs of America, said to number 4,800 voices, singing "Adeste Fideles" and "John Peel" for the first popular record under the new format, and by the fall the major labels had gone over to the new process.)

Gene Austin was among the first vocalists to switch to employing an unforced tenor rather than bellowing. His earliest recordings for Victor were not made electrically, but most of his catalog was, helping him become the most successful singer of the second half of the 1920s. Austin was born Eugene Lucas in Gainesville, Texas, in June 1900. After service in World War I, he went to the University of Maryland while leading a dance band on the side, and soon his taste for show business overcame his academic aspirations; by 1923 he was performing in vaudeville. In 1924 he cowrote "When My Sugar Walks Down the Street" with Jimmy McHugh and publisher Irving Mills, and recorded it as a duet with Aileen Stanley for Victor on January 30, 1925. It became a hit, and Austin followed it with his first solo recording, "Yearning (Just for You)," which did even better. By September, he had his first number-one hit, the frolicsome "Yes Sir, That's My Baby."

In addition to "Yes Sir, That's My Baby" and "All Alone," 1925 featured several song standards among its top hits. Irving Caesar and Vincent Youmans's "Tea for Two," recorded by Marion Harris for

Brunswick, was one of the two big hits from the musical *No, No, Nanette* (the other was "I Want to Be Happy," given its most popular recording as an instrumental by Vincent Lopez and His Orchestra on OKeh). The show took a long and circuitous route to Broadway, and the songs were hits long before the New York opening in September 1925, which helped the box office. Meanwhile, Isham Jones and his lyric partner, Gus Kahn, quietly continued to turn out evergreens from their base in Chicago, their biggest hit for the year being "I'll See You in My Dreams," which Jones, leading Ray Miller's Orchestra, recorded as an instrumental for Brunswick. (Marion Harris, also on Brunswick, had the most successful vocal version.) Ben Bernie helped his own cause by cowriting "Sweet Georgia Brown" with Maceo Pinkard and Ken Casey and recording a best-selling instrumental version. (Ethel Waters had a popular vocal recording on Columbia.) Al Jolson was the first to perform "If You Knew Susie," but he discarded it; it was taken up by Eddie Cantor, for whom it became a number-one hit and a signature song.

The Broadway songwriting team of Richard Rodgers (music) and Lorenz Hart (lyrics) had a long gestation period before scoring a success with the first edition of *The Garrick Gaieties* in May 1925. Their first hit song, taken from that show, was "Manhattan" ("I'll take Manhattan / The Bronx and Staten Island, too"), which "the Knickerbockers" (actually Ben Selvin and His Orchestra) recorded as an instrumental for a chart-topping hit on Columbia. And Irving Berlin continued to score with wistful songs, marking the end of the year with the melancholy ballad "Remember," recorded as an instrumental by Isham Jones for Brunswick, with successful vocal renditions by Jean Goldkette and His Orchestra (as sung by Seymour Simons), on Victor, and Cliff Edwards.

Whitburn lists five instrumental recordings among the top-ten hits of 1925, following five in 1924, four in 1923, five in 1922, seven in 1921, and five in 1920. But in 1926 there was only one: Vincent Lopez's OKeh disc of Irving Berlin's "Always," which was not as successful as the one by newcomer George Olsen and His Orchestra for Victor featuring a vocal trio. Clearly, things had changed. Paul Whiteman maintained his status as the decade's most successful recording artist by quickly adapting to the new vocal trend, using a variety of singers to keep scoring top hits. He had 1926's top record, "Valencia (A Song of Spain)," from the musical *Great Temptations*; it was the first of his number-one hits to feature a vocalist, Franklyn Baur. In December he returned to the top of the charts with "The Birth of the Blues," introduced by Harry Richman in *George White's Scandals*, which featured a vocal trio. Other bandleaders took a similar tack: Jan Garber employed Benny Davis, the song's lyricist, to sing "Baby Face" on Victor, and was rewarded with the year's second-biggest hit. And Ben Bernie used Arthur Fields on "Sleepy Time Gal" for a number-one hit on Brunswick.

The major singers of the year also performed such schmaltzy, good-time songs. Gene Austin made hits out of the eventual evergreens "Bye Bye Blackbird" and "Five Foot Two, Eyes of Blue (Has Anybody Seen My Gal)." Al Jolson, toning down his usual vocal pyrotechnics somewhat, swung his way through the previously mentioned chart-toppers "I'm Sitting on Top of the World" and "When the Red, Red Robin Comes Bob, Bob, Bobbin' Along." Characteristic of the quieter style of singers was the popular success of the vocalist billed as "Whispering" Jack Smith, who topped the charts in June with "'Gimme' a Little Kiss (Will 'Ya'? Huh?)" on Victor.

The relationship between Broadway and the record business was growing stronger, primarily through the musical theater providing a source of songs recorded for hits, but also by way of performers. One such performer was bandleader George Olsen, whose recording of "Always" was his second-biggest hit of 1926, the year he reached national recognition. Olsen was unusual in that his band often served as the pit orchestra for musicals, beginning when Fanny Brice arranged for it to appear in Eddie Cantor's show *Kid Boots*, which opened December 12, 1923. Starting on September 23, 1925, Olsen and his band played at the New Amsterdam Theatre for *Sunny*, a musical with songs composed by Jerome Kern with lyrics by Oscar Hammerstein II and Otto Harbach. Olsen recorded "Who?" from the score, using a male vocal trio, and it became a million seller.

Two long-term record sellers made their chart debuts in 1926. If jazz was imprecisely defined in the 1920s, that is not to say that jazz as we now know it was not being played; in fact, some of the genre's great innovators first began to be heard during the decade. Many jazz fans would date the start of modern jazz at 11 p.m. on the night of July 8, 1922. That was the moment a train arrived in Chicago from New Orleans carrying twenty-year-old Crescent City native Louis Armstrong, summoned by bandleader King Oliver to add his cornet to Oliver's jazz band. Two years later Armstrong moved to New York, and in November 1925 he began recording under his own name for OKeh, first hitting the charts in July 1926 with an instrumental version of "Muskrat Ramble" played by his Hot Five. Before the end of the decade, he had waxed such classics as "Struttin' with Some Barbecue," "West End Blues," and the Andy Razaf/Fats Waller classic "Ain't Misbehavin'" (from the musical revue *Hot Chocolates*).

Armstrong was always known as a joyous performer, but Ruth Etting, who followed him into the charts for the first time in August 1926, was the classic torch singer. Born in David City, Nebraska, in November 1896, she first gained notice in nightclubs in Chicago under the guidance of her manager-husband Martin (Moe the Gimp) Snyder, a gangster who later shot, but did not kill, her pianist (and second husband) Mryl Anderson. (The colorful story is told, with Hollywood glitz, in the 1955 movie musical *Love Me or Leave Me* starring Doris Day and James Cagney.) Before that happened, Etting went to New York, signed to Columbia Records, and debuted on the charts with "Let's Talk About My Sweetie," although she really made her mark by appearing in the *Ziegfeld Follies of 1927*, starting August 16, 1927, and singing songs like Irving Berlin's "Shaking the Blues Away."

Record sales appear to have peaked in 1927 at a figure of around 140 million copies, but that is a deceptive number, because the unit sales were inflated by the dumping of records from the acoustic era at discount prices by the major labels. The industry's gross revenues, $69.9 million, tells a more accurate story, considering that the figure for 1921, the real peak for the decade, was $106 million. Revenues dropped steadily through 1925, then recovered in 1926 and increased slightly but steadily through the end of the decade.

One song driving sales in late 1927 was Gene Austin's megahit "My Blue Heaven." His Victor record had sales estimated to be as high as 5 million copies, making it the second best-selling disc until it was unseated by "White Christmas" fifteen years later (unless the estimates for "The Prisoner's Song" are correct). Austin earlier topped the charts in 1927 with "Tonight You Belong to Me" and "Forgive Me." Paul Whiteman nearly kept pace with Austin for the year, hitting number one with his own instrumental version of "My Blue Heaven" and with "In a Little Spanish Town ('Twas on a Night Like This)," which featured a vocal by Jack Fulton, plus two number-two hits and three number-three hits. Although jazz fans rightly scoff at Whiteman's billing as the "King of Jazz," he was stocking his outfit with future jazz stars at this point. Saxophonist Jimmy Dorsey was already in the band, soon joined by his brother, trombonist Tommy Dorsey. Cornetist Bix Beiderbecke came to the band in 1928. And among the vocalists Whiteman was carrying by 1927 was a member of the Rhythm Boys trio, Bing Crosby.

Among the other notable songs to become record hits in 1927 were a revival of "Some of These Days" remade by Sophie Tucker (who had scored the original 1911 hit) backed by Ted Lewis and His Band on Columbia; "Me and My Shadow," recorded by "Whispering" Jack Smith for Victor; "Ain't She Sweet" recorded by Ben Bernie with vocals by Scrappy Lambert and Billy Hillpot; "Russian Lullaby," recorded by Roger Wolfe Kahn and His Orchestra with vocals by Henri Garden for Victor; the reported million-selling revival of the 1903 copyright "Ida! Sweet as Apple Cider" as an instrumental by Red Nichols and His Five Pennies for Brunswick; Irving Berlin's "Blue Skies," written for Belle Baker to sing in the musical *Betsy*, recorded by "the Knickerbockers" (the Ben Selvin orchestra), with another popular version by George Olsen; "I'm Looking Over a Four-Leaf Clover," recorded by Nick Lucas, and by Ben Bernie, with vocals by Scrappy Lambert, both for Brunswick; and the classic George and Ira Gershwin ballad "Someone to Watch Over Me," introduced by Gertrude Lawrence in the 1926 musical *Oh, Kay!* and recorded by her for Victor, with a popular instrumental version by George Olsen.

The most auspicious chart debut of 1927 was that of Guy Lombardo and His Royal Canadians, who scored a long-running number-one hit the first time out with "Charmaine!," with vocals by Weston Vaughan, on Columbia. Lombardo, born Gaetano Alberto Lombardo in London, Ontario, in June 1902, studied violin as a child (as a bandleader, he didn't play). He formed his first band, featuring two of his brothers, at the age of twelve. It was based in Cleveland as of 1924, the year it made its first recordings for Gennett. Three years later came the Columbia contract, beginning forty years of chart appearances.

An equally long run of chart appearances was enjoyed by the major jazz-related act to debut with a hit in 1927, Duke Ellington, whose instrumental "East St. Louis Toodle-oo" (music by Bubber Miley and Ellington), credited to "Duke Ellington and His Washingtonians," appeared in July on Columbia. Ellington, born in Washington, D.C., in April 1899, studied piano and became a professional musician in his teens. He moved to New York with the Washingtonians in September 1923 and began recording in 1924. On December 4, 1927, he and his band opened at the Cotton Club in Harlem, beginning a five-year residency that would establish them as a major force in jazz.

The technological innovation that had the greatest impact on recorded music toward the end of the 1920s was the arrival of talking motion pictures. It had been technically possible to synchronize sound to film many years before the talkies came, but the large motion picture studios weren't interested. Finally, upstart studio Warner Bros. launched the sound era with *The Jazz Singer*, starring Al Jolson, in October 1927. The film's success demonstrated the public's interest, and before long the movies were talking and, frequently, singing.

Jolson's second film, *The Singing Fool*, provided him with two number-one hits on the same million-selling Brunswick disc, the maudlin "Sonny Boy" and the exuberant "There's a Rainbow 'Round My Shoulder," demonstrating the promotional power of motion pictures on popular music. Gene Austin, without a movie deal (although he did turn to film acting later, as his singing career declined), managed to keep pace with Jolson for the year, scoring two number-one hits of his own with the gold-selling "Ramona," a song written to promote the silent film of the same name, and "Jeannine (I Dream of) Lilac Time," the theme song of the film *Lilac Time*. But Paul Whiteman outdistanced both of them, managing five of the year's ten highest-charting records, including his version of "Ramona," with vocals by Austin Young; and the Jerome Kern–Oscar Hammerstein II classic "Ol' Man River" from the 1927 musical *Show Boat*, the first major hit to be given a solo vocal by Bing Crosby.

Among the other memorable songs to emerge on record in 1928 were Dorothy Fields and Jimmy McHughs's jazz classic "I Can't Give You Anything but Love" from the musical *Blackbirds of 1928*, given a number-one treatment by Cliff Edwards (billed as Ukelele Ike) on Columbia; "I Wanna Be Loved by You" from the musical *Good Boy*, in which it was sung by Helen Kane, who added the nonsense phrase "boop-boop-a-doop" every eight bars, making her name, and recorded it for Victor; "Sweet Sue—Just You," in two versions, one by Ben Pollack, with Franklyn Baur on vocals, for Victor, and the other by Earl Burtnett and His Los Angeles Biltmore Hotel Orchestra, with vocals by the Biltmore Trio, for Columbia; "When You're Smiling," recorded by Seger Ellis and His Orchestra for Columbia; and the P.G. Wodehouse and Jerome Kern ballad "Bill," interpolated into *Show Boat*, by Helen Morgan, who introduced it onstage, for Victor.

By 1929 the era of instrumental dance hits was practically over; Whitburn lists only one instrumental, Ted Lewis's Columbia revival of the 1922 song "Farewell Blues," among the year's forty top record hits. Bandleaders were still able to score number-one hits, but they all did so with vocalists. Many of these hits were drawn from popular films of the day, showing the move beyond vaudeville and Broadway as the only popularizers of song hits. The Copley Plaza Orchestra had "Pagan Love Song," from the film *The Pagan*, with vocals by Frank Munn, on Brunswick; Leo Reisman had "The Wedding of the Painted Doll," from the film *The Broadway Melody*, with vocals by Lew Conrad; Guy Lombardo had "Sweethearts on Parade," with vocals by the song's lyricist, his brother Carmen; Paul Whiteman had "Great Day," from the musical of the same name, with vocals by Bing

Crosby, on Columbia (Whiteman having switched from Victor during 1928); and George Olsen had "A Precious Little Thing Called Love," from the film *Shopworn Angel*, with vocals by Ethel Shutta. But the top records of the year were all by solo singers like Nick Lucas, who sang Joe Burke and Al Dubin's "Tip-Toe thru the Tulips with Me," which he had introduced in the film *Gold Diggers of Broadway*, on Brunswick; Gene Austin, who sang "Carolina Moon" on Victor; and Al Jolson, who sang the heart-tugging "Little Pal," which he had introduced in the film *Say It with Songs*.

There was one notable addition to this list of solo singers, even though he was nominally a bandleader. Rudy Vallée, born in Island Pond, Vermont, in July 1901, grew up in Maine and developed his talents at singing and playing the saxophone in his youth. He paid for his tuition at Yale with his band work. After graduating in 1927 he put together a band to open at the Heigh-Ho Club in New York in January 1928. A radio wire made Vallée and his group, the Connecticut Yankees, popular nationally. Starting in 1929 he had a string of hits, first on Harmony Records and then on Victor; "Honey" (music by Richard A. Whiting, lyrics by Seymour Simons and Haven Gillespie) became one of the biggest hits of the year.

The final year of the 1920s produced several other songs that remain memorable, including the number-one hits, Nacio Herb Brown and Arthur Freed's "Singin' in the Rain," introduced by Cliff Edwards in the film *Hollywood Revue of 1929*; and Gene Clarke and Herb Akst's "Am I Blue?," introduced by Ethel Waters in the film *On with the Show*, both of whom also made the hit records. Other song hits of the year include "Makin' Whoopee," introduced in the musical *Whoopee* by Eddie Cantor and recorded by him for Victor; "You're the Cream in My Coffee," introduced in the musical *Hold Everything* and recorded by Ben Selvin, with vocals by Jack Palmer; "Ain't Misbehavin'," recorded by Leo Reisman, with Lew Conrad on vocals, for Victor; "I'll Get By as Long as I Have You," recorded by Ruth Etting; Sigmund Romberg and Oscar Hammerstein II's "Lover, Come Back to Me," introduced in the musical *The New Moon*, recorded by Paul Whiteman, with Jack Fulton on vocals; "She's Funny That Way," recorded by Gene Austin; Rodgers and Hart's "With a Song in My

Heart," introduced in the musical *Spring Is Here*, recorded by Leo Reisman, with Ran Weeks on vocals; and DeSylva and Brown and Henderson's "Button Up Your Overcoat," introduced in the musical *Follow Thru*, recorded by Helen Kane.

Even before the stock market crash of October 24, 1929, that devastated the record business along with the economy of the world, the last year of the decade marked significant changes. Record sales stood at 65 million copies, with gross revenues of $75.1 million, which culminated a three-year upward trend. Yet the industry was being overtaken by the radio business, as RCA's acquisition of the country's largest record company, Victor, indicated. Meanwhile, Edison Records quietly closed its doors. But the music-publishing companies were having even more trouble, and in 1929 many of them were purchased by the movie studios, providing the studios with a pipeline for songs to use in their many film musicals.

In retrospect, the decade of the 1920s initiated trends that would be played out during the rest of the century. Both radio and sound films would be boons to the record industry, serving as a means of promoting music that consumers would want to acquire. Individual stars would succeed in several media, becoming far more important than the songs they sang. And subgenres of popular music, like country and blues, would continue to influence more mainstream music when not simply outselling it. Little of this was apparent at the time, however, and, in any case, it was all about to be sidetracked by the Depression, which threatened the record business's very survival.

STORMY WEATHER

Cotton Club
presents

ETHEL WATERS
GEORGE DEWEY WASHINGTON

in

COTTON CLUB PARADE

22nd EDITION

with

DUKE ELLINGTON
AND HIS FAMOUS ORCHESTRA

STORMY WEATHER
HAPPY AS THE DAY IS LONG
RAISIN' THE RENT
GET YOURSELF A NEW BROOM
AND SWEEP THE BLUES AWAY
CALICO DAYS
MUGGIN' LIGHTLY

lyrics and music by
TED KOEHLER
HAROLD ARLEN

STAGED BY
DAN HEALY
DANCES BY
ELIDA WEBB • LEONARD HARPER

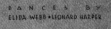

MILLS MUSIC
Music Publishers
1619 Broadway • New York N.Y.

4

THE 1930s

BROTHER, CAN YOU SPARE A DIME?

The 1930s began two months after the stock market crash that signaled the start of the Great Depression and ended four months after the European powers declared war on each other for the second time in the century. These two events shaped the decade, affecting all aspects of life in the United States, including the recording industry. The business had reached its peak in the early years of the 1920s and by the end of that decade was holding its own against the insurgence of radio as well as talking—and singing—motion pictures. Both those competing media would prove more resilient against the effects of the Depression, however. By 1930 there were 12 million radios in American homes, broadcasting music and entertainment without charge (although they subjected the listener to advertisements), an important factor when money became tight for everyone. In Hollywood, movie musicals were all the rage, with dozens of these films in production in 1930 and Broadway songwriters like Rodgers and Hart and the Gershwin brothers traveling west to write songs for them. But when none of these films became a box-office hit, the studios just as quickly turned away from movie musicals, not returning to them until one became successful in 1933.

Now that they had gone over to using vocalists, bandleaders were able to reassert their dominance of popular music. In 1929 five solo singers—Nick Lucas, Gene Austin, Al Jolson, Cliff "Ukelele Ike" Edwards, and Ethel Waters—had number-one hits. In 1930, for the second year in a row, there was only one instrumental record among the forty biggest hits, Paul Whiteman's revival of the 1924 song "Nobody's Sweetheart." But for fifty-one out of fifty-two weeks, the number-one spot was occupied by a vocal record credited to a bandleader, the sole exception being the week of March 1, when "Puttin' on the Ritz" (music and lyrics by Irving Berlin), introduced by Harry Richman in the film of the same name and recorded by him for Brunswick, reigned. Of course, one might argue that Rudy Vallée, the nominal leader of the Connecticut Yankees, who wielded a baton but really wasn't much more than a vocalist, was really a solo singer and that the ten weeks he spent at number one with the biggest record of the year, an unlikely revival of the twenty-year-old "Stein Song," the official song of the University of Maine, should be counted against the bandleaders. If so, that still leaves fifty-one weeks of dominance.

The most successful newly written song of the year was "Dancing with Tears in My Eyes," written for, but ultimately not used in, the film *Dancing Sweeties*. Nat Shilkret, employing vocalist Frank Munn, had the biggest hit with it, and there was also a popular recording by the Regent Club Orchestra on Brunswick. Paul Whiteman's only number-one hit of 1930, sung by Jack Fulton, came with "Body and Soul," an English import introduced by Gertrude Lawrence on the BBC and previously recorded by single-named British bandleader Ambrose. Whiteman's hit came in October just as it was being interpolated into the Broadway revue *Three's a Crowd*. Libby Holman, who sang it in the show, also had a hit version on Brunswick.

In an economy measure, Whiteman had dispensed with one of his vocal trios, the Rhythm Boys, consisting of Harry Barris, Bing Crosby, and Al Rinker, after completion of his movie musical *King of Jazz*. The Rhythm Boys stayed on in Hollywood, however, and found a one-time job with Duke Ellington, recording the vocals for "Three Little Words" (music by Harry Ruby, lyrics by Bert Kalmar) to be used in the Amos 'n' Andy film *Check and Double Check*. (The white Rhythm Boys were not seen onscreen; instead, the vocals seemed to be coming from black members of Ellington's band.) When RCA Victor released the recording, it went to number one in late November.

Another major song and eventual standard from 1930 was "Little White Lies" (music and lyrics by Walter Donaldson), most successfully recorded by Fred Waring's Pennsylvanians. There was a compet-

ing version by Ted Wallace and His Campus Boys, with Elmer
Feldkamp on vocals, for Columbia, which was that band's biggest hit.
Walter Donaldson, again writing both words and music, also gave
Guy Lombardo and His Royal Canadians their number-one hit for
the year with "You're Driving Me Crazy! (What Did I Do?)." (Rudy
Vallée's version peaked at number three in January 1931.)

Two songs each generated two number-one hit recordings in 1930.
"When It's Springtime in the Rockies" got two weeks at the top from
the recording by the Hilo Hawaiian Orchestra, with vocals by Frank
Luther and Carson Robison, on RCA Victor, and another three from
Ben Selvin. Selvin, the only recording artist to have two number-one
hits in 1930, also spent two weeks at the top with a song forever ironically associated with the start of the Depression, "Happy Days Are
Here Again" (music by Milton Ager, lyrics by Jack Yellen). Written
for the film *Chasing Rainbows*, it was given its most successful recording by Benny Meroff and His Orchestra, with vocals by Dusty
Rhodes, on Brunswick; a third version, by Leo Reisman, with Larry
Levin on vocals, was also popular. In 1932 New York governor Franklin D. Roosevelt used it as a campaign song in his successful run for
the presidency. Another number-one hit to emerge from the movies
was "Chant of the Jungle," introduced in the Joan Crawford picture
Untamed. Roy Ingraham and His Orchestra took it to the top for
Brunswick, outdistancing a competing version by Nat Shilkret, who
had Frank Munn sing it.

Both of the notable debut artists of the year were bandleaders.
Ozzie Nelson, born in March 1906 in Jersey City, New Jersey, began
a dance band after graduating from Rutgers University, featuring
himself on vocals and saxophone. By 1930 he was contracted to Brunswick, getting a hit with "I Still Get a Thrill (Thinking of You)," the
first of thirty-eight chart entries he would score through 1940. In
1930 he was still two years away from hiring Harriet Hilliard as his
vocalist and five years away from marrying her, leading to the successful radio and TV series *The Adventures of Ozzie and Harriet* and, in
the 1950s, the stardom of their son Ricky. Wayne King, the "Waltz
King," born in Savanah, Illinois, around 1901, worked in various jobs
outside music before finding a berth as a clarinetist with the Del

Lampe Orchestra. Starting his own band, he concentrated on waltzes while based at Chicago's Aragon Ballroom. The first of his thirty-six chart entries came with his instrumental RCA Victor revival of the 1915 tune "Song of the Islands" in March 1930.

The Depression was only in its first year in 1930, but the record business quickly felt the sting. Revenues fell from $75 million in 1929 to $46 million, a decline of nearly 40 percent. It was only the beginning.

Don Azpiazu and His Havana Casino Orchestra's had 1931's biggest hit with their sole chart record, the rhumba song "The Peanut Vendor" (a.k.a. "El Manisero"), with vocals by Antonio Machin, on Victor. Otherwise, the year belonged to more well-known names. Wayne King had the best year of his career on records, placing eight titles in the charts. The most successful of them, which nearly matched "The Peanut Vendor" in popularity, was the British song "Goodnight, Sweetheart," sung for King by Ernie Birchill. Guy Lombardo's version, with vocals by Carmen Lombardo, gave the tune enough weeks at number one to consider it the song of the year, especially because solo singer Russ Columbo also had a popular recording of it for RCA Victor. King's other number one hit for the year was the evergreen "Dream a Little Dream of Me," also with an Ernie Birchill vocal.

But two number-one hits were not enough to make King the top bandleader of 1931, not when Guy Lombardo had three number ones and seven of the forty biggest hits of the year. In addition to his "Goodnight, Sweetheart," Lombardo also topped the charts with "By the River St. Marie" and "(There Ought to Be a) Moonlight Saving Time," both also featuring Carmen Lombardo vocals. Hal Kemp and His Orchestra, with vocals by Skinnay Ennis, also had a hit recording of the latter song on Brunswick, the first substantial success for a bandleader who would have most of his big hits in 1936 and 1937.

Yet Lombardo's impressive performance did not make him the most successful recording artist of the year. That honor went to a debut artist, albeit one who had topped the charts earlier in other guises. He would go on to be the biggest pop singer of the 1930s *and* the 1940s. Harry Lillis "Bing" Crosby, born in May 1903 in Tacoma,

Washington, had grown up in the Northwest and headed to Los Angeles with his friend Al Rinker in 1925, where they eventually hooked up with Paul Whiteman, who added Harry Barris to create the Rhythm Boys vocal trio. They sang in various combinations on Whiteman's records, including many hits from 1927 to 1930, and then made their single appearance with Ellington on his chart-topping "Three Little Words." Meanwhile, they were also singing with Gus Arnheim's Orchestra at the Cocoanut Grove in the Ambassador Hotel in Los Angeles and recording with him for RCA Victor. In early 1931 Crosby was featured on Arnheim's recording of "I Surrender, Dear," which became a number-three hit. With that, Crosby was ready to make his move.

In February, Crosby signed a solo recording contract with Brunswick, and by May he was at number one with his solo single "Out of Nowhere." Significantly, at a time when record sales were falling, Crosby did not rely only on his recordings, but branched into other fields of entertainment. At the end of 1930 he had appeared briefly in the film *Reaching for the Moon*, a picture that had started out with a full Irving Berlin score, only to have all but one of the songs cut when the studio decided musicals were out of public favor. Unbilled, Crosby sang the one remaining song, "When the Folks High Up Do the Mean Low Down." In April 1931 he began filming the first of six short films for director Mack Sennett (the 1930s equivalents of music videos). In August, after scoring a second number-one hit, "Just One More Chance," he was hired by the CBS radio network and given his own show, premiering on September 2, which began his decades of broadcasting. Meanwhile, Crosby's third Brunswick single, "I Found a Million-Dollar Baby," from the musical *Crazy Quilt*, peaked at number two, outdistanced by the number-one recording of Fred Waring (vocals by Clare Hanlon), but Crosby returned to number one with "At Your Command" (which he took co-credit for writing along with ex-partner Harry Barris, and Harry Tobias). In all, Crosby placed eight recordings among the forty biggest hits of the year.

Oddly, Gus Arnheim's only number-one hit for the year, and the biggest hit of his career, did not feature a Crosby vocal. It was "Sweet and Lovely" (music and lyrics by Arnheim, Harry Tobias, and Jules

Lemare), and its vocalist was Donald Novis. In addition to Crosby and the one-hit wonder Don Azpiazu, the only other act to debut among the ten top records of the year was another long-lived Brunswick signee, the Mills Brothers, who revived "Tiger Rag" in their inimitable harmony style for a four-week run at number one at the end of 1931. The African-American vocal quartet of John Mills Jr., Herbert Mills, Harry F. Mills, and Donald F. Mills hailed from Piqua, Ohio, where they were born between 1911 and 1915 and began singing as children. They got their professional start on the radio in Cincinnati in the late 1920s and moved up to CBS and their Brunswick contract in 1931. Their records were still reaching the charts thirty-eight years later.

A third Brunswick newcomer scoring his first number-one hit in 1931 wasn't quite a chart debut, having placed a minor showing for a revival of "St. Louis Blues" under the billing of the Jungle Band in late 1930, but he was making his first entry under his own name. That was Cab Calloway, topping the charts with his signature song, "Minnie the Moocher (The Ho De Ho Song)" (music and lyrics by Cab Calloway, Clarence Gaskill, and Irving Mills). Born in Rochester, New York, on Christmas Day, 1907, Calloway was raised in Baltimore and Chicago, and he was leading a band while still attending high school and later led groups in Chicago and New York. He made his Broadway debut in *Hot Chocolates* in June 1929 and began recording for Brunswick in 1930. In February 1931 he and his band replaced Duke Ellington as the resident orchestra at the Cotton Club, where he introduced "Minnie the Moocher."

Two other musical artists who had their first successes on records in 1931 are worth mentioning. In addition to being the coauthor of "Goodnight, Sweetheart," Ray Noble was a British bandleader born in Brighton in December 1903. He initially intended to become a doctor like his father and studied medicine at Cambridge before moving to the Royal Academy of Music. His songwriting and arranging abilities eventually led to a job with HMV Records as head of light music (the British term for popular, as opposed to classical, music), which in turn put him in charge of a studio band called the New Mayfair Orchestra. RCA Victor, HMV's American affiliate, began to release his recordings with the orchestra in the United States, and his first chart record came in September 1931 with "Lady of Spain."

Because of his enormous success on the screen, one tends to think of Fred Astaire as a dancing movie star, but he was one of the biggest musical theater stars of the 1920s and among the ten most successful recording stars of the 1930s. He was born in Omaha, Nebraska, in May 1899, and the course of his life was largely determined by his older sister, Adele, whom he accompanied to dancing school. The two danced in vaudeville and then crossed over to the legitimate stage in the Broadway revue *Over the Top* in 1917. In 1923 they made their recording debut in London, singing songs from their show *Stop Flirting*. They also recorded songs from two shows in which they starred in London that featured the music of George Gershwin, *Lady, Be Good!* (1924) and *Funny Face* (1927). "My One and Only" (music by George Gershwin, lyrics by Ira Gershwin) was Astaire's first American chart entry when it was issued by Columbia in 1929. In 1931 he and his sister were appearing in their last show together before her marriage and retirement, the Broadway revue *The Band Wagon*, when Astaire made his first American recordings of two songs from the show, "I Love Louisa" and "New Sun in the Sky" (both music by Arthur Schwartz, lyrics by Howard Dietz), acting as the vocalist for Leo Reisman's Orchestra for RCA Victor, and they both reached the top ten.

The most successful song from *The Band Wagon* is one of several standards that became record hits in 1931. The Dietz-Schwartz standard "Dancing in the Dark" was given number-three recordings by both Bing Crosby and Fred Waring, the vocal on the latter by, as they were billed, "Three Waring Girls." Other notable songs of the year included "Just a Gigolo," given a number-one recording by Ted Lewis and also recorded by Ben Bernie; "When the Moon Comes Over the Mountain," the first big hit by Kate Smith (who also took writing credits along with Howard Johnson and Harry Woods) on Columbia; Hoagy Carmichael's immortal "Stardust," originally composed by him in 1927, with lyrics later added by Mitchell Parish and given a number-one instrumental recording by Isham Jones;

and the Depression-denying "Life Is Just a Bowl of Cherries," from the 1931 edition of *George White's Scandals*, recorded by Rudy Vallée.

The rise of singers like Vallée, Crosby, and Astaire, and the decline of singers like Al Jolson (who would give up recording for fourteen years after 1932) heralded the popularity of a more intimate vocal style, dubbed "crooning," that responded to the sensitivity of the recording microphones introduced in 1925, and of the conversational requirements of radio. It was significant that the crooners were finding their greatest exposure on radio. Record sales, meanwhile, continued to plummet. They dropped another 60 percent from 1930 to 1931 alone; a successful record that only a couple of years earlier might have approached sales of a million copies now struggled to sell 50,000. Sales would fall another 40 percent from 1931 to 1932, reaching revenues of $11 million on 10 million records sold. Record companies reacted by canceling most long-term contracts and hiring artists on a session-by-session basis, for which they paid flat fees, no royalties.

Although popular music tends to hew to romantic and upbeat subjects, the Depression began to creep into song lyrics. One of the most successful songs of 1932 was "In a Shanty in Old Shanty Town," introduced by Little Jack Little and His Orchestra and given a hit recording by Ted Lewis and His Band (with a competing one by Ted Black and His Orchestra, Chick Bullock on vocals, for RCA Victor), and another was "Let's Put Out the Lights and Go to Bed" (amended to "… Go to Sleep" in recordings), from *George White's Music Hall Follies* and recorded for hits by Rudy Vallée and by Paul Whiteman with Red McKenzie on vocals for RCA Victor, which noted, "No more money in the bank." But the virtual theme song of the Depression was lyricist E.Y. Harburg and composer Jay Gorney's "Brother, Can You Spare a Dime?," introduced in the Broadway show *Americana* in October and quickly recorded by Rudy Vallée (who began with a spoken disclaimer) and Bing Crosby for number-one hits in 1932. The plaintive cry of a "forgotten man" who had fought in World War I and built American prosperity in the 1920s, only to find himself out of work in the '30s, it was one of the few genuine protest songs to achieve massive and long-lasting popularity.

But it was already becoming clear by the end of 1932 that Broadway, Hollywood, and the music business had an alternate response to the Depression, one that would play much better than references to shanties and begging for handouts in song. The biggest hit of 1932 emerged at the end of the year. It was Cole Porter's "Night and Day," from the Broadway musical *Gay Divorce* starring Fred Astaire in his first—and only—stage appearance without his sister. As with "I Love Louisa," Astaire sang the vocal refrain on the hit recording by Leo Reisman's Orchestra. The song's success was an indication that a nation petrified by the fear of destitution still could react favorably to romantic fantasies expressed in a sophisticated manner. Astaire, of course, went to Hollywood, where, despite initial misgivings, he proved to be a major star, creating a happy-go-lucky persona dressed in a tuxedo, gliding across polished dance floors with Ginger Rogers.

The artists who shared the shrinking pie of record sales in 1932 included many of the same names that had dominated 1931. In addition to "Night and Day," Leo Reisman scored a number-one hit with "Paradise" from the film *A Woman Commands*, a song that also provided one of Guy Lombardo's four number-one hits. The other three were: "We Just Couldn't Say Goodbye," which also generated a hit recording by Paul Whiteman, with vocals by Mildred Bailey; "Too Many Tears"; and, the only one not to feature the singing of Carmen Lombardo, "River, Stay 'Way from My Door," cobilled to Kate Smith.

In addition to "Brother, Can You Spare a Dime?," Bing Crosby topped the charts with "Please" and a revival of the 1925 song "Dinah," performed with the Mills Brothers. Crosby sang both songs in his first starring role in a feature film, *The Big Broadcast*, the success of which led to a long-term contract with Paramount Pictures. And George Olsen had two number-one hits, Irving Berlin's plaintive ballad "Say It Isn't So," with Paul Small on vocals, and "Lullaby of the Leaves." Along with "Brother, Can You Spare a Dime?" and "Paradise," one other 1932 song generated two number-one renditions: the long-lived standard "All of Me" (music and lyrics by Seymour Simons and Gerald Marks), recorded by Paul Whiteman, with Mildred Bailey on vocals, and by Louis Armstrong.

Both of the notable debut artists of the year were emerging out of existing units. Pianist Eddy Duchin started out with Leo Reisman, with whom he gained renown before launching his own orchestra. Signed to Columbia, he debuted on the charts with "Snuggled on Your Shoulder (Cuddled in Your Arms)" in 1932, and his instrumental version of "Night and Day" went to number two in early 1933. Connie Boswell was the leading light of the Boswell Sisters but she also began recording solo and, oddly, in doing so changed the spelling of her first name to "Connee." Signed to Brunswick, she had a top-ten version of "Say It Isn't So" in 1932.

After releasing a flurry of movie musicals in the years immediately after the onset of talkies, Hollywood had abandoned the genre when the glut (or the low quality) kept audiences away. But that changed in 1933. The breakthrough came with *42nd Street*, which opened in March and told the already familiar backstage story of a chorus girl who becomes a Broadway star. It marked the film debut of Ruby Keeler and brought recognition to choreographer Busby Berkeley, who designed its elaborate dance sequences. Its score, by composer Harry Warren and lyricist Al Dubin, included "You're Getting to Be a Habit with Me," "Young and Healthy," and "Shuffle Off to Buffalo," all of which became hits. "You're Getting to Be a Habit with Me" went to number one for Guy Lombardo with Bing Crosby on vocals, a teaming of the two biggest stars of the day, with Crosby's number-two recording of "Young and Healthy" on the B-side; and "Forty-Second Street" topped the charts for Don Bestor and His Orchestra, with Dudley Mecum, an RCA Victor single that placed a number-two recording of "Shuffle Off to Buffalo," with a vocal by Maurice Cross, on the B-side (there was also a number-two recording by Hal Kemp, with Skinnay Ennis on vocals). *42nd Street* showed that audiences were interested in movie musicals with fantasy plots and big production numbers, and Hollywood proceeded to supply them.

The most popular song of 1933, generating no less than five recordings that placed at numbers one, two, or three, was the surprise hit "The Last Round Up," a cowboy song introduced by

George Olsen with Joe Morrison on vocals. Two versions reached number one, Olsen's recording and Guy Lombardo's with vocals by his brother Carmen, trailed by Don Bestor with Neil Buckley on vocals, Bing Crosby, and Victor Young and His Orchestra with the Songsmiths on vocals for Brunswick. The only other song to generate multiple number-one recordings was Ted Koehler and Harold Arlen's classic "Stormy Weather." The song later came to be associated with Lena Horne, who sang it in a film of the same name released a decade later, but the first time around composer Arlen himself, fronting Leo Reisman's Orchestra, had the biggest hit, followed by Ethel Waters, who had introduced it at the Cotton Club, and, further down the chart, Duke Ellington in an instrumental treatment, both for Brunswick.

Nineteen thirty-three also saw the first hit recordings of a number of well-remembered songs including "Lazybones" (music and lyrics by Johnny Mercer and Hoagy Carmichael), a number-one hit for Ted Lewis; "Did You Ever See a Dream Walking?" (from the film *Sitting Pretty*), a number-one hit for Eddy Duchin with Lew Sherwood on vocals and a number-two hit for Guy Lombardo with Carmen Lombardo on vocals; "Who's Afraid of the Big Bad Wolf?" (from the animated film *The Three Little Pigs*), a number-two hit for Don Bestor with Florence Case, Frank Sherry, and Charles Yontz on vocals and a number-three hit for Victor Young; "Just an Echo in the Valley," a number-two hit for Bing Crosby, who introduced it on radio and interpolated it into his film *Going Hollywood*, and a number-three hit for Rudy Vallée; "Willow Weep for Me" (music and lyrics by Ann Ronell), a number-two hit for Paul Whiteman with Irene Taylor on vocals; "Lover" (music by Richard Rodgers, lyrics by Lorenz Hart, from the film *Love Me Tonight*), a number-three hit for Paul Whiteman with Jack Fulton on vocals; "Yesterdays" (music by Jerome Kern, lyrics by Otto Harbach, from the musical *Roberta*), a number-three hit for Leo Reisman with Frank Luther on vocals; "I Cover the Waterfront" (written to promote the film of the same name and later incorporated on the soundtrack), a number-three hit for Eddy Duchin with Lew Sherwood on vocals; and "Sophisticated Lady" (music by

Duke Ellington, lyrics later added by Mitchell Parish), a number-three instrumental hit for Ellington.

All of the notable chart debuts for 1933 were by bands. The Casa Loma Orchestra, a collective, was named after the Toronto nightclub where it started. The first of its sixty-four chart records was the instrumental "Casa Loma Stomp" on OKeh in 1931, but "Under a Blanket of Blue" on Brunswick was its first top-ten hit. After 1934 saxophonist Glen Gray fronted the band, and the records usually billed him as the star. Freddy Martin, born in Cleveland in December 1906, learned to play music while growing up in an orphanage. He took over the band of Arnold Johnson and opened at the Hotel Bossert in Brooklyn in October 1931. Signed to Columbia in 1932, he had his first top-ten hit with "In the Park in Paree" (from the film *A Bedtime Story*) with Elmer Feldkamp on vocals; the disc was credited to the Hotel Bossert Orchestra. Then Martin switched to Brunswick and began recording under his own name.

None of the good music made in 1933 was enough to keep the record business from teetering on the brink of extinction. For the year, only $6 million was generated, a decline of more than 94 percent since the peak of 1921. It would be another twelve years before revenues recovered to and passed the 1921 figure, but 1933 would at least prove to be the bottom. One major development that helped begin to turn things around was the repeal of Prohibition, which occurred on December 5, 1933. With alcohol legal again in the United States, bars and clubs began to open, and many of them started to use jukeboxes. The coin-operated record-playing machines began to have an important impact on the record industry, which supplied the discs. By 1936 there were 150,000 of them operating in the country, and they were accounting for 40 percent of all records sold.

Record labels and trade magazines had maintained and published sales charts haphazardly for decades, but in the mid-1930s regular rankings of popular songs began to become available. On September 5, 1933, *Variety* began publishing a weekly list of the ten most popular songs in the country. And on April 20, 1935, the weekly *Your Hit Parade* radio show went on the air, counting down the top hits. In addition to measuring popularity, these charts also served to promote the songs they listed, tending to focus attention on a few songs and recordings.

By 1934 the wave of solo singers had largely subsided, with one exception. At the top of the pop music world, dividing up the bulk of the meager $7 million in record sales for the year, were a group of dance bands … and Bing Crosby. Crosby, reigning in the movies, where he made three pictures a year (in 1934, he starred in the features *We're Not Dressing, She Loves Me Not*, and *Here Is My Heart*), and on radio, where he appeared weekly on the CBS series *The Woodbury Soap Show*, attracting as much as 25 percent of the listening audience, also ranked as the country's top record seller. In 1934 he had three number-one hits, "Little Dutch Mill," "Love in Bloom" (from *She Loves Me Not*), and "June in January" (from *Here Is My Heart*), and two number twos, "Good Night, Lovely Little Lady" and "Love Thy Neighbor" (both from *We're Not Dressing*). The only other songs to place among the forty top hits of the year not made by bands were "One Night of Love," introduced by opera singer Grace Moore in the film of the same name and recorded by her for a number-one hit on Brunswick; "Sleepy Head" from the film *Operator 13*, recorded for a number-two hit by the Mills Brothers; and "Hands Across the Table," introduced by French cabaret performer Lucienne Boyer in the musical *Continental Varieties* and recorded by him for a number-two hit on Columbia.

Crosby's dominance, and his unusual position as a solo singer, made it all the more significant when he suddenly switched record labels in 1934. In September, Jack Kapp, former recording director of Brunswick Records, started an American branch of the British-based Decca Records. Kapp was able to get the new label off the ground immediately because he had developed personal relationships with his artists at Brunswick and brought many of them over to the new venture, not only Crosby, but also Guy Lombardo and the Mills Brothers. Also, he took the action the record industry had tried to avoid since the start of the Depression: Decca cut prices, selling its records for 35 cents instead of the customary 75 cents. That made it harder to make a profit, of course, but eventually Decca moved up to join the ranks of the major labels. (Brunswick, meanwhile, went into decline, and its catalog was later divvied up between Decca and Columbia.)

The big bands that dominated popular music in 1934 were relatively well balanced in terms of their success. Ray Noble, Paul Whiteman, and Ted Fiorito each scored two number-one recordings. Noble spent eight weeks at number one with "The Old Spinning Wheel" and "The Very Thought of You," both sung by Al Bowlly; Whiteman occupied the top spot for seven weeks with "(When Your Heart's on Fire) Smoke Gets in Your Eyes" (music by Jerome Kern, lyrics by Otto Harbach, from the musical *Roberta*) and "Wagon Wheels" (from the *Ziegfeld Follies of 1933–1934*), both sung by Bob Lawrence; and Fiorito had six weeks in charge with "My Little Grass Shack in Kealakekua, Hawaii" and "I'll String Along with You" (from the film *Twenty Million Sweethearts*), both sung by Muzzy Marcellino, for Brunswick. Three other bandleaders, Jimmie Grier, Duke Ellington, and Eddy Duchin, each spent five weeks at number one.

The year produced many other standards. Guy Lombardo with brother Carmen on vocals had three hits, "Stars Fell on Alabama," "Riptide," written to promote the film of the same name, and the Christmas favorite "Winter Wonderland," for Decca. There were two competing versions of "The Continental," the first Academy Award–winning song, from the Fred Astaire and Ginger Rogers picture *The Gay Divorcée*, an instrumental version recorded by Leo Reisman, and a vocal duet by Roy Storm and Harold Van Emburgh, backed by Jolly Coburn and His Orchestra, for RCA Victor. Other notable hits were two instrumental versions of "Carioca," from another Astaire and Rogers pairing, *Flying Down to Rio*; "Cocktails for Two," from the film *Murder at the Vanities*, recorded by Duke Ellington as an instrumental for RCA Victor; "Let's Fall in Love," from the film of the same name, recorded by Eddy Duchin with Lew Sherwood on vocals; "Stay as Sweet as You Are," from the film *College Rhythm*, recorded by Jimmie Grier and His Orchestra with Harry Foster on vocals for Brunswick; "You're the Top" from the Cole Porter musical *Anything Goes*, recorded by Paul Whiteman with Peggy Healy and John Hauser on vocals; "Two Cigarettes in the Dark," from the film *Kill That Story*, recorded by Johnny Green and His

Orchestra with George Bouler on vocals for Columbia; "You Oughta Be in Pictures," from the *Ziegfeld Follies of 1933–1934*, recorded by Little Jack Little and His Orchestra for Columbia; and "I Only Have Eyes for You," from the film *Dames*, recorded by Ben Selvin with Howard Phillips on vocals.

Two important musicians made their popular debuts on records in 1934. Neither was really a newcomer. Fats Waller was born in May 1904 in New York and was taught to play keyboard instruments as a child by his mother. He began writing songs in his teens and first recorded in 1922. He made his Broadway debut by writing songs and playing in the pit for the all-black revue *Keep Shufflin'* in 1928. *Hot Chocolates* (1929) introduced his song "Ain't Misbehavin'," which he recorded as an instrumental for Victor, as well as "Honeysuckle Rose" (music also by Harry Brooks, lyrics by Andy Razaf), and over the next few years he composed such hits as "Keepin' Out of Mischief Now" (lyrics by Andy Razaf) while appearing frequently on radio. In May 1934 he was signed again to RCA Victor and quickly blossomed into a successful recording artist, starting with the top-ten disc "I Wish I Were Twins" (music by Joseph Meyer, lyrics by Frank Loesser and Eddie DeLange).

Benny Goodman, soon to be crowned the "King of Swing," was born in May 1909 in Chicago and began taking clarinet lessons at a synagogue at the age of ten. At fourteen, he dropped out of high school to become a full-time musician. He joined Ben Pollack's band in 1925, staying four years and leaving in September 1929 to settle in New York as a session musician. His first chart record came with a studio band in 1931, "He's Not Worth Your Tears" with Scrappy Lambert on vocals for Melotone. In 1933 he began recording for Columbia under the auspices of jazz promoter John Hammond. "Ain'tcha Glad?" (music by Fats Waller, lyrics by Andy Razaf), with Jack Teagarden on vocals, gave him his first top-ten hit in early 1934. In July, he had his first number-one hit with an instrumental treatment of "Moonglow." By then, he had organized a permanent band for live performances.

Goodman wasn't the only studio musician testing his wings in this way. The repeal of Prohibition served as a signal to a generation of musicians who had been biding their time in New York recording sessions and Broadway pit bands that the time had come to make their move. Tommy and Jimmy Dorsey had been cutting the occasional side as the Dorsey Brothers Orchestra since the late 1920s, but in 1934 they launched their band as a permanent touring outfit, using their friend Glenn Miller as arranger. Hiring Bing Crosby's younger brother Bob as their vocalist, they enjoyed rapid success, topping the charts in May 1935 with Al Dubin and Harry Warren's classic "Lullaby of Broadway" (from the film *Golddiggers of 1935*) on Decca and in June with "Chasing Shadows," featuring new vocalist Bob Eberly, who replaced Bob Crosby when Crosby accepted an invitation to front his own band. (Crosby's first chart-topper came with "In a Little Gypsy Tea Room" on Decca in July.) Unfortunately, by June 1935 the Dorsey Brothers Orchestra had ceased to exist. The feuding brothers had split up at the end of May, with Tommy going off to start his own band and Jimmy eventually turning the remaining ensemble into Jimmy Dorsey and His Orchestra.

Fred Astaire, partnered with Ginger Rogers in a supporting role in *Flying Down to Rio* in 1933, had attained Hollywood stardom with her in 1934's *The Gay Divorcée*, and that success was repeated in the screen adaptation of *Roberta*, released in February 1935. But the Astaire-Rogers screen partnership arguably reached a peak, at least as far as music was concerned, with their fourth picture, *Top Hat*, which featured five newly written songs by Irving Berlin. Brunswick Records, having lost Bing Crosby, may have been trying to replace him by signing up Astaire, and they had him record studio versions of the film songs. All five made the top ten, and "Cheek to Cheek" spent eleven weeks at number one, making it the song and record of the year for 1935. It inspired two other versions, by bandleaders Eddie Duchin and Guy Lombardo, both of which reached number two on the charts. Astaire's "Top Hat, White Tie, and Tails" also got to number two.

In a sense, Astaire occupied the position for 1935 that Crosby had in 1934, the major solo singer for the year. Of course, Crosby himself was still around, in fact scoring three number-one hits—with Richard Rodgers and Lorenz Hart's songs "It's Easy to Remember" and

"Soon," both of which he introduced in the film *Mississippi*, and "Red Sails in the Sunset"—but they gave him only a total of five weeks at number one. (He also hit number two with "I Wished on the Moon," which he had introduced in *The Big Broadcast of 1936*.) Ruth Etting spent a couple of weeks at the top with "Life Is a Song" on Columbia, as did the Boswell Sisters with "The Object of My Affection" on Brunswick. But that was it for solo singers; thirty-two of the forty top hits of the year were by bands.

The most successful of those bands were Eddy Duchin's and Russ Noble's. With vocalist Lew Sherwood, Duchin had three number-one hits and two number twos. The top hits were "Lovely to Look At" and "I Won't Dance" (from the film *Roberta*) and "You Are My Lucky Star" (from the film *Broadway Melody of 1936*). Noble also had three chart-toppers: "Isle of Capri" and "Paris in the Spring" (from the film of the same name), both with vocals by Al Bowlly; and, in between, "Let's Swing It," with vocals by the Freshmen. Trailing these leaders were Glen Gray and the Casa Loma Orchestra and Guy Lombardo and His Royal Canadians, both scoring two number ones. With vocalist Kenny Sargent, Gray's top hits were "Blue Moon" (music by Richard Rodgers, lyrics by Lorenz Hart) and "When I Grow Too Old to Dream" (music by Sigmund Romberg, lyrics by Oscar Hammerstein II, from the film *The Night Is Young*). Carmen Lombardo sang with brother Guy for their top hits, "What's the Reason" (from the film *Times Square Lady*) and "Red Sails in the Sunset."

Not surprisingly, the notable newcomers of 1935 were also mostly bandleaders. Tommy Dorsey, having split from his brother, managed to put together a working unit and get into the charts on RCA Victor before the end of the year. Trombonist Tommy was born in Shenandoah, Pennsylvania, in November 1905, the son of a band director, and trained in brass instruments from a young age. With his older brother Jimmy, who played reeds, he began forming bands as early as 1920. Throughout the 1920s, they played in various bands including the Paul Whiteman Orchestra. In the late '20s, they settled in New York as session musicians. After the split-up, Tommy Dorsey arranged to take over a band formerly led by Joe Haymes. His first chart record was also his first number-one hit, "On Treasure Island," with vocals by Edythe Wright.

Russ Morgan, another trombonist turned bandleader, didn't debut quite so high with his first chart record in 1935, the instrumental "Tidal Wave," released by Columbia, but he did make the top ten. Morgan was also a Pennsylvania native, born in Scranton in April 1904. He learned various instruments in his youth in an attempt to escape the region's coal mines. By 1921 he was playing in bands. Morgan worked as both a musician and arranger for various bands during the 1920s. He was playing in Freddy Martin's band in 1935 when he had the opportunity to start his own unit, which got a residency at the Biltmore Hotel in New York, and earned the Columbia contract. Although he charted records throughout the rest of the 1930s and '40s, Morgan's biggest hits would come at the end of the '40s.

Annunzio Paolo Mantovani, who first reached the charts with an instrumental cover of "Red Sails in the Sunset" on Columbia in November 1935, was another bandleader who would gain his greatest success in later decades. Born in Venice, Italy, in November 1905, he was the son of a classical violinist who moved to London in 1912. He studied violin at Trinity College and made his professional debut at sixteen. But he was attracted to popular music and soon was leading bands. After his initial success in the 1930s, he wouldn't reach the charts again until the early '50s.

Brunswick 7498, "What a Little Moonlight Can Do," marks the chart debut both for its band and, separately, for its singer. Pianist Teddy Wilson was born in November 1912 in Austin, Texas, and studied music at Tuskegee Institute and Talladega College before adopting the career of a traveling musician. He was in New York from 1933, playing with Benny Carter and others, and by 1935 was appearing with Benny Goodman. He was credited as the bandleader on "What a Little Moonlight Can Do," backing vocalist Billie Holiday. The story of Holiday's difficult childhood after her illegitimate birth in Philadelphia in April 1915 has been much recounted. By 1929 she was living in New York and starting to work as a singer. She made her first recordings as the vocalist on recordings by Benny Goodman, including "Riffin' the Scotch," which became a top-ten hit on Columbia in early 1934. But her Brunswick sessions with Wilson, which began in July 1935, were her first as a top-billed artist.

On February 3, 1935, Martin Block began broadcasting a radio show on WNEW in New York called *Make Believe Ballroom*, on which he spun records while pretending they were coming from a live performance by bandleader Clyde McCoy. He even pretended to speak to McCoy. Three years earlier, Al Jarvis had begun playing records on a Los Angeles station, his show called *The World's Largest Make-Believe Ballroom*, but the Block show set a pattern for what came to be called disc jockeys. The record labels had resisted the playing of their records over the air, fearing (as always) a loss of sales due to free dissemination of their product. In 1938 Paul Whiteman even sued WNEW to prevent it from playing his records (a precursor to Metallica's fight against Napster more than sixty years later). But over time, radio became the chief means of promoting record sales by playing records.

The other major event in popular music for the year 1935 occurred on August 21 at the Palomar Ballroom in Los Angeles. Benny Goodman and His Orchestra had been touring the United States to a decidedly lukewarm response. But in Los Angeles, the band's late-night New York radio show, *Let's Dance*, had been heard in prime time, creating an audience for its sound. And when Goodman resignedly decided to go down swinging at the Palomar, instructing his musicians to play some of the hot charts he had bought from black bandleader Fletcher Henderson, the crowd went wild. It was the birth of the Swing Era.

Goodman's triumph was reflected in the record charts of 1936. He had five number-one hits, amassing eighteen weeks at the top of the charts, all with vocals by Helen Ward: "Goody-Goody," "It's Been So Long," "The Glory of Love," "These Foolish Things Remind Me of You" (from the London musical *Spread It Around*), and "You Turned the Tables on Me" (from the film *Sing, Baby, Sing*). Confirming the prominence of the new swing sound, Tommy Dorsey was the year's runner-up with three chart-toppers: "The Music Goes 'Round and 'Round" and "You" (from the film *The Great Ziegfeld*), both with Edythe Wright on vocals; and, in between, "Alone" (from the Marx Brothers film *A Night at the Opera*), with vocals by Cliff Weston.

As usual, Fred Astaire and Bing Crosby were the only solo singers to score major hits. Astaire hit number one with three releases: Irving Berlin's "I'm Putting All My Eggs in One Basket," from his fifth movie with Ginger Rogers, *Follow the Fleet*; and the Dorothy Fields and Jerome Kern classics "A Fine Romance (A Sarcastic Love Song)" and "The Way You Look Tonight," both from the sixth Astaire-Rogers picture, *Swing Time*. Crosby, meanwhile, had to content himself with having the biggest record of the year, with ten weeks at number one, "Pennies from Heaven," which he had introduced in the film of the same name.

The arrival of the swing bands tended to push aside the recordings of the society dance orchestras that had dominated pop music for over a decade, but Eddy Duchin managed a final flourish, scoring four number-one hits in 1936, plus one released late in the year that topped the charts at the start of 1937: "Moon over Miami" and "Lights Out," both with vocals by Lew Sherwood; "Take My Heart," with vocals by Jerry Cooper; "I'll Sing You a Thousand Love Songs" (from the film *Cain and Mabel*), with vocals by Jimmy Newill; and Cole Porter's "It's De Lovely" (from the musical *Red, Hot and Blue!*), with vocals by Jerry Cooper.

The notable acts premiering on the charts in 1936 were of course all swing bands, and by now swing was so big it had broken into two types, "hot" and "sweet," the hot bands including more jazz improvisation, the sweet ones less. The distinctions were sometimes fine, but they have affected how the bands are viewed historically. Jimmy Dorsey, born in Shenandoah, Pennsylvania, in February 1904 and with a background similar to his brother's, straddled the sweet and hot designations. After his brother walked out on him, he managed his first big hit with the chart-topper "Is It True What They Say About Dixie?," with Bob Eberly on vocals, for Decca, although his biggest successes would come in the early 1940s.

Artie Shaw would never have accepted the "sweet" tag. The clarinetist, born in New York in May 1910, began playing his instrument at the age of twelve and worked in various bands until 1936, when the swing fad made it possible for him to become a leader. He first reached the top ten with "There's Frost on the Moon" for Brunswick in December 1936, but later reorganized and really hit his stride on RCA Victor's discount-priced Bluebird label in 1938.

On the other hand, Shep Fields—who topped the charts for the first time in August 1936 with "Did I Remember" (from the film *Suzy*), with vocals by Charles Chester, for Bluebird—had no problem with being called sweet. He and his Rippling Rhythm Orchestra scored thirty-eight hits through 1943. Even more successful in the sweet category was Kay Kyser, who began charting for Brunswick in 1935, but got his first top-ten hit, a revival of the 1927 song "Did You Mean It?," in 1936. Kyser was born in Rocky Mount, North Carolina, in June 1905, the child of pharmacists. He intended to follow his parents' profession, but went astray while attending the University of North Carolina at Chapel Hill and formed a dance band. Kyser's flair for comedy found an outlet on radio, and that in turn stimulated his record sales.

By 1937 individual records were starting to sell in big numbers for the first time since the late 1920s. Jeanette MacDonald and Nelson Eddy's recording of "Indian Love Call," which they had sung in the movie version of the operetta *Rose Marie*, became a hit in late 1936 and is thought to have sold a million copies. So did Tommy Dorsey's imaginative arrangement of Irving Berlin's "Marie" (which he obtained from a black band) and Bing Crosby's Academy Award–winning "Sweet Leilani" (from his film *Waikiki Wedding*), both of which were recorded in the early months of 1937.

Crosby was holding his own against the onslaught of swing, but only a handful of other male singers continued to score hits. In the winter of 1937–38, however, a female trio entered the rarefied ranks of nonband hitmakers with a seemingly unlikely song, the Yiddish show tune "Bei Mir Bist Du Schoen," which, they helpfully sang, "means that you're grand." LaVerne, Maxene, and Patty Andrews were an anomaly, and it was natural that most of their hits were novelty songs, but they enjoyed a long, successful career.

The Swing Era hit something of a peak on January 16, 1938, when Benny Goodman played Carnegie Hall. (The show was recorded and

later released on LP.) Goodman may already have been past his popular peak, and his band was about to fragment, with star trumpeter
Harry James already recording separately and drummer Gene Krupa
about to start his own band. But Goodman was also a victim of his
own success, which created extensive competition, notably Artie
Shaw, whose new band swept all before it in 1938 with its recording
of Cole Porter's "Begin the Beguine."

Like Shaw, Glenn Miller failed with his first attempt to lead a
band. His second attempt, beginning in 1938, was only a qualified
success until the spring of 1939, when he began recording for Bluebird and scored a summer residency at the Glen Island Casino in New
Rochelle, New York, from which he made radio broadcasts. The
result was the kind of recording success that has occurred only rarely
in history. Miller scored seven consecutive number-one hits, remaining at the top of the charts for twenty-five weeks in a row with
"Wishing (Will Make It So)," "Stairway to the Stars," "Moon Love,"
"Sunrise Serenade," the Yip Harburg and Harold Arlen classic "Over
the Rainbow" from the film *The Wizard of Oz*, "The Man with the
Mandolin," and Hoagy Carmichael's "Blue Orchids."

As 1939, and with it the 1930s, came to a close, the record industry
had recovered much, but not all of the ground it had lost in the first
years of the decade, selling nearly 70 million units. The decade to
come would present different challenges, foreshadowed by two events
before the close of the year. Over the Labor Day weekend, war broke
out in Europe. The United States was neutral in the struggle, but the
new war would come to dominate the first half of the 1940s. Within
the music business, the founding on October 14 of Broadcast Music
Incorporated (BMI), a music licensing organization specifically
designed to compete with ASCAP, presaged both a period of conflict
in the industry that would include public squabbles between musicians and record labels, and an influx of non–Tin Pan Alley compositions into the mass market that would transform popular music in the
second half of the twentieth century.

But all that was yet to come. As 1939 ended, the nation continued to swing, buoyed by Glenn Miller's biggest hit yet, "In the
Mood."

5

THE 1940s

WAR AT HOME, WAR ABROAD

The obvious thing to say about the 1940s, the decade during which most of World War II was fought, is that it was a time of conflict. The war had a powerful effect on the music business, robbing it of manpower and materials, and making travel, a musician's necessity, more difficult. (Not all of the effects were negative; when a G.I., at the end of the war, brought back from Germany an early tape recorder, it was the beginning of a major technological innovation in radio and recording.) But conflict was the constant of the industry in the 1940s not just because of the war, but also because of a series of contentions within various aspects of the business that helped alter its structure as well as the direction of popular music.

What were these lesser wars that were fought in the world of music during the decade? To take them in roughly chronological order, the battles were: ASCAP versus radio, along with radio's ally, BMI; the American Federation of Musicians (AFM) versus the record companies, a war that was fought twice within the ten years; the major record companies versus a growing crop of small independents; record companies versus radio; traditional mainstream popular music versus rising genres such as hillbilly (a.k.a. country) and race (a.k.a. R&B) music; and big bands versus solo singers. These were not, of course, all separate battles; many of them were interrelated. The war between ASCAP and radio, for example, helped lead to the rise of country and R&B (and, eventually, rock 'n' roll), while the fight between the AFM and the record companies contributed to the triumph of the solo singers over the big bands in the second half of the decade.

At the start of the 1940s, the only war being fought was the one in Europe, about which the United States was claiming neutrality. In the music business, things were going well. The Depression was fading, and the rise of swing music in the mid-1930s had served as a stimulus to record sales and the concert business. Sales had not yet returned to their levels of the early 1920s, but they were growing steadily. Nineteen thirty-nine had seen the rise of a new star, orchestra leader Glenn Miller, and he continued to dominate the music business during 1940, starting with his massive instrumental hit "In the Mood" (music by Joe Garland, lyrics added later by Andy Razaf). According to the questionable ratings of the radio series *Your Hit Parade*, the tune never got higher than number nine, but *Billboard*'s jukebox chart had it as a long-running chart-topper, and it is remembered as one of Miller's most successful recordings, reportedly selling over a million copies. Miller also hit number one in 1940 with the instrumental "Tuxedo Junction" and "The Woodpecker Song," with Marion Hutton on vocals, and he was by far the most successful recording artist of the year.

Miller's style of music, big band swing, was at a peak of popularity. Of the twelve records that topped *Billboard*'s jukebox or Best Selling Retail Records charts (the latter instituted on July 27) in 1940, all but two were by big bands. Notable among them were Artie Shaw's instrumental "Frenesi," which, like "In the Mood," stayed at number one for thirteen weeks, and Tommy Dorsey's "I'll Never Smile Again," with Frank Sinatra and the Pied Pipers on vocals, which had a twelve-week run at the top. The success of these three records, combining for thirty-eight weeks at number one, made for the smallest number of new chart-toppers in a single year since 1933.

The two exceptions to the big band rule were a revival of the 1916 song "Sierra Sue" and "Only Forever," both by Bing Crosby, who introduced the latter in his film *Rhythm on the River*. Crosby, the top recording star of the 1930s, was something of an anomaly by the start of the 1940s. According to Joel Whitburn, Crosby, the third-biggest recording artist of 1940, behind Miller and Tommy Dorsey, was one of only two solo singers among the top twenty, the other being Dick Todd (number twelve), who made the list by virtue of his number-four hit "The Gaucho Serenade" on Bluebird. The list also included two vocal groups, the Ink Spots (number four) and the Andrews Sisters (number eight), but sixteen of the twenty were bandleaders.

Glenn Miller, naturally, had his pick of the best material, and he made hits out of several songs that became standards, including "When You Wish upon a Star" from the animated film *Pinocchio*; "Blueberry Hill"; "A Nightingale Sang in Berkeley Square," from the London musical *New Faces*; and "Fools Rush In (Where Angels Fear to Tread)," all with vocals by Ray Eberle (brother of Bob Eberly of the Jimmy Dorsey band who, unlike his sibling, had not changed the spelling of his name to make the pronunciation clearer). Tommy Dorsey, meanwhile, had the hit version of "All the Things You Are" from the musical *Very Warm for May*, with Jack Leonard on vocals. And Will Bradley and His Orchestra Featuring Ray McKinley and Freddie Slack took advantage of the boogie-woogie craze with their hit version of "Beat Me Daddy (Eight to the Bar)," its two parts spread across the two sides of Columbia single 35530, the band's chart debut.

Of the two major artists to enjoy their first hits in 1940, one was a solo vocalist and the other, while leading a band, was essentially a singer fronting an orchestra. Tony Martin (actually Alvin Morris), born on Christmas Day in 1912 in San Francisco, was a saxophone player for bandleader Tom Gerun, who then began to sing and act. He started appearing in films in 1936 and had his first chart entry in 1938, though his first top ten-hit came in April 1940 on Decca with "It's a Blue World," which he introduced in the movie *Music in My Heart*. Vaughn Monroe was born in October 1911 in Akron, Ohio. He grew up in Wisconsin, where he won a statewide trumpet contest at fifteen. He paid for college by playing and singing in bands, then dropped out to turn professional. By 1939 he was leading his own band, which earned him an RCA Victor contract, and he first reached the top ten with "There I Go" in December 1940.

The big bands were even more dominant in 1941, when, except for Crosby (number four), the list of the top twenty recording artists consisted entirely of groups. Once again, Miller was on top, this time followed by Jimmy Dorsey, with Tommy Dorsey coming in third. (These are Whitburn's rankings, based on chart positions. Russell

Sanjek tells a different story; "Miller's total sales were surpassed by both the Dorsey brothers," he writes of this period.)

Examining the hits of 1941, one notices a curious phenomenon, a preponderance of foreign adaptations—including the year's biggest hit, Jimmy Dorsey's million-selling recording of "Amapola (Pretty Little Poppy)" with Bob Eberly and Helen O'Connell on vocals—and of adaptations of classical music, including the year's third-biggest hit, Freddy Martin's instrumental recording of "Piano Concerto in B Flat," based on the music of Tchaikovsky (and later the basis for a vocal version, "Tonight We Love," with lyrics by Bobby Worth), another million seller. While popular music has always welcomed novelties, there was a specific reason for the success of this material. The song licensing organization ASCAP, which extracted performance fees from radio, attempted to raise its rates when its new contract came up at the start of 1941. Seeing the increase coming, radio had helped the formation of a rival organization, BMI, in 1939. Nevertheless, ASCAP controlled the work of all the major, established songwriters of the day. Radio held firm, however, and on January 1, 1941, all ASCAP songs were banned from radio broadcast. Suddenly, the songs of nineteenth-century songwriter Stephen Foster were all over the radio, along with much unusual material.

Jimmy Dorsey enjoyed the biggest year of his career in 1941. In addition to the million-selling "Amapola," he topped the charts with four more exotic (i.e., non-ASCAP) songs: "My Sister and I"; two more million sellers, "Maria Elena" and "Green Eyes (Aquellos Ojos Verdes)"; and "Blue Champagne." Bob Eberly provided vocals on all four, joined by Helen O'Connell on "Green Eyes."

But despite that success, Dorsey was edged out of being the year's top artist by Glenn Miller, who placed nineteen songs in the charts, including three number ones: the instrumental "Song of the Volga Boatmen" (another non-ASCAP item); "Chattanooga Choo Choo," which the Miller band introduced in the film *Sun Valley Serenade*, with Tex Beneke, Paula Kelly, and the Modernaires on vocals; and "Elmer's Tune," sung by Ray Eberle. (The last two came toward the end of the year, after the ASCAP ban ended.) On February 10, 1942, RCA Victor sprayed gold paint on a disc and presented Miller with the first "gold record" for sales of 1 million copies of "Chattanooga Choo Choo." It was only a promotional gimmick, and there would not be a means for certifying record sales for another sixteen years, but it was indicative of the continuing resonance of the million-sale mark in the record business.

Nineteen forty-one was not a good year for new artists, but one important singer got her first hit early on. Dinah (actually Frances Rose) Shore had been born in March 1917 in Winchester, Tennessee, and raised in Nashville. She sang locally while attending Vanderbilt University and made a first stab at a career in New York in 1937 before returning home to finish her studies. Then she returned and got a job on WNEW. By August 1939 she had her own radio series, and she began recording with Xavier Cugat's band. Her solo records on Bluebird began coming out in 1940, and in January 1941 she had her first top-ten hit, "Yes, My Darling Daughter."

It took ASCAP and radio until the fall of 1941 to come to terms, and by that time BMI was well established and a lot of music outside of the strict pop traditions favored by ASCAP had had a hearing. With Tin Pan Alley, Broadway, and Hollywood writers largely sewn up by ASCAP, BMI was forced to look further afield, and it began, for the first time, to license the work of country and R&B writers, which it then had an interest in promoting. Over time, this had the effect of transforming the sound of popular music.

No sooner had the ASCAP war ended than the United States entered World War II following the Japanese attack on Pearl Harbor on December 7, 1941. The music industry had already begun to feel the effects of the war with the institution of a peacetime draft in 1940. Now, with the country not just on a war footing, but actually at war, things became even more difficult. Having produced 130 million records in 1941, the best sales since 1921, the record companies faced a shortage of materials—particularly the shellac used in manufacturing discs—that led to old records being ground up to make new ones.

And there was yet another problem unrelated to the war effort. AFM president James Petrillo was concerned about the increased use of recordings on radio in place of live musicians and, defying the government's no-strike policy, called out his union, at least as far as recordings were concerned, in an effort to wring concessions from the record companies with regard to royalties. As of August 1, 1942, musicians stopped going into recording studios to make new records.

The result of the war and the strike was that 1942 marked the end of an era in the music business. In one way, things looked much the same. Once again, 130 million records were produced, and most of them were big band recordings. With the end of the ASCAP ban, the major songwriters were back in charge, the year's biggest hit being Irving Berlin's "White Christmas," recorded for a million seller (and, eventually, many more millions) by Bing Crosby, who introduced it on radio and in the film *Holiday Inn*. Of the top twenty artists, sixteen were big bands, the exceptions being Crosby, Shore, the Andrews Sisters, and Kate Smith. Glenn Miller was on top yet again. He had three of the year's eight number-one hits (the smallest number of new chart-toppers since 1905, in Whitburn's estimation): the instrumental "A String of Pearls," "Moonlight Cocktail," with vocals by Ray Eberle, and the million-selling "(I've Got a Gal in) Kalamazoo," which the Miller band introduced in the film *Orchestra Wives*, with vocals by Tex Beneke, Marion Hutton, and the Modernaires.

The remaining number-one hits of the year were Woody Herman's reading of the standard "Blues in the Night (My Mama Done Tol' Me)," from the film of the same name, on Decca; "Tangerine" by Jimmy Dorsey with vocals by Bob Eberly and Helen O'Connell, which the Dorsey band introduced in the film *The Fleet's In*; the Harry James instrumental "Sleepy Lagoon" on Columbia; and Kay Kyser's million-selling "Jingle Jangle Jingle," from the film *The Forest Rangers*.

Not surprisingly, the American entry into the war led to several war-themed songs in the top ten. Kay Kyser particularly jumped on the patriotic bandwagon, recording the million-selling "Praise the Lord and Pass the Ammunition!," "He Wears a Pair of Silver Wings" and "(There'll Be Blue Birds over) The White Cliffs of Dover" (both with Harry Babbitt on vocals; the latter was also recorded by Glenn Miller with Ray Eberle on vocals and by Kate Smith), and "Johnny Doughboy Found a Rose in Ireland" (also cut by Guy Lombardo with Kenny Gardner on vocals). Other wartime favorites on the charts included "Don't Sit Under the Apple Tree (with Anyone Else but Me)" by Glenn Miller with Marion Hutton and Tex Beneke on vocals; "When the Lights Go On Again (All Over the World)" by Vaughn Monroe; the novelty "Der Fuehrer's Face," from the animated film *Donald Duck in Nutsy Land*, by Spike Jones with Carl Grayson on vocals for Bluebird; "I Left My Heart at the Stage Door Canteen," from Irving Berlin's musical *This Is the Army*, by Sammy Kaye with Don Cornell on vocals and by Charlie Spivak and His Orchestra with Garry Stevens on vocals for Columbia; and "Remember Pearl Harbor" by Sammy Kaye. In addition to these songs specifically addressing war issues, there was a rise in songs of romantic parting, resulting in top-ten placings for "I Don't Want to Walk Without You," from the film *Sweater Girl*, by Harry James with Helen Forrest on vocals and by Bing Crosby, and "Just as Though You Were Here" by Tommy Dorsey with Frank Sinatra and the Pied Pipers on vocals.

So, if, in general terms, everything seemed the same, in fact everything was different. Miller, following the lead of other bandleaders, including Artie Shaw, and many musicians, quit the band business to join the service in September 1942. (He later died overseas.) The bands that carried on not only had personnel and travel problems, but also were unable to make records. And at the end of the year, they were challenged by a new musical style embodied in one man, Frank Sinatra.

Sinatra's name has already turned up here as a singer in Tommy Dorsey's band, which he had joined in February 1940. He had also sung with Harry James in 1939, the first big break for the Hoboken, New Jersey, native born in December 1915 who had longed for a career in the music business from a young age. In September 1942 Sinatra took a step that had not worked for any male singer since the Swing Era began: he went solo. It would be hard to exaggerate the result. From December 30, 1942, when he began an engagement as opening act for Benny Goodman at the Paramount Theatre in New York, Sinatra was a sensation. He quickly built a career on personal appearances, radio, and film. Records, given the ongoing strike, were of course another story. Dorsey, who had stockpiled some recordings before the start of the recording ban when Sinatra was still with him, scored number-one hits in 1943 with "There Are Such Things," which went gold, and "In the Blue of the Evening," on which Sinatra sang. Columbia Records even rebilled and reissued Sinatra's recordings with Harry James, enjoying a gold-selling, number-two hit with the four-year-old "All or Nothing at All." And the record labels thought up a loophole to the musicians strike, bringing singers into the studio with *a cappella* groups. The union soon cried foul and got the sessions stopped, but not before Sinatra, signed to Columbia, scored a series of hits, starting with the number-two chart entry "You'll Never Know" from the film *Hello, Frisco, Hello.*

Sinatra's version of the song was actually outpaced by one recorded in a similar manner by his immediate rival, Dick Haymes. Haymes, born in Buenos Aires to a Scottish father and an Irish mother in September 1918, had dogged Sinatra's path for years, following him into both the Harry James and Tommy Dorsey bands, and had just recently sung with Benny Goodman before following Sinatra once again into solo singing. Although he had sung in his youth, Haymes's entry into professional vocalizing was inadvertent; when he pitched some of the songs he had written to James by singing them, James said he'd hire the singer rather than record the songs. Haymes left Tommy Dorsey in May 1943 with a solo offer from Decca Records; by July, his first single, "It Can't Be Wrong," a song version of the theme from the film *Now, Voyager*, was number two.

The success of Sinatra and Haymes was an early indication of a trend toward solo singers. In 1943, only twelve of the top twenty recording artists were bandleaders. Of course, the most successful of the singers remained Bing Crosby. Crosby said that Sinatra was the sort of performer who came along only once in a lifetime, adding "but why did it have to be my lifetime?" Although Crosby comically decried the rise of Sinatra, the growing trend toward solo singers actually benefited him. He had, of course, been consistently successful, but now he hit a new peak of popularity, returning to the top of the list among recording artists for 1943, his biggest hit being the million-selling "Sunday, Monday or Always," which he had introduced in the film *Dixie*, sung, as with the Sinatra and Haymes records, with only a vocal group backing. Other Crosby hits for the year included "I'll Be Home for Christmas (If Only in My Dreams)," another war-era holiday song with a theme of separation, selling a million copies the first time out; and lyricist Johnny Burke and composer James Van Heusen's "Moonlight Becomes You," which Crosby introduced in the Hope-Crosby "road" picture *Road to Morocco*. (Glenn Miller also scored a top-ten hit with it, using Skip Nelson as vocalist.)

An important factor in Crosby's renewed success was that Decca Records and the smaller record labels settled with the AFM on September 18, 1943, while RCA Victor and Columbia held out until November 11, 1944. Decca, naturally, rushed its artists into the recording studio and, with a fresh bunch of records, began a fourteen-month dominance of record stores that quickly included the Mills Brothers' gold-selling "Paper Doll," hitting number one for twelve weeks beginning in early November. Decca was also able to take advantage of a novelty song hit of late 1943, "Pistol Packin' Mama." Al Dexter, who wrote the song, had a number-one, gold-selling hit with it on OKeh, but Decca's cover version, by Bing Crosby and the Andrews Sisters, went to number two and also sold a million copies.

Decca's settlement with the AFM came late enough in the year that the other majors, Columbia and RCA Victor, were still able to make a good showing for 1943. Drawing on material made just before the start of the recording ban, Harry James had two number-one hits, including the biggest hit of the year, the million-selling "I've Heard That Song Before," from the film *Youth on Parade*, and "I Had the Craziest Dream," another million seller that James introduced in the film *Springtime in the Rockies*, both with Helen Forrest on vocals. Other early-1943 hits recorded before the ban included Benny Goodman's "Taking a Chance on Love," from the musical *Cabin in the Sky*, which, due to the musical chairs of band personnel, also had Helen Forrest on vocals; and Glenn Miller's "That Old Black Magic" (music by Harold Arlen, lyrics by Johnny Mercer), from the film *Star Spangled Rhythm*, with Skip Nelson on vocals.

There were a number of other new songs that went on to become standards, and 1943 also boasted a couple of notable revivals. Among the newly minted hits were the war-related "Comin' In on a Wing and a Prayer," a number-one disc for the Song Spinners on Decca (another of those *a cappella* recordings); the Portuguese samba import "Brazil (Aquarela do Brasil)," from the animated film *Saludos Amigos*, a hit instrumental for Xavier Cugat on Columbia; Duke Ellington's "Don't Get Around Much Anymore," which began its life as the instrumental "Never No Lament," to which Bob Russell added lyrics and a new title, reaching the top ten in an *a cappella* version by the Ink Spots and in a big band recording by Glen Gray and the Casa Loma Orchestra, both on Decca; Cole Porter's "You'd Be So Nice to Come Home To," from the film *Something to Shout About*, a hit for Dinah Shore; the bluesy "Why Don't You Do Right?," played by Benny Goodman and sung by his new female vocalist Peggy Lee in the film *Stage Door Canteen*, in addition to being recorded by them for a hit; and "Let's Get Lost," introduced by Mary Martin in the film *Happy Go Lucky*, a hit by Kay Kyser with Harry Babbitt and Julie Conway on vocals.

The revival of the year was Herman Hupfeld's "As Time Goes By." The 1931 song was introduced in the film *Everybody's Welcome* and recorded by Rudy Vallée at the time, but it didn't catch on until Dooley Wilson sang it as an important plot point in the classic film *Casablanca* in the fall of 1942. By then, no one was able to record a new version, so the 1931 Vallée disc and another of the same vintage by Jacques Renard and His Orchestra with Frank Munn on vocals for Brunswick each became top-ten hits. The year's other significant revival also owed its success to the movies. "For Me and My Gal" dated back to 1917, when there were a number of successful recordings, and was brought back to life by film stars Judy Garland and Gene Kelly, who sang it in a motion picture of the same name and recorded it for Decca.

The most important Broadway musical of 1943, and arguably the most significant show since *Show Boat* in 1927, was *Oklahoma!*, written by the newly created team of musical theater veterans Richard Rodgers and Oscar Hammerstein II. Until this time, Rodgers had written music for the lyrics of the talented, but increasingly unreliable, Lorenz Hart. Hammerstein, the lyricist and librettist of *Show Boat*, had written extensively with Jerome Kern, *Show Boat*'s composer, and others. Hart turned down the opportunity to create a musical version of the stage play *Green Grow the Lilacs*, and so a new musical theater pairing was born. *Oklahoma!* may not, as has been claimed, have been the first "integrated" musical in which the songs contributed to plot and characterization, but it made integration the goal of musical theater creators after it became an immense hit upon its Broadway opening on March 31, 1943, on its way to a run of 2,248 performances, making it the longest-running show in Broadway history up to its time.

The show had an equally revolutionary impact on the recording industry. Of course, it produced songs that became hits, notably "People Will Say We're in Love," given top-ten renditions by the duet team of Bing Crosby and Trudy Erwin and by Frank Sinatra in an *a cappella* treatment, and "Oh! What a Beautiful Mornin'," another duet between Crosby and Erwin. More important, when Decca Records took members of the Broadway cast (notably Alfred Drake and Joan Roberts, who played the starring roles of Curly and Laurey) into a recording studio to make an album of the show's songs, that marked the beginning of the "original cast album" as a popular seller. Containing six 78 rpm records and twelve musical selections, Decca 359, which, in the absence of an album chart, reached the top ten of the *Billboard* singles chart in December 1943 on its way to selling a million copies, was not the first cast album. That title may be claimed by Brunswick 20114/5/6/7 (later released as Columbia AC-55), the four-disc collection of songs from *Show Boat* recorded in 1932 and featuring Paul Robeson and Helen Morgan of that year's Broadway revival. But the *Oklahoma!* album was the first one to be a big seller, and it increased not only the major record labels' interest in recording other Broadway shows, but also their interest in recording multidisc albums of nonclassical music in general.

With major rivals Columbia and RCA Victor still locked out of the recording studios, Decca had a clear field to dominate record sales in 1944. No less than thirty of the forty most successful records of the year were released on the label. The top three recording artists were all contracted to Decca: Bing Crosby, repeating from 1943; the Andrews Sisters, several of whose hits were recorded with him; and Jimmy

Dorsey. Eight of the top ten artists recorded for Decca, the only exceptions being Columbia's Harry James and Frank Sinatra. Crosby had the number-one record during thirty-seven of the year's weeks, fourteen of those weeks shared with the Andrews Sisters, who also had nine weeks at the top by themselves. Solo, Crosby had the biggest hit of the year with the million-selling "Swinging on a Star" (music by James Van Heusen, lyrics by Johnny Burke), which he introduced in the film *Going My Way*. He also hit number one with "San Fernando Valley," "I Love You," from the Cole Porter musical *Mexican Hayride*, and a revival of the 1938 song "I'll Be Seeing You" from the musical *Right This Way*. ("I'll Be Seeing You," which also gave Tommy Dorsey and his former vocalist Frank Sinatra a top-ten hit with a reissue of a four-year-old recording, benefited from an unintended association with romantic separations caused by the war.) With the Andrews Sisters, Crosby had additional chart-toppers with the million-selling Cole Porter song "Don't Fence Me In" and the war-themed "(There'll Be a) Hot Time in the Town of Berlin (When the Yanks Go Marching In)." And the Andrews Sisters went to number one on their own with "Shoo-Shoo Baby."

As "Hot Time in the Town of Berlin" suggested, songwriters were still writing about the war, and with the tide turned in favor of the Allies the tone of the songs was increasingly jaunty. Louis Jordan went to number one with Johnny Mercer's "G.I. Jive" (the exuberant Jordan also reached number two with his co-composition, "Is You Is or Is You Ain't [Ma Baby]," written with Billy Austin, in close competition with a cover by Crosby and the Andrews Sisters); and Jimmy Dorsey, with Kitty Kallen on vocals, had a hit with the comic lament "They're Either Too Young or Too Old," from the film *Thank Your Lucky Stars*. There were more hits about separated lovers on the order of "I'll Be Seeing You," often with similar titles, notably the 1928 song "I'll Get By (As Long as I Have You)," revived by Harry James with Dick Haymes on vocals in a reissue recorded in 1941, and "I'll Walk Alone," introduced by Dinah Shore in the film *Follow the Boys*, with hit versions by her and by Martha Tilton on the recently formed Capitol Records label. (Capitol had been founded in 1942 by songwriter Johnny Mercer, songwriter turned film executive B.G. De Sylva, and Los Angeles record store owner Glenn Wallichs.)

As usual, there were several songs of no particular category that became evergreens. The novelty "Mairzy Doats," given a number-one rendition by the Merry Macs for Decca, looked forward to the silly songs of the late 1940s and early '50s; film composer and conductor David Rose and His Orchestra's million-selling "Holiday for Strings" on RCA Victor was one of the diminishing number of instrumental hits of the day; "The Trolley Song," from the film *Meet Me in St. Louis*, was a hit for both Judy Garland, who sang it in the picture, and the Pied Pipers on Capitol; and "Long Ago (and Far Away)," from the film *Cover Girl*, was one of the last great ballad hits composed by Jerome Kern, to Ira Gershwin's lyrics. The most popular record was by the team of Helen Forrest and Dick Haymes.

For the year, thirteen of the top twenty recording artists were vocal performers, not bandleaders. Among them were the African-American acts the Ink Spots, Ella Fitzgerald, Louis Jordan, and the Mills Brothers. (*Billboard*, in recognition of the sales of such performers, had begun a separate chart for them in 1942; in 1944, the magazine added a chart for country artists.) Not surprisingly, the major artists to score their first hits in 1944 were all singers. Perry Como, born in May 1912 in Canonsburg, Pennsylvania, started out as a barber before joining the band of Freddie Carlone in 1933, and then Ted Weems in 1935. Weems disbanded to join the Merchant Marines in late 1942, and Como planned to go back to haircutting, but the sudden success of Frank Sinatra inspired him to try for a solo career. Como was signed to RCA Victor in June 1943, and first reached the top ten with a cover of "Long Ago (and Far Away)" in 1944. Jo Stafford was another big band vocalist turned solo act. She was born in Caolinga, California, in November 1917, and formed a vocal group with her sisters that found work in the movies doing backgrounds. She moved on to being the sole female voice in the Pied Pipers, who were hired by Tommy Dorsey initially in 1938, and on a full-time basis in late 1939. They stayed with him until November 1942, then went off on their own, signing to Capitol Records, which recorded them as a group and Stafford solo. She, too, had her first top-ten hit with "Long Ago (and Far Away)" in 1944, and soon the Pied Pipers found a replacement as she concentrated on solo work.

The third notable top-ten debut artist of 1944 was the "King Cole Trio," as it was credited on disc, but its focal point was Nat "King" Cole. Born in March 1919 in Montgomery, Alabama, Cole was raised in Chicago, where he took piano lessons and was playing in local bands by his teen years. He first recorded with the Solid Swingers in 1936. By the late 1930s he was based in Los Angeles, where he began working with his trio. It was a jazz group, but featured vocals, and gradually Cole took over as sole singer. There were various recordings in the late 1930s and early '40s, including a stint on Decca. Their first session for Capitol in November 1943 produced "Straighten Up and Fly Right" (co-credited to Cole and publisher Irving Mills), Cole's first major hit.

With the war winding down and the complete settlement of the musicians strike, the music industry looked forward to a profitable postwar period; 1944's revenues of $109 million exceeded those of 1921, finally erasing the impact of the Depression. The new solo singers had been able to use the feelings provoked by the war to make an emotional connection with listeners that the big bands, so good at stirring the feet, never could. Many of the hits of 1944 had spoken of the longing for loved ones far away in the war zone. The hits of 1945 spoke of triumph ("Ac-Cent-Tchu-Ate the Positive," "I'm Beginning to See the Light") and reconciliation ("Sentimental Journey," "It's Been a Long, Long Time"). The big bands actually made a comeback among the top twenty artists, with twelve bandleaders versus eight vocalists. But with Crosby (at number one for the third straight year), Sinatra, and Perry Como all in the top five, the bands were on their way out.

"Ac-Cent-Tchu-Ate the Positive" was given its most successful recording by its lyricist, Johnny Mercer (the music was by Harold Arlen), but Bing Crosby, who sang it in the film *Here Come the Waves* and recorded it with the Andrews Sisters, ran a close second. "I'm Beginning to See the Light" was also given its best-selling treatment by its coauthor, Harry James, with Kitty Kallen on vocals. James shared his writing credits with Duke Ellington, Don George, and Johnny Hodges. Finally, "Sentimental Journey," co-composed by Les Brown and Ben Homer, with lyrics by Bud Green, was a major hit in its recording by Brown with vocalist Doris Day. (Two other versions—one by Hal McIntyre with Frankie Lester on vocals for RCA Victor and another by the Merry Macs—were also successful.) "It's Been a Long, Long Time," on the other hand, was the product of the reliable songwriting team of composer Jule Styne and lyricist Sammy Cahn. Harry James, again with Kitty Kallen, had a number-one version, and so did Bing Crosby, singing with guitarist Les Paul.

The year produced several other memorable songs. The Andrews Sisters had the biggest hit of 1945 with the gold-selling "Rum and Coca-Cola," which topped the charts for ten weeks. Perry Como also had ten weeks at the top with his first number-one hit, "Till the End of Time" (music adapted from "Polonaise in A Flat Major," Opus 53, by Frederic Chopin), which also inspired hit recordings by Les Brown, with Doris Day on vocals, and by Dick Haymes. The movie song of the year was "On the Atchison, Topeka and the Santa Fe" (music by Harry Warren, lyrics by Johnny Mercer) from the film *The Harvey Girls*. Mercer himself had the number-one version, beating out Bing Crosby's number-three rendition. Rodgers and Hammerstein continued to provide pop singers with hits, as Perry Como extracted "If I Loved You" from their second stage musical, *Carousel*, for a number-three hit. And dreams, a lyrical perennial in romantic pop songs, were more ubiquitous than ever in the year's hits with "My Dreams Are Getting Better All the Time" (from the film *In Society*), given a seven-week run at number one by Les Brown with Doris Day on vocals, along with two other versions, both of which reached number three (one by Johnny Long and His Orchestra with Dick Robertson on vocals for Decca and the other by the Phil Moore Four on RCA Victor); "I'll Buy That Dream" (from the film *Sing Your Way Home*), inspiring number-two recordings by the team of Helen Forrest and Dick Haymes and by Harry James with Kitty Kallen on vocals; and just plain "Dream," a number-one hit for the Pied Pipers.

The one major debut artist of the year was another former band singer: Peggy Lee, born Norma Egstrom in Jamestown, North

Dakota, in May 1920. She was singing in a band by the age of four-teen, and after high school appeared with territory bands in the upper Midwest. In 1941 she was discovered by Benny Goodman in Chicago and sang with him until March 1943, when she married guitarist Dave Barbour and retired to raise a family. Capitol Records, however, talked her into cutting some solo tracks, and "Waitin' for the Train to Come In" reached the charts in November 1945, on its way to the top ten. After that, her retirement was over.

Nineteen forty-five marked the beginning of another new *Billboard* chart, one for albums. (Still collections of two-sided 78 rpm singles, they were housed in hard cardboard folding containers like photo albums, hence the name.) Albums were just starting to have a com-mercial impact in popular music, as fans had more disposable income. The first number one on *Billboard*'s album chart for March 24, 1945, was Capitol's four-disc, eight-song *The King Cole Trio*, and other chart-toppers for the first year included two Bing Crosby albums, *Going My Way*, which featured his studio recordings of songs from his film of the same name, and the holiday collection *Merry Christmas*, as well as two original Broadway cast albums, *Song of Norway* and *Car-ousel*, both on Decca. But the biggest album of 1945 was a compila-tion called *Glenn Miller*, memorializing the bandleader who had been lost in the war the year before.

Nineteen forty-six exceeded all expectations, becoming by far the industry's biggest year yet, with sales doubling, to 350 million records. Whitburn's list of the top twenty artists shows twelve bandleaders and eight vocalists, but this is deceptive. Four of the top five—Crosby (on top for the fourth year in a row), Sinatra, Como, and Shore—were singers, and even the band recordings usually featured vocals. Also, the more jazz-oriented bands had given way to softer sweet bands like those of Sammy Kaye and Les Brown. Not only declining record sales, but also declining tour revenues plagued the bandleaders, and in December 1946 eight of them—Woody Herman, Harry James, Benny Goodman, Les Brown, Tommy Dorsey, Benny Carter, Jack Teagarden, and Ina Ray Hutton—disbanded their groups. Several reorganized within months, but the end of 1946 still marks the end of the Swing Era and its replacement by a "Sing Era" that dominated popular music until the rise of rock 'n' roll. Meanwhile, upcoming jazz musicians were also turning away from swing and toward a more innovative style that came to be called bebop. Many jazz fans hailed this new development, but it had the effect of divorcing jazz from mainstream popular music. From this point on, relatively few jazz performers would achieve popularity beyond their genre, and jazz, like classical music, despite garnering significant press attention and, eventually, institutional support, would account for less than 5 percent of sales by the end of the century.

Of the 350 million records sold in 1946, 300 million were sold by Columbia, RCA Victor, Decca, and Capitol, the other 50 million by independents. The increase in sales made for growth in competition that could be seen among the most popular records of the year. In a business that had begun with the song being emphasized over the singer, it had never been unusual for there to be multiple recorded versions of a particular popular song; when one label enjoyed a hit with a song, the other labels would cover it with an artist of their own, enjoying reduced, but sometimes still substantial sales. By 1946, however, labels were quickly jumping on each other with cover versions and cutting into each other's sales. A good example could be found in the year's biggest hit, "The Gypsy," a British song. Dinah Shore, recently switching from RCA Victor to Columbia, released a version that reached the charts on April 27, 1946. The Ink Spots' recording on Decca entered the charts a week later on May 4, followed by Sammy Kaye's on RCA Victor and Hildegarde's with Guy Lombardo, also on Decca, the following week on May 11. The Ink Spots' version was the most popular, with thirteen weeks at number one, but Shore had another five weeks at the top, and Kaye made number three. Hildegarde and Lombardo got to number seven, and subsequent versions on smaller labels by Hal McIntyre on Cosmo Records and by Jan Garber on Black & White Records also charted.

Similar successful piling-on could be seen with other song hits. "To Each His Own" (music by Jay Livingston, lyrics by Ray Evans), written to publicize the movie of the same name, was given its most successful treatment, a number-one million seller, by Eddy Howard and His Orchestra, sung by Howard himself for Majestic Records. (It was the first hit for Howard, born in Woodland, California, in September 1914. He had previously made his mark as a singer with the Dick Jurgens band. He would have another forty-one chart singles through 1955.) But Freddy Martin, with vocals by Stuart Wade (on RCA Victor), and the Ink Spots (on Decca) also took it to number one, the Modernaires with Paula Kelly (on Columbia) went to number three, and Tony Martin (on Mercury Records), got to number four. The Ink Spots and Tony Martin versions were also million sellers. Nor are these isolated examples. In total, the forty biggest records of 1946 featured only twenty-five different songs.

Among them were several songs that have lived on. The King Cole Trio sounded more than ever like Nat "King" Cole as a solo crooner on their first number-one hit, "(I Love You) For Sentimental Reasons," and created a seasonal standard with "The Christmas Song (Merry Christmas to You)," the generic title of which always obliges one to note its opening line, "Chestnuts roasting on an open fire." Vaughn Monroe also joined the list of originators of Christmas perennials and got himself a number-one hit by recording lyricist Sammy Cahn and composer Jule Styne's "Let It Snow! Let It Snow! Let It Snow!" And Hoagy Carmichael, who was acting as a precursor to the 1960s rock generation by establishing himself as a singer-songwriter, went to number two with "Ole Buttermilk Sky" (co-credited to Jack Brooks), which he had introduced in the film *Canyon Passage*, on ARA Records—but Kay Kyser, with Michael (later Mike) Douglas on vocals, took it all the way to number one. Meanwhile, Irving Berlin just missed topping the album charts with the cast album for his most successful Broadway musical, *Annie Get Your Gun*, on Decca, but two of its songs ranked among the year's best sellers, each in two different versions: the ballad "They Say It's Wonderful" was recorded by Frank Sinatra and by Perry Como; the novelty "Doin' What Comes Natur'lly" was a hit for both Freddy Martin, with Glenn Hughes on vocals, and Dinah Shore recording with Spade Cooley.

In addition to Eddy Howard, the most notable recording artist to debut on the charts in 1946 was Margaret Whiting. Whiting, the daughter of songwriter Richard A. Whiting, was born in Detroit in

July 1924, but moved to Hollywood, California, four years later. She showed an early interest in singing, and after her father's death in 1938, fellow songwriter Johnny Mercer became her mentor. Naturally, she joined Capitol Records when Mercer cofounded it in 1942, initially working with bands led by Freddie Slack and Billy Butterfield. Finally, in 1946, she began making solo records, first charting with a single that combined two songs from the film *Centennial Summer*, both composed by Jerome Kern for his last work before his death: "All Through the Day" (lyrics by Oscar Hammerstein II) and "In Love in Vain" (lyrics by Leo Robin).

Kern had died suddenly in November 1945 before he could begin work on the musical that became *Annie Get Your Gun*. MGM quickly told his story (after a fashion) in the biographical film *Till the Clouds Roll By*, which was released a year later. Packed with Kern songs sung by MGM stars, the film occasioned the movie studio's entry into the record business with its own MGM Records, and it also marked the invention of the original soundtrack album, a logical corollary to the original cast album. As noted, Bing Crosby's *Going My Way* had topped the album charts in 1945, and it was followed in 1946 by a Crosby album of *The Bells of St. Mary's* (the film sequel to *Going My Way*) as well as a *State Fair* album by Dick Haymes. (*State Fair* was a movie musical with songs by Rodgers and Hammerstein.) But none of these albums contained the actual soundtrack recordings; they all consisted of separate studio recordings of the songs heard in the films. *Till the Clouds Roll By*, on the other hand, featured the performances recorded on the soundstage at MGM by Judy Garland, Lena Horne, and others.

Nineteen forty-seven was another record year, with sales estimated at 375 million copies. It was also a year in which vocalists continued to outdistance bands, with eleven of them ranking among the top twenty artists. Veterans like Crosby (number eight) and Sinatra (number four) seemed to be fading slightly, while Perry Como held his own (number three again) and some new names appeared. Among them was the year's top recording artist, Eddy Howard (technically a bandleader, although really a singer), whose biggest hit was "I Wonder, I Wonder, I Wonder." Also new to the top twenty were Buddy

Clark (number eleven), whose tragic death in 1949 would cut short a promising career; Margaret Whiting (number fifteen); and former Benny Goodman Orchestra singer Art Lund (number nineteen).

It was another year in which the biggest hits were frequently covered by multiple artists; once again, the forty most successful records consisted of only twenty-five different songs. The year's biggest hit, with a record-breaking seventeen weeks at the top of the *Billboard* chart, was "Near You," as recorded by composer Francis Craig and His Orchestra, with Bob Lamm on vocals, for the Nashville-based independent Bullet Records. There was also a number-two version by the Andrews Sisters and number-three versions by Larry Green and His Orchestra for RCA Victor and Alvino Rey and His Orchestra, with Jimmy Joyce on vocals, for Capitol. The 1913 song "Peg o' My Heart" was revived for no less than three number-one versions: the Harmonicats had a million seller on Vitacoustic Records; Buddy Clark covered with a vocal version for Columbia; and the Three Suns had another instrumental for RCA Victor. "Managua, Nicaragua" produced two chart-topping versions, one by Freddy Martin with vocals by Stuart Wade and the other by Guy Lombardo with Don Rodney on vocals. "Mam'selle," the instrumental theme from the film *The Razor's Edge* with words added, gave Art Lund a million-selling number-one hit for MGM, while Frank Sinatra also topped the charts with it. The Three Flames for Columbia and Count Basie and His Orchestra, with Harry Edison and Bill Johnson on vocals, for RCA Victor, each scored number-one hits with the novelty "Open the Door, Richard." And "Anniversary Song," the sole new number in the wildly successful film biography *The Jolson Story*, was recorded for a number-one hit by Dinah Shore; number-two discs by Jolson himself, who took cowriter credit with Saul Chaplin (a million seller for Decca) and Guy Lombardo, with Kenny Gardner on vocals; and a number-three version by Tex Beneke and the Glenn Miller Orchestra, with Garry Stevens on vocals, for RCA Victor. The success of *The Jolson Story* carried over to the album charts, where a virtual soundtrack album, *Al Jolson in Songs He Made Famous*, consisting of the veteran singer's re-recordings of his old hits to be dubbed into the mouth of Larry Parks, who portrayed the young Jolson on film, spent almost six months at number one, with a follow-up, *Al Jolson Souvenir Album*, reigning for ten weeks, and *Al Jolson—Volume Three* spending fourteen weeks on top in 1948.

The year brought two important debut artists: Frankie Laine and Vic Damone. Laine was born Francesco Paolo Lo Vecchio in Chicago in March 1913. He began singing as a child, but it took him a long time to find his way into the entertainment business. He was already in his thirties when Hoagy Carmichael heard him singing in a Hollywood nightclub and got him a job there. A contract with Mercury Records followed, and he scored his first hit with a revival of the 1931 song "That's My Desire," which sold a million copies. Vic Damone was another son of Italy, born Vito Farinola in Brooklyn in June 1928. Also signed to Mercury Records, he demonstrated his love of his heritage with his first hit, "I Have but One Heart" ("O Marinariello"), which he sang in both English and Italian for a top-ten hit.

The future of the music business was thrown into uncertainty again come January 1, 1948, when the AFM instituted another recording ban. This one, which lasted almost a year, was not as serious as the first one because the record companies, with advance warning, had time to stockpile recordings, and because they cheated the ban not only by making more *a cappella* recordings, but also by having instrumental tracks recorded in Mexico and Great Britain and then importing them for American singers to record over. As a result, the ban had a negligible effect.

Along with the continuing rise of singers, 1948 saw an increase in novelty songs over romantic ballads that would continue into the early 1950s. The year's biggest hit was Jay Livingston and Ray Evans's Western-themed "Buttons and Bows," an Academy Award winner from the film *Paleface*, recorded by Dinah Shore for a million seller, with a cover version by the Dinning Sisters for Capitol. The runner-up was Peggy Lee's Mexican-styled "Mañana (Is Soon Enough for Me)," another million seller. Also hitting number one during the year were Nat "King" Cole's singular "Nature Boy," a gold record; "Woody Wood-Pecker," by Kay Kyser and His Orchestra with Gloria Wood on vocals; a revival of the 1927 song "I'm Looking over a Four Leaf Clover," by Art Mooney for MGM; "Now Is the Hour (Maori Farewell Song)" by Bing Crosby; and "All I Want for Christmas (Is My Two Front Teeth)" by Spike Jones, with George Rock on vocals for RCA Victor. A new age of silliness seemed to have arrived.

The year's most significant debut artist was another former band singer with a successful track record. Doris Day, born Doris Mary Anne von Kappelhoff in Cincinnati in April 1922, had turned to singing after an automobile accident scuttled her dancing ambitions. She was singing in bands by her late teens, most notably Les Brown and His Band of Renown, with which she scored such hits as "Sentimental Journey." She left Brown in 1947 and earned both a singing contract with Columbia and an acting one with Warner Bros. Pictures. Her first single, "Love Somebody," a duet with Buddy Clark, hit the charts in May 1948 on its way to number one and gold-record status. Her first film, *Romance on the High Seas*, followed in June.

That same month, for the first time in decades, the record business had a new format. On June 18, 1948, Columbia Records demonstrated a new "microgroove" disc capable of playing up to forty-five minutes of music by running at 33 $1/_3$ instead of 78 rpm. The new disc required a new record player to play it on, and it needed industry concurrence, which was not forthcoming from rival RCA Victor. Instead, RCA introduced its own new format, a 7-inch disc with a large hole that ran at 45 rpm. Decca adopted both new formats while retaining 78s, and so, over time, did the rest of the industry, although 78s were gradually phased out during the 1950s. The introduction of the 33 $1/_3$ rpm. "long-playing" (LP) disc naturally stimulated sales of albums, especially original cast recordings like the one for the 1949 Rodgers and Hammerstein musical *South Pacific*, released on Columbia, which spent a record sixty-nine weeks at the top of the *Billboard* album charts and sold in the millions.

By the end of 1949, trends that had been at work in the music business for several years had come to dominate the industry. Sales were better than ever, and vocalists were driving those sales. Frankie Laine typified the current fashion, with his big dramatic voice and his Western-tinged hits like the million sellers "That Lucky Old Sun" and "Mule Train." No one could have foreseen the popularity of such music ten years earlier, when everyone was dancing to "In the Mood." And, of course, no one could predict the much stranger music people would be dancing to only a few years hence, though glances at the newly christened Rhythm and Blues chart, where Wynonie Harris's "All She Wants to Do Is Rock" (co-credited to Harris and Teddy McRae) was a number-one hit, and at the Country and Western chart, where the year's second-biggest hit was Hank Williams's "Lovesick Blues" (music by Cliff Friend, lyrics by Irving Mills), might have provided hints.

"C·R·Y"

Words and Music by CHURCHILL KOHLMAN

PRICE
40¢
IN U.S.A.

6

THE 1950s

ALL SHOOK UP

Though it marked the middle of the twentieth century and the beginning of what would turn out to be the century's decade of greatest change in popular music, 1950 seemed in some ways a throwback to past trends rather than a harbinger of new ones. According to Joel Whitburn's analysis of the *Billboard* Best-Selling Pop Singles chart, the year's number-one recording artist was Bing Crosby, a forty-six-year-old who had made his first recording in 1926 and ranked as the leading record seller of the first half of the century. (While Whitburn's statistical analyses have not been broken down by year for the 1930s, he does rank Crosby at the top for that decade as well as the 1940s, when the singer consistently figured in the top ten and was the top-selling artist of 1943, 1944, 1945, and 1946.)

Crosby's big hits for 1950 included "Dear Hearts and Gentle People"; "Chattanoogie Shoe Shine Boy," a pop cover of a country hit originally recorded by Red Foley (the year's number-one country artist), whose version for Decca was a million-selling, number-one pop hit as well; and two songs Crosby recorded as duets with his eldest son Gary, a revival of the 1914 Irving Berlin song "Play a Simple Melody" and "Sam's Song (The Happy Tune)," both clever novelties featuring countermelodies. Typically, Crosby triumphed by employing varied material, old and new, mainstream and genre-inspired. In his appropriation of Foley's country song for the pop market, he was looking ahead. But as popular music became increasingly diverse and balkanized, there would be less room for a generalist like Crosby. In 1951, he tumbled to eleventh place among recording artists, and that was the last time he figured in the top twenty.

The year's second most successful recording artist was another veteran, forty-seven-year-old bandleader Guy Lombardo, who had been recording with his Royal Canadians since 1924. Lombardo's biggest hits included three songs with vocals by Kenny Gardner: "Enjoy Yourself (It's Later than You Think)," "Dearie," and a revival of the 1937 song "Harbor Lights." Lombardo also enjoyed a million-selling, chart-topping version of the instrumental "The 3rd Man Theme" from the film (composed by zither player Anton Karas, whose own recording for London Records edged out Lombardo's in total sales), and the orchestra leader also scored with "All My Love (Bolero)" with vocals by Bill Flanagan. As a further nod to the past, among the top twenty artists were several others whose chart debuts stretched back more than ten years: the Andrews Sisters (number seven, 1938), Sammy Kaye (number thirteen, 1937), Tony Martin (number nineteen, 1938), and Russ Morgan (number twenty, 1935).

But 1950's biggest hit was by a relative newcomer. She was Patti Page, born Clara Ann Fowler in Muskogee, Oklahoma, in November 1927. Growing up in Tulsa, she sang in church and with her sisters before finding a job on a radio station. By 1948 she had been signed to Mercury Records and scored her first chart record, "Confess." More singles followed, including, in the first half of 1950, a gold-selling revival of the 1934 song "With My Eyes Wide Open I'm Dreaming" (from the film *Shoot the Works*), her first top-ten hit, Mack David's "I Don't Care if the Sun Don't Shine," and a million-selling, number-one version of "All My Love (Bolero)." In the fall of 1950, however, Page had her greatest success with her cover of "The Tennessee Waltz," which had been a hit in the country charts for Pee Wee King, who cowrote it with Redd Stewart, in 1948. The song, recorded in her trademark multitracked vocal style, produced a disc that spent thirteen weeks at number one, longer than any single since 1947.

Right behind "The Tennessee Waltz," also racking up thirteen weeks on top, was an even more unlikely hit, "Goodnight Irene." This single was credited to Gordon Jenkins and His Orchestra and the Weavers. Jenkins was a conductor at Decca Records. The Weavers were an urban folk quartet led by Pete Seeger. And "Goodnight

Irene" was an adaptation of an old folk song by the recently deceased folk and blues singer Lead Belly. The Weavers would flourish for the next couple of years, scoring two more top-ten hits, but they ran up against one of the prevailing forces of the politics of the early 1950s, a militant anti-Communist sentiment that devastated the careers of many left-leaning entertainers. An informant who branded some members of the group Communists later recanted his claims, but not before forcing the Weavers to disband. Yet "The Tennessee Waltz" and "Goodnight Irene" ranked as the two biggest chart hits of the entire 1950s, and no record would reign at the top of the *Billboard* pop singles chart for as long as thirteen weeks for another forty-two years.

In addition to folk and country trends, 1950's most popular music continued a fashion for extremely lighthearted material that had begun to come to the fore in the late 1940s. The year's other biggest hits included such novelty fluff as "If I Knew You Were Comin' (I'd've Baked a Cake)," recorded by Eileen Barton for National Records; "The Thing," recorded by Phil Harris for RCA Victor; "Music! Music! Music!," recorded by Teresa Brewer for London; "Rag Mop" (music and lyrics by Western swing star Johnnie Lee Wills and Deacon Anderson), recorded by the Ames Brothers for Decca subsidary Coral Records; and "Hoop-Dee-Doo," recorded by Perry Como with the Fontane Sisters. The Fontanes were a trio from New Milford, New Jersey, who made their own separate chart debut within months singing a revival of the 1933 song "I Wanna Be Loved" on RCA Victor (actually a cover of the Andrews Sisters' chart-topping revival).

Among the other significant artists making their first commercial impact in 1950 were a moonlighting music-industry executive, Mitch Miller, and a new male singer, Eddie Fisher. Mitchell William Miller, one of the less likely recording stars of the twentieth century, was born in July 1911 in Rochester, New York. He began playing the oboe as a child and was a member of the Rochester Philharmonic Orchestra in the early 1930s. From 1936 to 1947, he played in the CBS Symphony Orchestra, leaving in 1947 to become musical director of Mercury Records' classical division. In 1948 he took over the pop division, where he was the producer (though that word was not yet in

vogue) of the recordings of Frankie Laine, Patti Page, and Vic
Damone. He moved to Columbia Records in 1950, lured by a deal
that also allowed him to make his own recordings. That July, his cover
of the Weavers' hit "Tzena Tzena Tzena," billed to "Mitch Miller and
His Orchestra & Chorus," peaked at number three.

In sharp contrast to the bearded, academic-looking Miller was teen
idol Eddie Fisher, who also scored his first hit in 1950. Fisher, born in
Philadelphia in August 1928, was singing in nightclubs by his teens.
That led to band work and radio, and in 1948 he was in the charts,
second-billed to the Marlin Sisters, on the Columbia single "You
Can't Be True, Dear." Two years later, he had his own top-ten hit on
RCA Victor, a revival of the 1927 song "Thinking of You" made
timely by the release of the film biography of the songwriters Harry
Ruby and Bert Kalmar, *Three Little Words*.

Beyond questions of musical style and new artists, various technological and business issues drove popular music in 1950. If the singles
chart was getting sillier, one reason may have been that there was now
an increasingly divided market for music. The introduction of the LP
and the 45 rpm single in the late 1940s had begun a division in the
record-buying public in which adults tended to buy the more expensive albums (most of which were still released in the 10-inch format),
while young people, with less money to spend, bought singles. In
contrast to the singles chart, the LP chart for 1950 continued to be
dominated by the 1949 original Broadway cast album of *South Pacific*,
with other number ones including the original soundtrack albums of
Annie Get Your Gun (MGM) and *Three Little Words* (MGM), and
Harry James and Doris Day's album of songs from the film *Young
Man with a Horn*, all adult fare.

Broadway and Hollywood may have driven album sales, but other
media fueled the popularity of singles. And radio was changing from
a varied live medium dominated by variety shows and serials into one
that played records picked by increasingly influential disc jockeys.
And radio's place as a broadcaster of narrative material was being
taken over by television; in 1950 there were already 4 million TV sets
in the United States, a number that would mushroom quickly. Some
recording artists, such as Perry Como and Dinah Shore, had made or

were about to make transitions to the new medium. The move to more country and R&B material was fueled by the rivalry between the song licensing agencies ASCAP and BMI. By far the older of the two, ASCAP represented the Tin Pan Alley, theater, and film writers who had dominated popular music since the beginning of the century. Rival BMI was forced to look elsewhere for clients, and ended up encouraging the country and R&B writers ASCAP had always ignored. This was a major factor not only in the increased success of country and R&B in the early 1950s, but also of the rise of rock 'n' roll, which effected a marriage between the two genres.

Another major factor in changing the sound of popular music was the advent of tape recording. Developed by the Germans during World War II, tape recording was brought to the United States after the war and encouraged by Bing Crosby Enterprises, the entertainer's corporate entity. Soon, the process of recording had changed drastically and become much easier, which encouraged the founding of more small record companies that began to compete with the majors, Columbia, RCA Victor, Decca, and Capitol. According to show business historian Robert C. Toll, the number of recording companies jumped from eleven to two hundred between 1949 and 1954. Like BMI, the new independents tended to look for talent in places not already tapped by their better-established rivals. They became niche producers of genres like jazz, classical, and folk music, stimulating the popularity of these marginal styles.

Tape recording also made possible overdubbing like that heard on Patti Page's "The Tennessee Waltz" and paved the way for the top recording act of 1951, husband and wife Les Paul and Mary Ford, who had launched their vocal-and-guitar duo in 1950. Paul, an engineering genius as well as a talented guitarist, overdubbed his wife's vocals in a manner similar to the Page tracks and also made multiple passes on his guitar to create full-bodied recordings. Their rich, unique pop sound was captured on three gold-selling hits that year: "Mockin' Bird Hill"; a revival of the 1940 song "How High the Moon" (from the musical *Two for the Money*); and a revival of the 1919 song "The World Is Waiting for the Sunrise," all on Capitol.

The year's second-biggest recording artist also emerged for the first time at the end of 1950. He was Guy Mitchell, the first of a series of protégés of Mitch Miller. Born Al Cernik in Detroit in February 1927, he briefly worked as a band singer before coming to Miller's attention. "My Heart Cries for You" gave him a million-selling hit that peaked at number two in January 1951 (the B-side, "The Roving Kind," reached number four). Before the year was out, Mitchell had scored another two top-ten hits and returned to number two with his second million seller, "My Truly, Truly Fair."

But Guy Mitchell was only one of Mitch Miller's success stories at Columbia in 1951. Frankie Laine, who owed much of his popularity to Miller's guidance when the two were at Mercury together (and who had suffered since), followed his producer to the new label and quickly returned to his winning ways with a million-selling single pairing the number-two hit "Jezebel" with the number-three hit "Rose, Rose, I Love You." In December, Laine was back at number three with a million-selling revival of the 1925 British song "Jealousy (Jalousie)," and he finished out the year as the third-biggest recording artist of 1951, a considerable comeback from his twelfth-place showing the year before.

Then there was Rosemary Clooney, who also achieved broad commercial success with Miller starting in 1951 (although she later disparaged the material he used to give her that success). Born in Maysville, Kentucky, in May 1928, she had first gained recognition as part of a duo with her sister Betty singing in Tony Pastor's band, then went solo when her sister retired. Signed to Columbia, Clooney had her first chart entry in a duo with Guy Mitchell on "You're Just in Love" (from the Irving Berlin musical *Call Me Madam*) in early 1951. Then her solo single of the traditional country song "Beautiful Brown Eyes" got to number eleven. She was not enamored of Miller's next suggestion, the ethnic novelty number "Come On-A My House" (music and lyrics by Ross Bagdasarian and William Saroyan, from Saroyan's Off-Broadway play *The Son*), which required her to affect an Italian accent. But Miller prevailed, and the record spent eight weeks at number one on the way to selling a million copies.

Tony Bennett also qualifies as a Mitch Miller discovery. He was born Anthony Benedetto in the borough of Queens in New York City, the son of a grocer, and became a professional singer after seeing combat in Europe in World War II. Miller signed him to Columbia and had him record "Because of You," a 1940 song given a new lease on life thanks to its inclusion in the film *I Was an American Spy*. The Bennett recording sold a million copies and spent ten weeks at number one, making it the second-biggest hit of 1951. It was followed by a second million-selling chart-topper, another song Miller had to convince one of his singers to record. Miller recognized the popularity of country music, which accounted for 40 percent of all sales of 78s in 1951, and strove to incorporate it into mainstream pop. In Bennett's case, he chose Hank Williams's classic honky tonk song "Cold, Cold Heart," which Williams took to number one in the country charts on MGM in May. Bennett's pop cover was number one in the pop charts by November.

The biggest hit of 1951 was also one recorded under Miller's aegis, "Cry" (by Churchill Kolman), the first hit for Johnnie Ray. (It got in just under the wire, reaching number one on December 29 and remaining there for eleven weeks.) The single's B-side, Ray's own composition "The Little White Cloud that Cried," got to number two. Ray, born in Dallas, Oregon, in January 1927, was singing on local radio by the age of fifteen despite suffering an injury that forced him to wear a hearing aid. He moved to Los Angeles to pursue a singing career in 1949 and played in clubs around the country until he was discovered by an executive at Columbia subsidiary OKeh in Detroit in the spring of 1951. The emotive "Cry" marked him as a precursor to the flamboyant rock 'n' roll singers who would follow later in the decade.

This infusion of new talent helped the record industry continue a recovery in sales, which had peaked at $224 million in 1947, then fallen to $189 million in 1948 and to $173 million in 1949. In 1950 sales rebounded to $189 million, reaching $199 million in 1951, and $214 million in 1952. The figure rose to $219 million in 1953, but that was a surprisingly modest increase that indicated all was not well. Some perspective on the volcanic eruption of rock 'n' roll that took place in mid-decade—no doubt the most remarkable shift in the nation's taste for popular music ever—is given by considering the relative weakness of the pop music that preceded it. The trend toward novelty music, while it produced many isolated hits, tended to reduce the loyalty of music fans rather than strengthen it. At the same time, it tended to drive out better-written material, which continued to be composed for the Broadway stage and even the diminishing number of movie musicals, but that turned up less frequently in the hit parade.

A scan of the popular songs of the years just before the onset of rock 'n' reveals very few standards that hold up as even remotely familiar fifty years later, unless they originated in the country or R&B realms (and some of them are songs that were not hits at the time). From 1952, the memorable songs include: "Don't Let the Stars Get in Your Eyes," recorded by Perry Como and by Giselle MacKenzie for Capitol; "The Glow-Worm," recorded by the Mills Brothers and by Johnny Mercer; "Hi-Lili, Hi-Lo," from the movie *Lili*; "I Believe," recorded by Frankie Laine and by Jane Froman; "Jambalaya (On the Bayou)," by Jo Stafford for Columbia; "Wimoweh," recorded by the Weavers and Gordon Jenkins; and "Your Cheatin' Heart," recorded by Joni James for MGM and by Frankie Laine. Of these, "Don't Let the Starts Get in Your Eyes," "Jambalaya (On the Bayou)," and "Your Cheatin' Heart" all originated as country hits; "The Glow-Worm" was a song from 1907 with new lyrics; and "Wimoweh" was a folk song based on a South African Zulu song. "Hi-Lili, Hi-Lo" was not a chart hit. The other memorable songs for the year stayed within subgenres: the country hits "It Wasn't God Who Made Honky Tonk Angels," recorded by Kitty Wells for Decca, and "You Win Again," recorded by Hank Williams; and the R&B hits "Lawdy Miss Clawdy," recorded by Lloyd Price for Specialty Records, and "Night Train," recorded by Jimmy Forrest as an instrumental for United Records.

A similar survey for 1953 produces similar results. For that year, the memorable songs include: "Baubles, Bangles, and Beads" and "Stranger in Paradise" from the musical *Kismet*, the latter recorded by Tony Bennett, by the Four Aces for Decca, and by Tony Martin for RCA Victor; "The Doggie in the Window," recorded by Patti Page (perhaps *infamous* is a better word than *memorable* in this case); "Ebb Tide," recorded as an instrumental by Frank Chacksfield and His Orchestra for London Records and in a vocal version by Vic Damone; "(Now and Then There's) a Fool Such as I," recorded by Jo Stafford; "That's Amore," recorded by Dean Martin for Capitol; and "That's Entertainment," from the movie musical *The Band Wagon.* Of these, the two songs from *Kismet* were based on the music of classical composer Alexander Borodin; and "(Now and Then There's) a Fool Such as I" originated as a country hit. "Baubles, Bangles, and Beads" was not a chart hit. One other memorable song for the year was heard only in the R&B field (for the moment), "Hound Dog," recorded by Big Mama Thornton for Peacock Records.

And in 1954, the pickings remained slim. The memorable songs for the year include: "Fly Me to the Moon (In Other Words)," first recorded by Felicia Sanders for Columbia; "Hey There" from the musical *The Pajama Game*, recorded by Rosemary Clooney and by Sammy Davis, Jr., for Decca; "The Man that Got Away," from the movie *A Star Is Born*; "Sh-Boom," recorded by the Crew-Cuts for Mercury; "Three Coins in the Fountain," recorded by the Four Aces and by Frank Sinatra for Capitol; and "Young at Heart," recorded by Frank Sinatra. Of these, "Sh-Boom" originated as an R&B hit. "Fly Me to the Moon (In Other Words)" and "The Man that Got Away" were not chart hits. One other memorable song for the year originated and stayed an R&B hit, "I'm Your Hoochie Coochie Man," recorded by Muddy Waters for Chess Records. Of these songs from 1952 through 1954, only "The Glow-Worm," "The Doggie in the Window," "Don't Let the Stars Get in Your Eyes," "Hey There," "Sh-Boom," and "Three Coins in the Fountain" topped the pop charts.

Admittedly, this list of notable songs is subjective, but there was a general consensus that great songs on a par with those of the classic pop songwriters of the 1920s, '30s, and '40s, people like Irving Berlin, George Gershwin, Cole Porter, and Rodgers and Hart, were not being written in the early '50s. It's no wonder that Frank Sinatra, who mounted a remarkable comeback during this period and began a string of eighteen consecutive top-ten albums with 1954's *Songs for Young Lovers*, did so largely by reviving the work of those songwriters of a generation earlier in striking new arrangements by Nelson Riddle and others. Sinatra commissioned the occasional new song by his personal lyricist, Sammy Cahn, but for the most part he relied on the catalogs of people who were writing songs in his youth. Sinatra was hardly alone in his taste for music of the recent past. The top of the LP charts from 1952 to 1954 included the soundtrack to *An American in Paris* (MGM), which consisted of the music of George Gershwin; Mantovani's *Music of Victor Herbert* (London), recalling the early twentieth-century operetta composer; the archival Benny Goodman album *1937–38 Jazz Concert No. 2* (Columbia), a follow-up to Goodman's 1950 *Carnegie Hall Jazz Concert* album of his famous 1938 performance; and the soundtrack to *The Glenn Miller Story* (Decca). It is a truism in the music business that new music and new artists are the lifeblood of the industry, and relatively few important new artists were emerging in this period. It shouldn't be surprising, therefore, that record sales declined in 1954, with total revenues dropping back to $213 million.

The obvious conclusion is that rock 'n' roll arrived just in time to rescue popular music, and in many ways that's true, even if established people in the business didn't see it that way at the time. But it's also worth examining the circumstances that allowed the rock revolution to occur. We have already noted the increasing incursions of country and R&B music into pop, and the institutions that benefited by encouraging them. It is also true that a new audience was growing in the baby boom generation emerging from World War II, a generation that hadn't yet put on its dancing shoes and for which the big bands and the dance halls of the 1930s and '40s no longer stood ready. That audience was more affluent than its parents had been, which made it a natural target for the music business. At the same time, certain developments in the media also prepared for a growth in the industry. By the start of 1955, the LP market had expanded such that, increasingly, 12-inch records were pushing out the shorter 10-inch discs to become the standard. Television, which had increased its coverage and its viewership remarkably during the first half of the 1950s, stood as a dominant medium by the middle of the decade and was becoming a natural means of promoting music. And the movie business had been rocked both by television and an antitrust consent decree that separated ownership of the film studios from the theater chains. That helped lead to the rise of cheap, independent films intended for market niches, not the broad audiences traditionally addressed by the major studios. There had always been B-movies (although they were being replaced by television); now there were exploitation movies.

If MGM's *The Blackboard Jungle*, which opened in February 1955, wasn't quite an exploitation movie, it wasn't far from the definition. Director Richard Brooks's adaptation of Evan Hunter's novel about the experiences of a teacher in an inner-city high school was one of those films in which the nominal message may reinforce traditional values, but the surface conflict overwhelms that point. Today, we remember it not so much for the decency of the teacher (played by Glenn Ford) as for the aggression of the rebellious student (Vic Morrow). But, of course, the main thing we remember it for is "(We're Gonna) Rock Around the Clock" (music and lyrics by James E. Myers, using the pseudonym Jimmy De Knight, and Max Freedman).

The song had been recorded by twenty-eight-year-old Bill Haley and his backup band the Comets on April 12, 1954, and initially released by Decca Records on May 10, when it failed to reach the charts. Haley was a northerner, born in July 1925 in Highland Park, Michigan, who led a series of Western swing bands in the late 1940s and early '50s before he hit upon the idea of combining his buoyant style with R&B. Changing his band's name from the Saddlemen to the Comets, he first reached the charts in May 1953 with the top-ten hit "Crazy Man, Crazy," his own composition, on Essex Records, which led to his contract with Decca. After the failure of "Rock Around the Clock" in 1954, Haley covered "Shake, Rattle and Roll," recently a number-one R&B hit for Joe Turner on Atlantic Records, and took it into the pop top five. The follow-ups "Dim, Dim the Lights (I Want Some Atmosphere)" (music and lyrics by Beverly Ross and Julius Dixon), "Birth of the Boogie," and "Mambo Rock" all peaked in the top twenty in the first quarter of 1955 before Decca re-released "Rock Around the Clock" to tie in with the success of *The Blackboard Jungle*. It became a massive hit, topping the charts in July and selling a million copies.

Various recordings dating back into the 1940s have been cited as the first rock 'n' roll record, but there is no dispute about what the first really successful rock 'n' roll record was. Yet "Rock Around the Clock" was not alone in 1955, as a number of records led the way to the new style. In many cases, they were songs that originated with black R&B performers and were covered by white pop performers, later a sore point among rock fans. While not entirely without justification, this resentment should be tempered by an understanding of common practice in the music industry up to this time. Simply put, the business had been founded and, even at this point, continued to rest on the song rather than the singer (or the record) as the primary element of creativity. The initial dominant force in the music business was song publishing, and singers and their records were viewed primarily as vehicles for selling sheet music. Hence, as a song became popular, it was not unusual for several cover versions to be released by different record companies, a practice encouraged by the publishers. Initial charts such as that of the *Your Hit Parade* radio series ranked songs, not particular recordings of them. (In both the original radio show and the later television version, *Your Hit Parade* employed a regular staff of singers to perform the hits each week, not the recording artists.) The proliferation of new record companies in the late 1940s and early '50s exacerbated the tendency toward multiple versions of popular songs. For example, there were seven different versions of "The Tennessee Waltz" in the *Billboard* singles chart in 1950 and 1951.

Of course, covering a country or R&B hit to achieve pop crossover was a slightly different phenomenon, but the principle was the same. As R&B and country music began to achieve broader commercial success in the early 1950s, record companies naturally looked to capitalize on that success with a tried-and-true method. The black vocal group the Penguins' recording of "Earth Angel (Will You Be Mine)" on DooTone Records entered the *Billboard* R&B chart on December 18, 1954, and rose to number one on January 15, 1955. A week after its appearance on the R&B chart, it broke into the pop chart. On February 5, it rose from number thirteen to number eight; the same week, a white group, the Crew-Cuts, entered the chart with their cover version. The Penguins' recording stalled, while the Crew-Cuts' record surpassed it and reached number three. That spring, African-American LaVern Baker's original Atlantic recording of "Tweedle Dee," an R&B top-five hit, was outdistanced on the pop chart by Caucasian singer Georgia Gibbs's cover for Mercury, and later in the year Fats Domino's R&B chart-topper "Ain't It a Shame" (a.k.a. "Ain't That a Shame"), which he cowrote with producer Dave Bartholomew, for Imperial Records gave way on the pop chart to a cover by Pat Boone on Dot Records. Sometimes, too, lyrics were bowdlerized to the point that titles had to be changed. The Midnighters' 1954 R&B chart-topper for Federal Records "Work with Me Annie" (music and lyrics by Hank Ballard) was transformed into "Wallflower" (music and lyrics by Johnny Otis, Hank Ballard, and Etta James) for a recording by Etta James on Modern Records before becoming a number-one pop hit for Georgia Gibbs under the title "Dance with Me Henry (Wallflower)." (Such efforts to sanitize risqué lyrics for mass consumption would have been familiar to Broadway songwriters like Cole Porter and Lorenz Hart, whose songs had been similarly cleaned up in earlier decades.) Songwriters and publishers had no reason to complain, even if the R&B artists felt slighted. Of course, the artists ultimately benefited from the exposure, not to mention the comparison.

What was clearly needed, however, was something that fell in between the authentic R&B sound of the originators and the pale imitations of the cover artists. The two major artists to emerge in the early days of rock 'n' roll were a black man who performed songs that addressed the concerns of teenagers (Chuck Berry), and a white man who could sing R&B convincingly (Elvis Presley). Berry topped the R&B charts and reached the pop top five with his first hit, "Maybellene" (music and lyrics by Chuck Berry, Russ Frato, and Alan Freed), in 1955. Although he recorded for Chess Records, a bastion of Chicago blues, Berry early on mixed R&B and country into rock 'n' roll; "Maybellene" was based on "Ida Red," a Western swing song cut by Bob Wills. Just weeks before it hit the charts, a performer unlike any country music had known reached the country charts for the first time when Elvis Presley's Sun Records single "Baby, Let's Play House" (a cover of an R&B hit for its author, Arthur Gunter, on Excello Records) made the listings on the way to a top five placing.

With these artists, 1955 was a turning point not only in the decade, but in the century. Not surprisingly, record sales, having dipped in 1954, took a big jump in 1955, rising 30 percent to a new high of $277 million. That rosy picture was marred, from the major labels' point of view, however, because the wrong style of music was selling and, even more important, it was being produced by the wrong companies. Of the 331 records that made the 1950 *Billboard* pop singles chart, 246, or nearly 75 percent, were released by Capitol, Columbia, Decca, or RCA Victor; of the 246 singles that reached the same chart in 1955, only 119, or less than 49 percent, were released by the big four. These figures do not count major label subsidiaries like Decca's Coral and Columbia's Epic, but they are still impressive.

Clearly, it was up to the majors to either join the teenage rock 'n' roll revolution or ignore it. Of the four, only RCA took the former path wholeheartedly and in a characteristic manner by simply buying an act that had shown promise on an independent label. RCA purchased Elvis Presley's contract from Sun Records for $25,000 on November 20, 1955. Thereafter, things happened rapidly for the young singer from Tupelo, Mississippi, by way of Memphis, Tennessee. On January 5, 1956, he entered RCA's Nashville studio and recorded "Heartbreak Hotel" three days before his twenty-first birthday. RCA released the single on January 17; it was not an immediate success. But the record company and Presley's manager, "Colonel" Tom Parker, hit upon a crucial promotional idea, inducing Tommy and Jimmy Dorsey to put Presley on their live Saturday-night variety program *Stage Show*, broadcast nationally on CBS, for six consecutive weeks, starting January 28. Presley didn't sing "Heartbreak Hotel" the first week, or the second, but he finally performed the song on February 11, and that got the ball rolling. The single broke into the pop charts for the week ending March 3 and hit number one for the week ending April 21.

This set a pattern that lasted through the year. Presley appeared on a succession of television shows including *The Milton Berle Show*, *The Steve Allen Show*, and *The Ed Sullivan Show*, and his records dominated the charts, hogging the number-one spot for twenty-five of the year's fifty-two weeks with "Heartbreak Hotel," "I Want You, I Need You, I Love You," the double-sided hit single "Don't Be Cruel"/ "Hound Dog," and "Love Me Tender," which Presley had introduced in the film of the same name, his movie debut. He even made incursions into the LP charts, hitting number one with the albums *Elvis Presley* and *Elvis*. In all, Presley sold over 10 million records in 1956, more than any individual recording artist had sold in a single year before. Nor was Presley the only rocker racking up big record sales in 1956, as Bill Haley & the Comets and Fats Domino also figured among the year's top twenty artists, joined by newcomer Little Richard on Specialty Records, while Memphis (in the form of Sun Records) also gave the world Johnny Cash and Roy Orbison. Little wonder that the record industry's gross revenues jumped to $377 million, an increase of more than 36 percent.

Nineteen fifty-seven was more of the same. Now making movies instead of appearing on TV, Presley was at number one for twenty-six weeks in the singles charts with "Too Much," "All Shook Up," "(Let Me Be Your) Teddy Bear," and "Jailhouse Rock," and at the top of the LP charts with *Loving You* and *Elvis' Christmas Album*. Meanwhile, Ricky Nelson (whose career was launched through his parents' TV series and who recorded for Verve Records, then Imperial), the Everly Brothers (Cadence Records), Jerry Lee Lewis (Sun Records), and Buddy Holly & the Crickets (Decca subsidiaries Brunswick and Coral) made their chart debuts, and gross revenues crossed the $400 million mark.

As quickly as rock 'n' roll had achieved this success, however, its initial wave began to recede. Despite the unprecedented sales the new musical style brought to the industry, the music business—at least the major labels that still dominated it—didn't really support rock 'n' roll. They did recognize, however, that it had ushered in a whole new, young audience that could be exploited. All along, nonrock music had still been selling. If 1956 was the year of "Heartbreak Hotel," it was also the year of Gogi Grant's "The Wayward Wind" on Era Records, Dean Martin's "Memories Are Made of This," and Nelson Riddle's instrumental "Lisbon Antigua" on Capitol, as well as the year when the LP charts were dominated by Harry Belafonte's *Calypso* on RCA Victor, which foreshadowed the folk boom, as well as the original Broadway cast album of *My Fair Lady* (Columbia) and the motion picture soundtracks to the musicals *Oklahoma!* and *The King and I* (both Capitol).

Pat Boone turned away from covering rock songs to scoring hits with ballads like a revival of the 1931 song "Love Letters in the Sand" and the title song from his film "April Love" in 1957, and he inspired a wave of clean-cut pop singers like Johnny Mathis (Columbia), Paul Anka (ABC-Paramount), Connie Francis (MGM), and the film stars Tab Hunter (Dot) and Debbie Reynolds (Coral). A signal moment in this trend occurred on August 5, 1957, when disc jockey Dick Clark took his local Philadelphia TV show *Bandstand* national, and *American Bandstand* began airing every weekday afternoon, promoting a softer, more conventional style of music. On October 12, 1957, in Sydney, Australia, rock 'n' roll suffered its first of a series of casualties when Little Richard renounced his musical career and announced his intention to become a minister.

Rock 'n' roll really began to collapse in 1958, however. On March 24, Elvis Presley was inducted into the U.S. Army, which didn't end his run at the top of the charts—he still managed to be the number-one recording artist of the year—but did slow him down. In May, Jerry Lee Lewis's career was wrecked by the scandal surrounding his marriage to his thirteen-year-old second cousin. Meanwhile, the year's artist debuts included Frankie Avalon (Chancellor), Dion and the Belmonts (Laurie), Jan & Dean (Dore), Bobby Darin (Atlantic subsidiary Atco), and Neil Sedaka (RCA Victor), continuing the trend toward softer music. The Kingston Trio's "Tom Dooley" on Capitol heralded the start of the folk boom. The soundtrack to *South Pacific* (RCA Victor) became the biggest-selling LP of the second half of the 1950s, and other chart-toppers among albums included the original Broadway cast album of *The Music Man* (Capitol); the soundtrack to the movie musical *Gigi* (MGM); the first greatest hits album, *Johnny's Greatest Hits* by Johnny Mathis; and two Frank Sinatra albums, *Come Fly with Me* and *Frank Sinatra Sings for Only the Lonely*. But the major new trend in LPs was Mitch Miller's series of choral records of traditional songs starting with *Sing Along with Mitch*, released in May. Record sales continued to climb, but the rate of increase slowed. At $511 million, gross revenues were up 11 percent over the previous year.

On February 3, 1959, Buddy Holly, Ritchie Valens, and the Big Bopper were killed in an airplane crash, an event that became symbolic of the decline of rock 'n' roll, remembered by Don McLean nearly thirteen years later as "the day the music died." And on December 23, 1959, Chuck Berry was arrested for violation of the Mann Act, which prohibited taking a minor across state lines for immoral purposes. That set in motion a series of legal complications that effectively put him out of action until his release from prison in 1964.

In its continuing efforts to turn back the tide of rock 'n' roll, the music industry set up the National Academy of Recording Arts and Sciences (NARAS), which, on May 4, 1959, awarded the first group of Grammy Awards to recording artists for recordings released during 1958. Henry Mancini's *The Music from Peter Gunn* (RCA Victor) was named Album of the Year, while Record of the Year and Song of the Year went to "Nel Blu Dipinto Di Blu" (a/k/a "Volare"), recorded by Domenico Modugno and released on Decca. The closest thing to a rock 'n' roll nominee was the Champs' instrumental "Tequila," which won the Grammy for Best Rhythm & Blues Performance. For years to come, the Grammys would lead the charge against rock.

Finally, in November 1959, New York district attorney Frank Hogan subpoenaed the financial records of several recording companies in an attempt to investigate their involvement in payola, setting off a national scandal that led to Congressional hearings and ruined the career of famed disc jockey Alan Freed, who had been an early advocate of rock 'n' roll. Although the scandal exposed illegal practices in the music business, it was also a vendetta against rock, the implication being that the music wouldn't sell unless impressionable teenagers were forced to listen to it. Of course, payoffs for the promotion of popular music had been going on as long as the music industry had existed, but the payola scandal was used against rock.

As the decade came to a close, teen pop continued to flourish, with Fabian (Chancellor) and Bobby Rydell (Cameo) among the year's new artists. But 1959 also saw the pop chart debuts of Chubby Checker (Parkway), the Isley Brothers (RCA Victor), and the Miracles (Chess), acts that would provide exciting music in the early 1960s. At the very least, popular music had become far more diverse in the 1950s and in so doing expanded its audience, with sales crossing over the $600 million mark by the end of the decade. That, of course, was only the beginning.

As Recorded by THE BEATLES on Capitol Records

I WANT TO HOLD YOUR HAND

Words and Music by JOHN LENNON and PAUL McCARTNEY

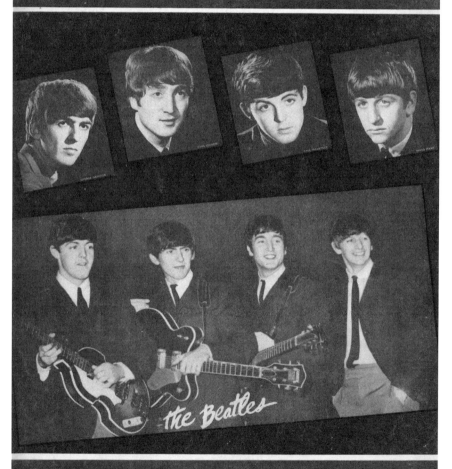

the Beatles

DUCHESS MUSIC CORPORATION .60 in U.S.A.

7

THE 1960s

THE ROCK INVASION

As historians are often painfully aware, the past, their field of study, doesn't really exist. It is only a collection of memories and ideas held by people living in the present, and those impressions are conditioned by succeeding events. When we look at a photograph taken of the New York City skyline any time between the early 1970s and September 10, 2001, for example, we now do so with a sense of poignancy the photographer had no reason to feel. The past is over and therefore should be immutable, but, since it is merely a concept, history—or the way we look at it, which is the same thing—actually changes depending upon what happens in the future.

When we look back at the 1960s, still remembered as a period of great social upheaval, we think of it, in terms of popular music, as a period that marked the consolidation and expansion of the rock era, primarily due to the Beatles. But the "Rock Era," even though it's usually thought to have begun in 1955, is a phrase that only makes sense in the wake of the Beatles, who did not achieve worldwide fame until 1964. The pop music observer of January 1, 1960, would have had no reason to think he or she was living in the midst of it. Rather, such a person would have been likely to consider rock 'n' roll one of the many passing trends in popular music, more significant, perhaps, than the fad for Hawaiian music in the 1910s, but far less important than the Swing Era. After a heady start in the mid-1950s that brought about a big jump in record sales, rock 'n' roll had receded in the late '50s due to a combination of attrition, as its stars encountered scandal (Jerry Lee Lewis, Chuck Berry), conversion (Little Richard), accidental death (Buddy Holly), and the draft (Elvis Presley); co-optation in the form of teen idols like Frankie Avalon; resistance from the major record labels; and government investigations into payola, which allegedly caused disc jockeys to favor rock over what had come to be called "good" music.

But the result of the anti-rock campaign was to stem the rise in record sales rock had brought. In 1959 singles sales were 25 percent lower than they had been in 1954, and in 1960, while singles sales rebounded with the return of Elvis Presley from the army, overall revenues declined for the first time since 1954. The record industry had long since become a two-part business, consisting of 45 rpm, 7-inch singles sold at a suggested retail price of about a dollar and $33^1/_3$ rpm, 12-inch albums sold for about four dollars (although, in practice, most stores sold them at discounts below these prices). Singles, bought largely by young people, tended more toward contemporary pop and often retained at least vestiges of rock 'n' roll, but the market was driven by albums, purchased largely by adults. By the end of the 1950s, with the decline in singles sales, the industry had begun to try to fuse the two. Previously, singles tended to contain songs not also featured on a current album by the same artist. Increasingly, there was a trend toward releasing as singles songs that were contained on albums in contemporaneous release, so that singles began to be thought of primarily as promotional items for the more profitable albums rather than as a source of revenue unto themselves. Eventually, this became the rule, and "one-off" singles released exclusively from albums became a rarity. The transition took place during the 1960s.

In 1960 Elvis Presley reclaimed his crown as the country's top singles artist, a position he had occupied from 1956 to 1958, pushing 1959's leader, Connie Francis, down to second place, followed by the resurgent Everly Brothers, who were now signed to Warner Bros. Records, which had been founded as an extension of the film studio in 1958. The signing of the Everlys marked a move into the pop mainstream for a label previously known mainly for comedy albums. Presley occupied the top of the charts for fifteen weeks with three hits: a revival of the 1927 song "Are You Lonesome To-night?," "It's Now or Never" (with a melody adapted from the Italian pop standard "O Sole Mio"), and "Stuck on You."

But an entirely different kind of entertainment was being enjoyed by an entirely different audience on the LP charts. There, the year's longest-running number-one hit, with sixteen weeks on top, was the original Broadway cast album of *The Sound of Music* (Columbia), Rodgers and Hammerstein's final effort (Hammerstein died of cancer during the year); followed by the comedy album *The Button-Down Mind of Bob Newhart* (Warner Bros.), at fourteen weeks; the instrumental release *Persuasive Percussion* by Enoch Light and the Light Brigade (billed as "Terry Snyder and the All-Stars") (Command Records), at thirteen weeks; the Kingston Trio's *Sold Out* (twelve weeks) and *String Along* (10 weeks); and Frank Sinatra's *Nice 'n' Easy* (9 weeks). Nothing even vaguely rocking got to the top of the LP list until December, when the soundtrack to Presley's comeback film *G.I. Blues* made a showing. But Presley was no longer the wild man of rock 'n' roll he had appeared to be in 1956. His return to action had been heralded by a TV special hosted by Sinatra, and his sound had been considerably softened as he turned to movie-making full-time.

And the hit parade had been softened up considerably in his absence. The biggest hit of the year was the string-filled instrumental "The Theme from *A Summer Place*" drawn from the 1959 film, by Percy Faith and His Orchestra on Columbia. Folk and country sounds prevailed in such number-one pop hits as the Everly Brothers' "Cathy's Clown," written by the duo; Johnny Preston's "Running Bear" (music and lyrics by J.P. Richardson, a.k.a. the Big Bopper) on Mercury; and Marty Robbins's performance of his own "El Paso" on Columbia. Female singers Brenda Lee ("I'm Sorry," "I Want to Be Wanted") on Decca and Connie Francis ("My Heart Has a Mind of Its Own," "Everybody's Somebody's Fool") contributed romantic ballads. The R&B-styled hits—"Save the Last Dance for Me" by the Drifters on Atlantic, "Stay" by Maurice Williams and the Zodiacs on Herald Records, and a revival of the 1930 song "Georgia on My Mind" by Ray Charles on ABC-Paramount—were all gentle, melodic efforts. And there were four silly novelties that topped the charts: "Teen Angel" by Mark Dinning on MGM, "Itsy Bitsy Teenie Weenie Yellow Polkadot Bikini" by Brian Hyland on Leader Records,

"Alley-Oop" by the Hollywood Argyles on Lute Records, and "Mr. Custer" by Larry Verne on Era.

But there was one exception among all this light fare. If the record business was content to forget that rock had ever existed, not all the fans were, and they showed it in the late summer of 1960 when Chubby Checker's cover of Hank Ballard and the Midnighters' 1959 B-side "The Twist," on Parkway Records, became a number-one hit and launched a dance fad. The music industry could exploit this and simultaneously dismiss it, but it kept the Big Beat going for a while longer. These subsequent hits—"Pony Time," "Let's Twist Again," and "The Fly"—propelled Checker into third place among singles artists in 1961, behind Presley and Brenda Lee. The Twist fad stimulated popularity for harder rocking songs like the year's biggest hit, "Tossin' and Turnin'," by Bobby Lewis on Beltone Records, and Del Shannon's "Runaway" (music cowritten by Shannon with Max Crook to Shannon's lyric) on Big Top Records, Dion's "Runaround Sue" (co-credited to Dion and Ernest Maresca), (Gary) U.S. Bonds's "Quarter to Three" on Legrand Records, and Ray Charles's "Hit the Road Jack" (written by Percy Mayfield), all of which topped the charts that year.

At the same time, other important new figures were emerging. The chart-topping success of the Shirelles' "Will You Love Me Tomorrow" on Scepter Records in January 1961 and Bobby Vee's "Take Good Care of My Baby" on Liberty Records in September, both of them written by Gerry Goffin and Carole King, signaled the rise to prominence of a new generation of Tin Pan Alley songwriters usually referred to by one of the New York City office buildings in which they worked, the Brill Building. For the next several years, writers from the Brill Building dominated popular music.

Also, songwriter Berry Gordy Jr.'s Motown Records label began to score crossover hits from the R&B charts, with the Miracles' "Shop Around" (co-credited to Gordy and Miracles lead singer Smokey Robinson) peaking at number two in February 1961 and the Marvelettes' "Please Mr. Postman" going all the way to number one in December. (Both titles were actually on the Motown subsidiary Tamla.) Motown would be another major force in 1960s pop music.

Of course, many hitmakers continued to succeed with smoother sounds in familiar styles. As in 1960, number-one hits were scored with orchestral instrumentals, country- and folk-inspired songs, R&B ballads, and softer rock. The craze for country and folkish sounds continued, exemplified by major hits including "Big Bad John" composed and performed by Jimmy Dean on Columbia; "The Lion Sleeps Tonight" (a Tin Pan Alley creation based on the same South African Zulu song that also served as the basis for the Weavers' "Wimoweh") by the Tokens on RCA Victor; "Michael" (a.k.a. "Michael, Row the Boat Ashore," adapted from the traditional folk song) by the Highwaymen on United Artists; and "Wooden Heart" (based on a German folk song) by Joe Dowell on Smash. Two R&B acts crossed over to the pop charts, although the doo-wop group the Marcels scored by covering the 1935 Rodgers and Hart classic "Blue Moon" on Colpix; only New Orleans singer Ernie K-Doe brought a tougher R&B sound to the chart, albeit with the novelty "Mother-in-Law," written by famed producer Alan Toussaint and released on the small Minit label. Meanwhile, 1950s-era rock stars sounded considerably less energetic with a series of softer hits, including the country-ish "Travelin' Man" by Ricky Nelson, the love ballad "Surrender" (based on an Italian pop song) by Elvis Presley, "Moody River" by Pat Boone, and "Running Scared" (co-credited to Orbison and Joe Melson) by Roy Orbison on Monument.

During 1961 little had changed in the album charts, with the year's three longest-running number-one hits being the soundtrack to Elvis Presley's *Blue Hawaii* (RCA Victor; 20 weeks), the soundtrack to *Exodus* (RCA Victor; 14 weeks), and Judy Garland's Grammy-winning double live album *Judy at Carnegie Hall* (Capitol; 13 weeks). But the new trends were enough to send sales back up, with gross revenues rising $6^2/_3$ percent to a new high of $640 million.

The new elements consolidated their success in 1962. By now, people were twisting in the White House, and Chubby Checker's "The Twist" actually returned to number one in January, followed by Joey Dee and the Starlighters' "Peppermint Twist—Part I" (co-credited to Dee and Henry Glover) on Roulette. Goffin and King were the year's most successful songwriters with hits like Little Eva's

"The Loco-Motion" on Dimension Records, and they were joined in the winner's circle by Brill Building members Barry Mann and Cynthia Weil (the Crystals' "Uptown" on Philles Records), Neil Sedaka and Howard Greenfield (Sedaka's "Breaking Up Is Hard to Do"), and, if not Brill Building, then just up the street, Burt Bacharach and Hal David (Gene Pitney's "Only Love Can Break a Heart" on Musicor Records). Motown made even more inroads, its hits including the Contours' "Do You Love Me," written by Berry Gordy Jr. himself and released on the Gordy Records subsidiary. And another new force was emerging, as producer Phil Spector, frequently employing the Brill Building writers, crafted hits for a series of groups on his Philles label, notably the Crystals' "He's a Rebel" (written by Gene Pitney).

In both teenagers' and adults' music, a breakthrough success was scored by Ray Charles, who delved into country music with his album *Modern Sounds in Country and Western Music*, which spent fourteen weeks on top of the *Billboard* chart, and who had the year's most successful single with a revival of the 1958 country song "I Can't Stop Loving You" (written by Nashville singer Don Gibson). Charles finished second to Elvis Presley as the year's top singles artist. Presley won out with one number-one hit ("Good Luck Charm") and two singles that peaked at number two ("Return to Sender" from his film *Girls! Girls! Girls!* and "Can't Help Falling in Love" from his film *Blue Hawaii*). Although they came in tenth on that list, New Jersey's vocal group the 4 Seasons, led by the startling falsetto of Frankie Valli, had the year's second- and third-biggest hits, "Big Girls Don't Cry" and "Sherry" on Vee-Jay.

On the album side, Ray Charles's fourteen weeks at number one was dwarfed by the year's biggest success, the soundtrack to the film adaptation of the Broadway musical *West Side Story* (Columbia), which eventually spent more than a year at number one. Henry Mancini's *Breakfast at Tiffany's*, drawn from his score for the film and featuring his number-eleven single of the Academy Award–winning song "Moon River" (with lyrics by Johnny Mercer), spent twelve weeks at number one. Mancini's deal at RCA Victor allowed him to record albums of his film scores such as this that were not technically "original soundtracks" and gave him far greater recognition than most film composers received.

Folk music, which had enjoyed broad popularity since the late 1950s, experienced a resurgence with the commercial breakthroughs of Joan Baez, each of whose first three albums, *Joan Baez, Joan Baez, Vol. 2*, and *Joan Baez in Concert* (all on Vanguard Records), were high in the charts during the year (on November 23, she made the cover of *Time* magazine), and Peter, Paul and Mary, whose self-titled debut album on Warner Bros. hit number one in October. Folk was already the subject of parody, with Allan Sherman taking *My Son, the Folk Singer* (Warner Bros.) to the top of the charts. But then, parody was the most successful form of comedy, exemplified by the chart-topping success of Vaughn Meader's take-off on President Kennedy and his relatives, *The First Family* (Cadence), another long-running number-one hit. This varied fare helped the record business to a sales increase of almost $7^1/_2$ percent, to $687 million.

As a general rule, we have tried in this book to introduce notable recording artists at the point in their careers when they made their commercial breakthroughs, not when they first appeared. But 1962 is so packed with important debuts that we will suspend this policy temporarily and note the following.

On February 17, 1962, "Surfin'" (music and lyrics by group members Brian Wilson and Mike Love) by the Beach Boys on Candix Records entered the *Billboard* Hot 100, launching the career of the most successful (at least in chart terms) American rock band in history. The group consisted of cousins Wilson (bass guitar and vocals) and Love (lead vocals), Wilson's younger brothers Dennis (drums and vocals) and Carl (lead guitar and vocals), and friend Al Jardine (rhythm guitar and vocals). Based in Hawthorne, California, the band melded an affection for vocal quartet harmonies influenced by the Four Freshmen to the guitar rock of Chuck Berry and, at the suggestion of the athletic Dennis Wilson, a lyrical interest in the southern California subculture of surfers. By the time of their second chart single, "Surfin' Safari" (also composed by Brian Wilson and Mike Love), which peaked at number fourteen in October, they had moved up to Capitol Records.

On March 19, 1962, Columbia Records released the LP *Bob Dylan* by Bob Dylan; it would sell so poorly at first that Dylan would be dubbed "Hammond's folly" after record executive John Hammond, who signed him. But people would stop laughing after Dylan penned the civil rights anthem "Blowin' in the Wind" later in the year. Born Robert Allen Zimmerman in May 1941 in Hibbing, Minnesota, Dylan became enamored of folksinger Woody Guthrie while attending the University of Minnesota and dropped out to look up his hero on the East Coast. On March 11, 1961, he made his New York stage debut at Gerde's Folk City in Greenwich Village, and by the fall Hammond had signed him to Columbia. (Forty years later, in the fall of 2001, Dylan's forty-third chart album, *Love and Theft*, debuted in the top five; soon after, it topped most critics' polls as the best album of the year.)

On July 21, 1962, the original Broadway cast album of *I Can Get It for You Wholesale* (Columbia) entered the LP charts, marking the first chart appearance of Barbra Streisand, who would go on to become the best-selling female singer of all time. She had been born Barbara Joan Streisand in Brooklyn in April 1942 and headed for New York upon graduating from high school, intent on becoming an actress. Instead, she began singing in nightclubs, where her remarkable voice soon attracted notice. *I Can Get It for You Wholesale* offered her the showy supporting role of Miss Marmelstein and a song named after her character. It would be a long time before she took another supporting part in anything.

On August 11, 1962, "Your Heart Belongs to Me," written by Smokey Robinson and recorded by the Supremes on Motown, entered the charts, beginning their dominant role as the most important girl group in history. Diana Ross, Mary Wilson, and Florence Ballard were Detroit teenagers signed up by Motown's Berry Gordy Jr., and "Your Heart Belongs to Me" was their first single on Motown following two on Tamla in 1961. They released five more singles before breaking through to widespread success with their ninth single, "Where Did Our Love Go" (composed by the Motown powerhouse songwriters Brian Holland, Eddie Holland, and Lamont Dozier) in 1964. It would be the first of five consecutive number-one hits.

On October 13, 1962, "Love Me Do" (music and lyrics by group members John Lennon and Paul McCartney) by the Beatles on Parlophone Records debuted in the British charts. They would have a large impact—needless to say—on the future of popular music; more on that soon.

Finally, on October 27, 1962, the instrumental "The Lonely Bull," financed and released by songwriter-trumpeter Herb Alpert and his partner Jerry Moss on their new A&M Records label, entered the charts credited to the Tijuana Brass, on its way to a top-ten ranking, beginning one of the 1960s' most remarkable success stories. Alpert, born in Los Angeles in March 1935, already had a considerable resume. He had begun playing trumpet at age eight. As a producer, he had worked with Jan and Dean. He was the coauthor of "Wonderful World" (co-credited to Alpert, producer Lou Adler, and Barbara Campbell), a perennial hit that peaked at number twelve for Sam Cooke on Keen Records (where Alpert worked as an A&R director) in 1960 and would be revived for a top-ten hit by Herman's Hermits on MGM in 1965 and again for a Top 40 hit by Art Garfunkel with James Taylor and Paul Simon on Columbia in 1978. (Identified by its opening line, "Don't know much about history," it is not to be confused with the 1968 song "What a Wonderful World" that was an international hit for Louis Armstrong, revived in 1986 when it was used in the film *Good Morning, Vietnam.*)

Quite a year, all things considered, and that's even without mentioning several other performers who debuted in the charts in 1962: Paul Simon (albeit as a part of the group Tico and the Triumphs and following the temporary demise of his partnership with Art Garfunkel), Carole King, Marvin Gaye, and Dionne Warwick.

The seeds of 1962 would sprout into quite a lot of foliage, but 1963, a turning-point year in the decade, forever associated with the assassination of President Kennedy and inevitably thought of in America as The Year Before the Beatles, marked one of those periodic sidesteps in popular music history. In the singles charts, the Beach Boys were the year's top recording artists, dominating with hits like "Surfin' U.S.A." (music and lyrics by Chuck Berry and Brian Wilson) and "Surfer Girl" (by Brian Wilson), both on Capitol, followed by

Dion (Jerry Leiber and Mike Stoller's "Ruby Baby"), on Columbia, the major label to which he had moved, and a resurgent Rick (no longer Ricky) Nelson, as Elvis Presley tumbled to fourteenth place. Goffin and King (Steve Lawrence's "Go Away Little Girl" on Columbia), Mann and Weil, and Bacharach and David were joined by Ellie Greenwich and Jeff Barry among the top songwriters, while the Beach Boys' Brian Wilson was writing hits for Jan and Dean (the number-one "Surf City" [co-credited to Jan Berry]) in addition to ones for his own band, and Bob Dylan's "Blowin' in the Wind" brought singles success to Peter, Paul and Mary (arguably the year's most successful act, with two number-one albums, their debut, *Peter, Paul and Mary*, from 1962, and their third LP, *In the Wind*). Inspired by Chuck Berry and Buddy Holly, Wilson and Dylan led the charge, soon joined by the Beatles, of songwriter-performers, a trend that would threaten the bank accounts of the residents of Tin Pan Alley and the Brill Building. Meanwhile, Motown continued to score, notably breaking Little Stevie Wonder with "Fingertips—Pt. 2" on Tamla, and Phil Spector reached number two with the Ronettes' "Be My Baby."

But 1963 was also a year of foreign novelty hits, with the Singing Nun's "Dominique" on Philips Records and Kyu Sakamoto's "Sukiyaki" on Capitol at number one, while Allan Sherman (*My Son, the Celebrity* and *My Son, the Nut*) amused and middle-of-the-road pop singers Frank Fontaine (*Songs I Sing on the Jackie Gleason Show*, for ABC-Paramount) and Andy Williams (*Days of Wine and Roses*, for Columbia) soothed adults at the top of the LP charts and Barbra Streisand scored her first important success with *The Barbra Streisand Album* (Columbia), which hit the top ten, went gold, and won the Grammy Award for Album of the Year. Sales continued to rise, but only by about $1\frac{1}{2}$ percent, to $698 million. On the whole, the American music scene seemed stale.

And then the Beatles happened.

Maybe we should have seen it coming. Music historian Russell Sanjek cites a telling statistic: although he emphasizes that the single most successful type of record in 1963 was the original Broadway cast album, Sanjek notes that, despite representing only 6 percent of the U.S. population, "11 million young girls" accounted for 56.3 percent of the entire amount expended on recorded music for the year. In America, those young girls might have been fixing their attention for the moment on thirteen-year-old Little Stevie Wonder or the Singing Nun, but in Great Britain, their counterparts had fallen in love with the Beatles, who sold 2.5 million records there during the year, the most ever sold by a single performer in a single year in U.K. history to that date. Of course, British stars rarely became successful in the United States, and Capitol Records, owned since 1955 by EMI, parent company of the Beatles' British label, Parlophone, had refused to issue their records, allowing them to be licensed to such labels as the Chicago R&B independent Vee-Jay, where they languished.

Finally, bowing to pressure and to indications from radio and television that the group might have a chance, Capitol agreed to release the Beatles' fifth single, "I Want to Hold Your Hand," on January 13, 1964, followed a week later with a modified version of the group's second Parlophone album, *With the Beatles*, renamed *Meet the Beatles!* The result dwarfed the breakthroughs of Benny Goodman in 1935, Frank Sinatra in 1943, and Elvis Presley in 1956. Thirty Beatles songs reached the Hot 100 during 1964, accompanied by eleven albums of one sort or another in the LP charts. The group's twenty weeks at number one in the singles chart with six different songs ("I Want to Hold Your Hand," "She Loves You," "Can't Buy Me Love," "Love Me Do," "A Hard Day's Night," and "I Feel Fine") may not have been as much as Presley in 1956, but they also had thirty weeks at number one on the LP chart with three different albums (*Meet the Beatles!*, *The Beatles' Second Album*, and, on United Artists Records, the soundtrack to their first film, *A Hard Day's Night*). And, of course, there was that famous week, April 4, 1964, when the top five titles on the Hot 100 were all Beatles records ("Can't Buy Me Love" at number one, a revival of the 1962 Isley Brothers hit "Twist and Shout" on Tollie Records at number two, "She Loves You" at number three, "I Want to Hold Your Hand" at number four, and "Please Please Me" on Vee-Jay at number five).

In the short term, the Beatles' impact on the American music industry was enormous both for itself and for what it brought in its immediate wake, an army of similarly coifed British musicians playing a similar amalgam of U.S. pop/rock styles. In the long term, their impact was so profound because it kept coming. There wasn't just one British Invasion, one Beatles-inspired transformation of popular music, but a series of them that ended by altering the business in previously unimaginable ways.

Back in 1964, however, the Beatles ushered in a slew of important new British performers including Dusty Springfield (Philips), the Dave Clark Five (Epic), the Searchers (Kapp), the Rolling Stones (London), Peter and Gordon (Capitol), the Hollies (Imperial), Gerry and the Pacemakers (Laurie), the Animals (MGM), Manfred Mann (Ascot), the Kinks (Warner Bros. subsidiary Reprise), Herman's Hermits (MGM), and Petula Clark (Warner Bros.), all of whom made their U.S. singles chart debuts the same year. These artists pushed aside many middle-level American performers, whose careers suddenly and permanently went into the shade.

Who survived? Well, the Beach Boys, with their harmonies and rock 'n' roll backing, didn't sound too different from the new trend, and they had hits such as "I Get Around" and "Fun, Fun, Fun" (both by Brian Wilson and Mike Love). The 4 Seasons, another harmony group with solid rock arrangements, continued to succeed on their old label, Vee-Jay, and their new one, Philips, their number-one hit for the year being "Rag Doll" on Philips; they managed to rank a distant second to the Beatles in the list of top recording artists of the year. The Motown Sound flourished, with the Supremes breaking through to three number-one hits (in addition to "Where Did Our Love Go," there were "Baby Love" and "Come See About Me"), Mary Wells (the number-one "My Guy") and Martha and the Vandellas (the number-two "Dancing in the Street" on the Gordy Records subsidiary) scoring, and the Temptations making their pop chart debut with the number-eleven hit "The Way You Do the Things You Do" on Gordy Records. The Brill Building writers suffered, as the Beatles furthered the trend of writer-performers, but Jeff Barry and Ellie Greenwich came up with three number-one hits, the Dixie Cups'

"Chapel of Love" (written with Phil Spector) on Red Bird, Manfred Mann's "Do Wah Diddy Diddy" (some British Invasion acts did need writers), and the Shangri-Las' "Leader of the Pack" (written with George "Shadow" Morton) on Red Bird.

Nineteen sixty-four also saw some odd jazz and pop breakouts, including hits by Louis Armstrong (Jerry Herman's "Hello, Dolly!," on Kapp Records, the title song of the year's biggest Broadway musical, which spawned a chart-topping cast album on RCA Victor), Dean Martin (a revival of the 1948 song "Everybody Loves Somebody") on Reprise, Al Hirt (the instrumental "Java") on RCA Victor, and the team of jazz saxophonist Stan Getz and Brazilian singer Astrud Gilberto ("The Girl from Ipanema") on Verve. Barbra Streisand not only survived, but flourished, making TV specials, starring in her own Broadway musical, *Funny Girl*, releasing more gold albums, and even enjoying a top-ten single with "People" from *Funny Girl*. But these were the exceptions; nearly everything else was swept away by the mop-topped Beatles and their British followers. Still, the American record business could hardly complain when revenues had gone up more than $8\frac{1}{2}$ percent, to $758 million, the biggest increase since 1959.

The Beatles' dominance in 1964 was partially due to the backlog of material they had, dating back to 1961. They again beat all comers in 1965, but not as badly, spending ten weeks at number one in the singles charts with four 45s ("Eight Days a Week," "Ticket to Ride," "Help!," and "Yesterday") and twenty-four weeks atop the LP charts with three albums (*Beatles '65*, *Beatles VI*, and the soundtrack to their second film, *Help!*). And the rest of the British Invasion continued, too, with Herman's Hermits, the Dave Clark Five, the Rolling Stones, Petula Clark, and Freddie and the Dreamers (with releases on Capitol subsidiary Tower and on Mercury) ranking among the top twenty pop singles artists. One act emerged from the Beatles' shadow by combining their own blues-rock sound with songs written by group members Mick Jagger and Keith Richards: the Rolling Stones had the year's top single with "(I Can't Get No) Satisfaction" and also topped the charts with "Get Off of My Cloud." Herman's Hermits, on the other hand, although they also enjoyed two number-one hits,

"Mrs. Brown You've Got a Lovely Daughter" and a revival of the 1911 music-hall song "I'm Henry VIII, I Am," quickly turned out to be a novelty act pegged to the good looks of teenage lead singer Peter Noone that would fade when fickle fans (or their younger sisters) turned to the next pretty face.

Meanwhile, a counterattack was launched by Americans who grew their hair long and adapted to the Merseybeat sound. The most successful of them were Gary Lewis and the Playboys (Liberty), the Byrds (Columbia), and Sonny and Cher (Atco), all from Los Angeles. The last two also bore the distinct influence of another American who had fused the Beatles' approach with his own, Bob Dylan. By 1964 Dylan had become the premier figure in folk music thanks to his songwriting, as, with songs like "Blowin' in the Wind" and its successors, he commented trenchantly on political and social issues that were stirring action nationally, particularly the civil rights movement on behalf of African Americans. But in the songs on his fourth album, *Another Side of Bob Dylan*, released in August 1964, particularly "My Back Pages," Dylan turned his back on simple political messages, and at the start of 1965 he strapped on an electric guitar and invented folk-rock on his fifth album, *Bringing It All Back Home*. The result was not only top-ten albums and singles for him (notably the number-two hit "Like a Rolling Stone"), but a stream of mostly West Coast artists who either covered his songs (electrified folkies the Byrds' "Mr. Tambourine Man," former surf band the Turtles' "It Ain't Me Babe" on White Whale) or imitated his sound and/or attitude (Phil Spector protégés Sonny and Cher's "I Got You Babe," written by Bono; ex–New Christy Minstrels member Barry McGuire's "Eve of Destruction" on Dunhill).

At the same time, the success of Motown, particularly the Supremes, the Four Tops, and the Temptations, continued. The Supremes' string of number-one hits was extended to five by "Stop! In the Name of Love" and "Back in My Arms Again," interrupted by the number-eleven showing of "Nothing but Heartaches," and resumed with "I Hear a Symphony." (All four were written by the production team by now known as Holland-Dozier-Holland.) The Four Tops, who had been singing professionally since 1953, broke through to mass success with the number-one hit "I Can't Help Myself" (another Holland-Dozier-Holland effort). And the Temptations also enjoyed their first number one with "My Girl" (cowritten by Smokey Robinson and Ronald White).

On the LP side, in addition to the Beatles, movie musical soundtracks still succeeded, notably *Mary Poppins* (Buena Vista) and *The Sound of Music* (RCA Victor), both featuring Julie Andrews, but the only original Broadway cast album to place in the top ten was *Fiddler on the Roof* (RCA Victor). This was the last year that such records, and albums by middle-of-the-road singers performing standards, enjoyed extensive popularity. "Between 1960 and 1965," writes Robert C. Toll, "the list of the Top Ten LPs contained twice as many Tin Pan Alley albums as the total of all the folk, rock, rhythm and blues, soul, and country and western albums combined." Then everything changed: "the record industry … sold more rock albums between 1966 and 1971 than all other major categories of music combined." For the year 1965, sales were up more than $13\frac{1}{2}$ percent, to $862 million.

The American counterattack against the British Invasion gathered steam in 1966. The Beatles ruled for a third year, spending seventeen weeks at the top of the LP chart with *Rubber Soul*, *"Yesterday" … and Today*, and *Revolver*, also being the top pop singles act with the number-one hits "We Can Work It Out" and "Paperback Writer," the number-two hit "Yellow Submarine," and four more Top 40 hits. Other British Invasion stars the Rolling Stones (with the number-one hit "Paint It, Black" and the number-two hit "19th Nervous Breakdown"), Herman's Hermits, Petula Clark (with the number-one hit "My Love"), and the Animals were all among the top twenty acts. But the Lovin' Spoonful on Kama Sutra Records (with the number-one hit "Summer in the City" and the number-two hits "Daydream" and "Did You Ever Have to Make Up Your Mind?"), the Mamas and the Papas on Dunhill (with the number-one hit "Monday, Monday" and the number-one album *If You Can Believe Your Eyes and Ears*), and Simon and Garfunkel on Columbia (with the number-one single "The Sounds of Silence"), all American folk-rock acts, were now also in the mix. The chart veterans the

Beach Boys continued to score, with the number-one hit "Good Vibrations" and the number-two revival of the 1961 song "Barbara Ann."

Another response to the Beatles' dominance was "the pre-fab four," the Monkees, a product of an alliance between TV and the pop music industry. The group was assembled by a TV network to appear on their own sitcom in the fall of the year. Teen pop producer Don Kirshner was hired to assemble Brill Building songwriters to provide the group with hits, and they were successfully launched with the biggest hit of the year, "I'm a Believer" (written by Neil Diamond), the number-one hit "Last Train to Clarksville" (by the pop songwriting team of Tommy Boyce and Bobby Hart), and the year's longest-running number-one album, *The Monkees*, all on Colgems Records.

Motown acts also held their own in the wake of the Beatles. The Supremes (with the number-one hits "You Can't Hurry Love" and "You Keep Me Hangin' On," and the number-one album *Supremes A' Go-Go*), the Temptations, and Stevie Wonder, among others, continued to fill the label's coffers. The year's three most successful songwriters on the Hot 100 were 1965's repeating champion Eddie Holland, whose name was on twenty-two chart entries, Brian Holland on eighteen, and Lamont Dozier on seventeen, beating out Paul McCartney with fifteen, and John Lennon with fourteen.

From earlier generations, Frank Sinatra on Reprise Records (with the number-one hit "Strangers in the Night" and the number-one album of the same name) and Ray Charles, enjoyed upticks of popularity, but Herb Alpert and the Tijuana Brass, who had two number-one albums during the year, *Going Places* and *What Now My Love*, dominated easy listening music, selling 13 million albums, which placed them second only to the Beatles in LP sales.

With revenues of $959 million, the record industry grew more than 11 percent and stood tantalizingly close to being a billion-dollar business. Feeding this growth in income were two new delivery formats, both involving tape. The industry had tried introducing pre-recorded reel-to-reel tapes in the 1950s, but consumers weren't interested. In 1966 came eight-track tape cartridges, primarily for use in cars, and the smaller cassette tape.

Yet the argument could be made that, despite this success, the major labels hadn't really accepted the second rock revolution yet. Columbia Records had Bob Dylan, Paul Revere and the Raiders, the Byrds, and Simon and Garfunkel; RCA had Elvis Presley; Capitol had the Beatles and the Beach Boys; Warner Bros., which had ascended to major-label status by buying Reprise Records from Frank Sinatra in 1963, had Petula Clark and the Kinks; and Decca had the Rolling Stones through its London subsidiary. But however profitable these acts might be, they were largely tokens. The majors hadn't committed to rock, but they finally would in 1967, due to the next new musical trend, the San Francisco Sound.

RCA Victor had gotten in on the ground floor of the psychedelic San Francisco dance band trend by signing Jefferson Airplane in 1966, but the group didn't really jell until it acquired a new female lead singer in Grace Slick, who brought in the breakout hit "Somebody to Love" (composed by her brother-in-law, Darby Slick). The song peaked in the top ten in mid-June 1967, coincident with that watershed '60s event, the Monterey Pop Festival. Gradually, the youth movement had become identifiable as a long-haired, anti–Vietnam War, drug-taking community that used rock music as an active part of its lifestyle. Its heroes were, perhaps, no more palatable to record company executives than the early rock 'n' rollers or the British Invasion mop tops had been, but successive waves must have broken down resistance, and the size of the audience had become impossible to ignore. The record business's double-digit sales increases were coming from young rock fans, and the time had come to get on the bandwagon wholeheartedly. Accordingly, the psychedelic bands that played at Monterey were either recent signees of major labels (the Grateful Dead, whose self-titled Warner Bros. debut had come out two months earlier) or about to be snapped up (Big Brother and the Holding Company by Columbia, the Anglo-American Jimi Hendrix Experience by Reprise). Meanwhile, the Beatles had metamorphosed into their own version of the psychedelic sound with their "Penny Lane"/"Strawberry Fields Forever" single and *Sgt. Pepper's Lonely Hearts Club Band* album, both number-one hits. Ironically, the group that was created to imitate the Beatles—the Monkees—sold more records in the United States in 1967 than anyone else, hitting number one on the singles chart with "Daydream Believer," number two with "A Little Bit Me, a Little Bit You," and number three with "Pleasant Valley Sunday," and spending twenty-four weeks at the top of the LP chart with *More of the Monkees*, *Headquarters*, and *Pisces, Aquarius, Capricorn and Jones Ltd.* But the Beatles, adding in the number-one hits "Hello Goodbye" and "All You Need Is Love," were a close second.

The effect of the music's evolution and its close association with the youth culture produced obvious benefits to the industry. The magical $1 billion figure was exceeded, with sales of $1.173 billion in 1967, more than a 22 percent increase in one year. No wonder the majors were moving in on rock. But the size of the increase was affected by a price increase. Since the 1950s, LPs had sold for about four dollars, and the price had even dipped slightly in the mid-'60s when the government eliminated an excise tax. Stereo records, introduced in 1958, sold for a dollar more. In May 1967, Columbia and RCA equalized the price of mono and stereo albums at about five dollars, which led to the demise of the former.

In commercial terms, the psychedelic and San Francisco bands generated more light than heat in the late 1960s. Jefferson Airplane's 1967 album *Surrealistic Pillow*, spurred by two top-ten singles ("Somebody to Love" and "White Rabbit"), went gold within six months of its release, but the band's subsequent releases didn't do as well. Big Brother and the Holding Company topped the charts in October 1968 with their Columbia debut *Cheap Thrills*, after which lead singer Janis Joplin went solo. The Grateful Dead quickly went into massive debt to Warner Bros. as they spent freely on recordings that achieved only modest sales. The rest of the San Francisco bands performed even more disappointingly. (The Jimi Hendrix Experience, however, achieved tremendous commercial success; their double-disc *Electric Ladyland* hit number one in November 1968.) But for the record companies, these groups afforded a transition to a new, bigger music scene. As FM radio began to be programmed independently from the AM stations to which it had previously been shackled, disc jockeys took to playing the longer tracks the new rock bands were recording on their albums without much concern for scoring hit singles, and LPs sold well on their own. Despite hitting number one on the album charts, neither Hendrix nor Big Brother ever got into the top ten in the singles charts.

Coming into the traumatic year of 1968, pop psychedelia gave way, on the one hand, to a heavier rock sound and, on the other, to a much lighter one. On the hard rock side, Hendrix and Big Brother were joined at the top of the LP charts by the apocalyptic Doors (*Waiting for the Sun* on Elektra) and the extended blues-rock improvisations of Cream (*Wheels of Fire* on Atco), led by guitarist Eric Clapton. On the lighter side, Bob Dylan, who had been sidelined for much of 1966 and 1967 by a motorcycle accident, returned with the quiet, allusive *John Wesley Harding* and took it into the top ten. The commercial phenomenon of the spring of 1968 was Simon and Garfunkel, with their fourth album, *Bookends*, and their participation in the soundtrack to *The Graduate* (Columbia), which in turn restimulated sales of their third album, *Parsley, Sage, Rosemary and Thyme*, giving them three top-ten albums at the same time. Black music had meanwhile become harder edged, particularly in the soulful sounds of the year's top pop singles artist Aretha Franklin (Atlantic) and James Brown (King), who came in third, and more socially conscious, with even Motown turning out hits like Diana Ross and the Supremes' "Love Child," about the fear of illegitimate pregnancy. (Ross had been promoted by Gordy to star billing in the group in 1967.)

Although their releases were coming less frequently, the Beatles continued to set the pace, absorbing trends and starting new ones. They began the year at the top of the LP charts with *Magical Mystery Tour* and ended it in the same place with their double-length "white album," *The Beatles*, in between scoring the year's biggest hit single with "Hey Jude." *The Beatles* and "Hey Jude" were early releases on the Beatles' custom label, Apple, distributed by Capitol, beginning a trend for rock artists to be given their own labels by the majors as a means of granting the artists further control over their recordings, though the labels were just imprints and the majors retained ownership of the recordings. Taken together, 1968's revenues came to $1,358,000,000, another big increase, of over $15\frac{1}{2}$ percent.

In 1969 the most successful single and album of the year came from a Broadway musical, but it was music utterly unlike that of *The Sound of Music*, Rodgers and Hammerstein's last show, which had dominated the sales of 1959–60. The single was the 5th Dimension's "Aquarius/Let the Sunshine In (The Flesh Failures)," and the album was the original Broadway cast recording of *Hair* (RCA Victor), which spent thirteen weeks at the top of the *Billboard* chart in the spring and summer. *Hair* merged Broadway with what was now known as the counterculture, combining show music with elements of folk, rock, and soul. It was emblematic of the growing diversity in popular music, which was now able to accept everything from the hard rock of the Rolling Stones' "Honky Tonk Women" to the bubblegum pop of the fictional cartoon-series group the Archies' "Sugar, Sugar" on Calendar Records, and from the Temptations' furious R&B stomp "I Can't Get Next to You" to Henry Mancini's tranquil "Love Theme from *Romeo and Juliet*" and even, on the comeback trail, Elvis Presley with "Suspicious Minds." All these songs hit number one during the year.

Much was made of the yin-yang quality of 1969's two famous rock festivals, the ecstatic Woodstock and the disastrous Altamont, but for the record business the spirit of such gatherings was less significant than their sheer size and what it said about the importance of popular music to a mass audience. Perhaps as one result, a business that had not risked a price increase for more than a decade between 1953 and 1967 went for another one only two years later, earning the wrath of Beatles fans by charging about six dollars for *Abbey Road* in the fall of 1969 and discovering that it didn't matter. (As of this writing, *Abbey Road* has sold better than any other Beatles album in the United States.) For the fifth straight year, revenues increased by double digits, over $16\frac{1}{2}$ percent, in fact, to more than 1.5 billion dollars.

The enormous growth in the record industry that had begun with the emergence of rock 'n' roll in 1955 paused in the relatively fallow years of the early 1960s, but resumed with the breakthrough of the Beatles in 1964. By 1969 what was now just called "rock" was an entertainment medium that pervaded the culture, not just the counterculture. In the last week of the year, *Led Zeppelin II* (Atlantic), a hard rock album in a style that was coming to be known as heavy metal, took over the top of the charts. Also in the top ten was *Crosby, Stills and Nash* (Atlantic), the latest development in folk-rock. Rock-influenced pop acts Tom Jones (on Decca subsidiary Parrot) and Three Dog Night (Dunhill/ABC) were also near the top of the charts, as was the jazz-rock fusion of Blood, Sweat and Tears (Columbia). The top ten was filled out by the latest albums by the Beatles, the Rolling Stones, and the Temptations. It was a diverse list, but it all answered to the term *rock*, and it was selling better than any music in history.

The Swing Era and the "Sing Era" that followed it each flourished for about ten years. By the end of the 1960s, rock was still going strong after fifteen. It had, in effect, *become* popular music. In doing so, it had absorbed much of what had gone before, and its definition had become so broad as to become vague. It had also begun to lose its inherent air of rebellion and to become a central part of a modified culture rather than simply the voice of youth. Though it would continue to grow as an entertainment medium in the coming years, the end of the 1960s musically, as politically, would prove to have been a high-water mark of a sort, and that would become apparent as early as the start of the 1970s. But the music business would be able to draw upon the talents of the musicians who emerged in the '60s and the lessons it had learned about how to do business for decades to come.

EAGLES
HEARTACHE TONIGHT

Words and Music by DON HENLEY, GLENN FREY, BOB SEGER and J.D. SOUTHER

Recorded by the EAGLES on Asylum Records

Exclusive Selling Agent for
the United States and Canada
WARNER BROS. PUBLICATIONS INC.
75 Rockefeller Plaza • New York, N.Y. 10019

CASS COUNTY MUSIC, RED CLOUD MUSIC, GEAR PUBLISHING
and ICE AGE MUSIC

$1.95
in U.S.A.

8

THE 1970s

THE BALKANIZATION
OF POPULAR MUSIC

A rule of thumb among historians holds that there is little point in trying to assess history that is less than thirty years in the past because it is still too soon to have the proper perspective. If we accept this notion, then what follows here, at least after 1974, is not to be trusted. And given the differing ways that the 1970s have been viewed in only the twenty-some years since they ended, that may be fair. Following the tumultuous 1960s, the '70s were considered something of a hangover even while they were going on, and the trend toward introspection was remarked. In an article published in *New York* magazine on August 23, 1976, when the decade was only a little more than half over, Tom Wolfe coined the term the "Me Decade" to describe these years. By the '80s, they were dismissed, though by the '90s the twenty-year cycle of nostalgia that has become common (and that had its birth in the surge of interest in the '50s during the early '70s) had lent them an affectionate glow, leading to commemorative books and CD box sets. Then in 2000, arch-conservative David Frum's book *How We Got Here: The '70s* argued that it was the 1970s, not the '60s, that marked the blossoming of a cultural and political radicalism that made the right-wing Reagan era of the '80s all but inevitable.

Luckily, we are only addressing the music business here! But, of course, the culture and the politics of any decade inevitably affect the music, too. By 1970, as a result of trends in the '60s, popular music was dominated by rock music in a way that it had never been by any previous genre. To use a potitical analogy, it was a little like the period

149

in France under President Charles de Gaulle in which everyone became a Gaullist, and then they began to break down into right Gaullists and left Gaullists. In 1970 all of popular music seemed definable as "rock music," but soon it had to be qualified as soft rock, hard rock, country rock, progressive rock, jazz rock, and so on. The triumph of the Beatles, the 1960s' most successful act, had been to synthesize a variety of styles of popular music; even early in their career, they were as likely to perform a Broadway show tune like "Till There Was You" from Meredith Willson's *The Music Man* as a raucous rocker like "Twist and Shout." Some pop musicians continued to aspire to this kind of eclecticism as the 1970s began, but the Beatles' breakup, which was announced in 1970, was symbolic of the balkanization of rock (and thus of popular music in general), which was already under way when the decade began.

Indeed, the Beatles' split was only the most visible of many in a year that seemed to explode the '60s notion of the value of music made by groups. Diana Ross and the Supremes, the second-biggest singles act of the '60s, broke up after a final appearance on January 14, 1970, with Ross going solo and being replaced in the group, which reverted to being called simply "The Supremes." The same month, Simon and Garfunkel released what would be their final new album, *Bridge over Troubled Water*, though they did not formally announce their split and indeed performed together as late as the summer. The LP was the year's biggest, and it spawned the most successful single of 1970 in the title track, resulting in six Grammy Awards including Album of the Year and Record of the Year. The Beatles' breakup was announced on April 11 with the release of Paul McCartney's first solo album, *McCartney* (Apple). Peter, Paul and Mary broke up with the release of *10 Years Together/ The Best of Peter, Paul and Mary* in May. (By the end of the decade, they had re-formed.) Lou Reed made his final appearance with the critically acclaimed, commercially negligible New York rock band the Velvet Underground on August 23, the same month that the volatile Crosby, Stills, Nash and Young, formed only in 1969, split up. (They would return in a variety of configurations.) Curtis Mayfield left the venerable Chicago-based soul group the Impressions on October 1. And the Doors made their final appearance with unpredictable lead singer Jim Morrison on November 12. (Morrison would die in the middle of the following year, making, after Jimi Hendrix on September 18, 1970, and Janis Joplin less than a month later on October 4, for three major deaths in rock within twelve months.)

The Beatles (with their 1969 LP *Abbey Road* and "Let It Be") and Simon and Garfunkel were the only performers to have both an album and a single among 1970's ten most successful. (You might also include the soundtrack to *Butch Cassidy and the Sundance Kid* on A&M and B.J. Thomas's "Raindrops Keep Fallin' on My Head," on Scepter Records, which came from it. That song won the 1969 Academy Award for its authors, Burt Bacharach and Hal David.) But there were other performers emerging who represented the kind of broad stylistic reach that they had embraced.

Chicago, initially known as Chicago Transit Authority, a seven-piece rock band with three horns formed in 1967 in the city for which it was named, had debuted on the charts in 1969. For 1970 the band placed its first two double-LPs on Columbia (*Chicago Transit Authority* and *Chicago*, a.k.a. *Chicago II*) among the top twenty-five best-sellers. They scored three top-ten singles ("Make Me Smile," "25 or 6 to 4," and "Does Anybody Really Know What Time It Is?") with a sense of popular music that even extended to elements of big band jazz.

Elton John, born Reginald Dwight in Pinner, Middlesex, England, in March 1947, studied piano, played in the band Bluesology, and worked as a sideman before hooking up with his lyric partner, Bernie Taupin, and starting to get his own record releases in the United Kingdom He first reached the American charts with "Border Song" on the Decca Records subsidiary Uni just before his U.S. debut at the Troubadour nightclub in Los Angeles on August 25, 1970. The appearance marked the release of his album *Elton John*, a string-filled ballad collection, but John's energetic shows revealed that he could rock out as well. The album broke into the charts in October, on its way to the top ten in January 1971, followed by the single "Your Song," a gentle, melodic ballad, which also became a top-ten hit. Like Chicago, John was able to alternate such light pop statements with full-blooded hard rock, appealing to a broad fan base.

Then, too, the former Beatles themselves wasted no time in getting their solo careers under way: John Lennon had the gold-selling top-ten Apple single "Instant Karma (We All Shine On)" in March 1970, even before the band's breakup was announced officially, and he followed in December with the top-ten album *John Lennon/Plastic Ono Band*; *McCartney* hit number one and went gold; Ringo Starr charted with two albums on Apple, the standards collection *Sentimental Journey* in May and the country disc *Beaucoups of Blues* in October; and George Harrison went gold and topped the charts on Apple with the triple-LP box set *All Things Must Pass* (released in November) and its first single, "My Sweet Lord"/"Isn't It a Pity."

But if there was any trend in popular music in 1970, it was toward soft rock. As if comforting listeners after the storms of the '60s, many of the biggest hits were grand ballads that offered reassurance, such as "Bridge over Troubled Water," "I'll Be There" (recorded by the Jackson 5 on Motown), and "Let It Be." The most notable chart-debut artists of the year in this sense were the Carpenters (on A&M), who hit number one with Hal David and Burt Bacharach's ballad "(They Long to Be) Close to You" and number two with "We've Only Just Begun"; Bread (on Elektra), who had a number-one single with "Make It with You"; and James Taylor (on Warner Bros.), who had a number-three single with his song "Fire and Rain" and a top-ten album with *Sweet Baby James*. These artists ushered in a new form of easy listening music that dealt the real death blow to the frontline careers of older middle-of-the-road singers like Andy Williams, Frank Sinatra (who would announce his retirement in 1971, only to return in 1973), and Tony Bennett. Although these singers had been pushed to the margins by the rock revolution of the '60s, they had maintained much of their audiences. But groups like the Carpenters offered fans of pop ballads a younger, relatively hipper alternative, and by 1972 the older generation of easy listening artists was falling off the charts and off the rosters of the major labels.

James Taylor, of course, represented the vanguard of the singer-songwriter movement, which included performers like Joni Mitchell (who had debuted on the charts with her self-titled first album on Reprise in 1968) and veteran Brill Building songwriter Carole King (on Ode Records), who pursued a confessional style of folk-rock that appealed to a more refined audience. In addition, the older generation was being edged aside by a new set of pop singers who could stand toe-to-toe with them on stages in Las Vegas and elsewhere, including Neil Diamond, 1970's second-biggest pop singles act, who hit number one with "Cracklin' Rosie" and could make a claim to be included in the singer-songwriter camp as well; Tom Jones, whose *Tom Jones Live in Las Vegas* (Parrot Records), released in the fall of 1969, was one of 1970's thirty best-selling albums and whose 1970 studio collections *Tom* and *I (Who Have Nothing)* went gold; and Engelbert Humperdinck, whose self-titled album on Parrot, released late in 1969, was another of the year's thirty best-sellers and who released the gold-selling follow-up *We Made It Happen* for the summer.

And then there was the unrefined audience for hard rock that put Led Zeppelin's *Led Zeppelin II*, Iron Butterfly's *In-A-Gadda-Da-Vida* on Atco, Grand Funk Railroad's *Grand Funk* on Capitol, Mountain's *Mountain Climbing!* (Windfall), and Steppenwolf's *Steppenwolf "Live"* (Dunhill/ABC) among the year's forty best-selling albums and launched the career of Black Sabbath on Warner Bros. Somewhat more discerning were fans of popular mainstream rock performers like Creedence Clearwater Revival, who had two double-sided number-two singles on Fantasy Records, "Travelin' Band"/"Who'll Stop the Rain" and "Lookin' Out My Back Door"/"Long as I Can See the Light," all composed by group leader-vocalist-guitarist John Fogerty, as well as the million-selling albums *Willie and the Poor Boys* (released in late 1969) and *Cosmo's Factory*; Latin rock band Santana, whose self-titled debut album on Columbia, released in the wake of the band's celebrated appearance at Woodstock in August 1969, continued to sell well in 1970; Joe Cocker, who also got a boost from Woodstock, with his late-1969 LP *Joe Cocker!* on A&M; Canadians the Guess

Who, whose top-ten album on RCA Victor was promoted by its number-one title track, "American Woman"; the Moody Blues, with their late-1969 top-twenty album *To Our Children's Children's Children* on the band's Threshold imprint through Decca and the top-ten follow-up LP *A Question of Balance*; and Bob Dylan's former backup group the Band, whose second, self-titled effort, released in the fall of 1969, hit the top ten in February 1970.

Meanwhile, R&B—or "soul" music, as it was now being called—continued to be dominated by Motown, particularly in the teeny pop style of the Jackson 5, the year's top pop singles artists, boasting four number-one hits, "I'll Be There," "ABC," "The Love You Save," and "I Want You Back." Veteran Motown acts also continued to enjoy success, including Diana Ross (who had the number-one hit, by Ashford and Simpson, "Ain't No Mountain High Enough"), Smokey Robinson and the Miracles (the belated number-one hit "The Tears of a Clown"), the Temptations (the number-three hit "Ball of Confusion [That's What the World Is Today]"), and Stevie Wonder (the number-three hit "Signed, Sealed, Delivered I'm Yours"). Among the major non-Motown soul acts of the year were Sly and the Family Stone (the number-one single "Thank You Falettinme Be Mice Elf Agin" and the 1969 album *Stand!*, still a strong seller in 1970), Isaac Hayes (with the still-popular 1969 album *Hot Buttered Soul* and 1970's top-ten hit *The Isaac Hayes Movement*, both on Enterprise), James Brown, and Aretha Franklin. Taken all together, these trends were enough to give the music industry a growth of more than $4\frac{1}{2}$ percent, to gross revenues of more than $1.6 billion for 1970.

From the record industry's point of view, steady growth had become a byword. Music was selling in a variety of formats, including LPs, 8-track tape cartridges, and cassette tapes, the last one growing quickly. The industry introduced a new format, the quadraphonic disc, containing four channels of sound to be played on four speakers, in May 1970, and records were manufactured in quad for the next few years. But the format did not catch on, and it was discontinued.

Meanwhile, the success of the business led to unforeseen consequences in the form of a new kind of bootlegging. Although counterfeiting of records had been a worldwide problem for a long time, the manufacture of albums containing otherwise unavailable performances by popular acts (given a certain cachet at a time when "underground" was considered a highly complimentary term) was something new, at least to popular music. In September 1970, it was reported that an unauthorized two-LP set of Bob Dylan recordings, *The Great White Wonder* (consisting partially of what were eventually dubbed *The Basement Tapes* and released legitimately by Columbia in 1975) had sold 350,000 copies. The record industry cried foul, but the popularity of bootlegs was a measure of the vehemence felt by a mass audience for popular music, and eventually the industry found ways to satisfy that demand.

In November 1970 Decca Records released the two-LP set *Jesus Christ Superstar*, a new rock opera composed by Andrew Lloyd Webber with lyrics by Tim Rice featuring a cast of British singers including Murray Head and Yvonne Elliman. Even in a period when interest in Christ approached faddish proportions, reflected in such top-ten hits as Norman Greenbaum's "Spirit in the Sky" on Reprise and Ocean's "Put Your Hand in the Hand" on Kama Sutra, *Jesus Christ Superstar* was still a surprise success, since the songwriters and performers were previously unknown and the idea of releasing what was in essence an original cast album prior to the mounting of a stage production that would promote it seemed counterintuitive. But it ranked at the top of the *Billboard* chart for 1971 (although Carole King's *Tapestry* spent more weeks at number one and outsold it in the long run). And a stage version finally opened on Broadway on October 12, 1971, launching Lloyd Webber and Rice to long careers in musical theater. Another Christ-related show, *Godspell*, had preceded it to the New York stage, with a cast album on Bell Records containing the hit "Day by Day."

Otherwise, the singer-songwriter movement was the main story in popular music in 1971. *Tapestry*, eventually certified for sales of 10 million copies, was ubiquitous, spawning a double-sided number-one single in "It's Too Late" (music by King, lyrics by Toni Stern)/"I Feel the Earth Move" (music and lyrics by King), and it was joined among the ten best-selling albums by James Taylor's still-popular *Sweet Baby*

James and Cat Stevens' *Tea for the Tillerman* (A&M), his American chart debut. Taylor also had a number-one single with his cover of King's "You've Got a Friend" from his number-two album *Mud Slide Slim and the Blue Horizon*. Notable new acts in 1971 included Carly Simon on Elektra and John Denver on RCA Victor (although Denver had previously performed as a member of the Mitchell Trio, replacing Chad Mitchell in what had previously been called the Chad Mitchell Trio, and his song, "Leaving on a Jet Plane," had been a number-one hit for Peter, Paul and Mary in 1969). Denver reached number two on the singles chart with "Take Me Home, Country Roads" (co-credited to Denver, Bill Danoff, and Taffy Nivert), and his album *Poems, Prayers and Promises* ranked fortieth among the year's best-sellers.

Hard rock continued to be popular, particularly in the hands of Led Zeppelin, which in the fall released its untitled fourth album, containing the power ballad "Stairway to Heaven" (music by Jimmy Page, lyrics by Robert Plant), which, at last count, had sold 22 million copies in the United States. Black Sabbath's second album, *Paranoid*, meanwhile, outsold its debut, and Grand Funk Railroad had two LPs among the year's biggest sellers, the late-1970 release *Live Album* and the spring studio recording *Survival*.

Mainstream rock also produced numerous hits, including further work by ex-Beatles Paul McCartney (the number-one single "Uncle Albert"/"Admiral Halsey" from the number-two album *Ram*) and John Lennon (the number-three single "Imagine" from the number-one album of the same name). Faces lead singer Rod Stewart was quickly eclipsing his band, with his number-one single "Maggie May" (co-credited to Stewart and Martin Quittenton) from the number-one album *Every Picture Tells a Story* on Mercury. Two posthumous stars scored hits, Jimi Hendrix with the number-three album *The Cry of Love*, and Janis Joplin, with the number-one single "Me and Bobby McGee" and the number-one album *Pearl*. The Rolling Stones were enjoying a career revival, with the single "Brown Sugar" and their album *Sticky Fingers* (Rolling Stones Records) both reaching number one. Other mainstream rock acts scoring success included Santana (the number-one 1970 album *Abraxas*); Chicago (the number-two album *Chicago III*); Neil Young (the top-ten 1970 album *After the Gold Rush* on Reprise); the disbanded Crosby, Stills, Nash and Young (the number-one live album *4 Way Street* on Atlantic); new British supergroup Emerson, Lake and Palmer (the gold-selling self-titled debut album on the Cotillion subsidiary of Atlantic); Creedence Clearwater Revival (the late-1970 album release *Pendulum*); and Jethro Tull (their first top-ten album *Aqualung*).

Among soul performers, the major artists again included Sly and the Family Stone (the number-one single "Family Affair"), Isaac Hayes (the Academy Award–winning number-one single "Theme from Shaft"), and Aretha Franklin (a number-two revival of the 1961 song "Spanish Harlem"). And while Motown's grasp on the soul market seemed to be slipping, 1971 was the year of Marvin Gaye's seminal *What's Going On* (with its number-two title track) and further successes by the Temptations (the number-one single "Just My Imagination [Running Away with Me]") and the Jackson 5 (the number-two hits "Never Can Say Goodbye" and "Mama's Pearl"). For the year, sales were up a healthy 5 percent industrywide.

The softening of rock continued in 1972, a year when the biggest artists were Roberta Flack on Atlantic (with the number-one 1970 album *First Take*, the late-1971 album *Quiet Fire*, the top-ten duet album *Roberta Flack & Donny Hathaway*, and the number-one single of the year "The First Time Ever I Saw Your Face"), Don McLean on United Artists (with *American Pie* and its number-one title song), Nilsson on RCA Victor (with the number-one single "Without You" and the late-1971 album *Nilsson Schmilsson*), and America on Warner Bros. (with the number-one album *America* and the number-one hit "A Horse with No Name"). Even rocker Neil Young turned to a softer sound, earning a number-one single with "Heart of Gold" and the biggest album of the year with his country-rock-flavored *Harvest*.

Among the still ascendant singer-songwriters, Carole King continued to sell lots of copies of *Tapestry* (enough to make it the second-best-selling album of 1972) as well as her chart-topping late-1971 follow-up album *Music*; Cat Stevens had another big seller with his follow-up to *Tea for the Tillerman*, *Teaser and the*

Firecat; and Paul Simon emerged from his partnership with Art Garfunkel by releasing a self-titled solo album that reached the top ten.

Mainstream rock was reasserting itself, however. The Allman Brothers Band on Capricorn Records, forging on after the October 1971 death of their leader, guitarist Duane Allman, scored their first top-ten album with *Eat a Peach*; Alice Cooper broke into the top ten on Warner Bros. with *School's Out*; Columbia Records signed Aerosmith and Bruce Springsteen; and the Rolling Stones toured North America for the first time since 1969. That tour, kicking off on June 3 and encompassing fifty-four shows in twenty-nine cities, demonstrated how touring had changed in only a few years. The Stones' 1969 tour had consisted of only twenty shows, plus the disastrous Altamont Festival. It had gone mostly to big cities. The 1972 tour exploited the rash of multipurpose arenas that had grown up all over the United States in the intervening years, as well as the all-pervasive reach of rock music. Now, there were plenty of shows in the South and the Midwest in towns that big tours usually missed in the past. The tour stimulated sales of the Stones' oldies collection, *Hot Rocks 1964–1971* (London), and their new chart-topping double album *Exile on Main St.* (Rolling Stones Records). Continuing to enjoy success on albums were Jethro Tull (*Thick as a Brick*) and Santana (*Santana III*), joined by British performers Yes on Atlantic (*Fragile*) and Humble Pie on A&M (*Smokin'*), while Chicago continued its winning ways with the number-three single "Saturday in the Park" and *Chicago V*.

The beginnings of a major development in soul music were forged in 1972 with the emergence of writer-producers Kenny Gamble and Leon Huff, who put nine singles in the pop charts through their Philadelphia International label, the most successful of them being Billy Paul's number-one hit "Me and Mrs. Jones" and Harold Melvin and the Blue Notes' number-three hit "If You Don't Know Me by Now." Gamble and Huff had a new, lush style more sophisticated than the Motown or Stax approaches that harked back to the 1960s and that would prove a precursor to disco. But the biggest R&B act of the year (and the top pop singles artist) was Memphis-based Al Green, with three top singles (the number-one "Let's Stay Together" and the number-threes "You Ought to Be with Me" and "I'm Still in Love with You" [all music and lyrics by Al Green, Al Jackson, and Willie Mitchell]), as well as the top-ten *Let's Stay Together* LP (Hi Records). Close on Green's heels among soul performers were the Staple Singers on Stax Records (the number-one single "I'll Take You There" and the album *Bealtitude: Respect Yourself*) and the Chi-Lites on Brunswick (the number-one single "Oh Girl" and the top-ten album *A Lonely Man*).

A major musical trend of the year worth noting was nostalgia. On February 14, 1972, the musical *Grease*, a satire on the 1950s, opened on Broadway. By the time it closed, after 3,388 performances, on April 13, 1980, it was the longest-running musical in Broadway history up to that time. Meanwhile, a surprising comeback was mounted by Chuck Berry, whose album *The London Chuck Berry Sessions* entered the top ten in October, spurred by the success of his suggestive novelty single "My Ding-a-Ling," which hit number one later that month, giving Berry the only chart-topping pop hit of his career. (He had hit number one on the R&B charts with "Maybellene," "School Day," and "Sweet Little Sixteen" in the 1950s.) The following week, Elvis Presley peaked at number two with his first major hit in three years, and the last of his career, "Burning Love." As major hits like Gilbert O'Sullivan's "Alone Again (Naturally)" on MAM Records and "American Pie" expressed depression and disillusionment, the past seemed more attractive. The nostalgia for the '50s would be goosed by director George Lucas's 1973 film *American Graffiti* (although it was set in the spring of 1962) and its top-ten double-LP soundtrack album of oldies; the movie in turn would inspire the sitcom *Happy Days*, also starring Ron Howard, which began its ten-year run on television in January 1974, its initial theme song being Bill Haley and the Comets' "Rock Around the Clock."

The retrospective trend in music didn't only relate to the 1950s, however. Among the year's most successful albums was the double-LP compilation *History of Eric Clapton* (Atco). Released at a time when the legendary guitarist was out of action due to heroin addiction, the album consolidated his legend by drawing tracks from the various group configurations in which he had participated; it was a top-ten, gold-selling hit. As previously mentioned, there was also the Rolling Stones compilation, *Hot Rocks 1964–1971*, which reached the top ten, and by the end of the year it was joined by a successful follow-up, *More Hot Rocks (Big Hits & Fazed Cookies)*. Although 1972 was not a big year for the Beatles, George Harrison's charity show *Concert for Bangla Desh*, a triple-LP set, reached number two. On it, Harrison sang old Beatles songs and Bob Dylan came out of retirement to perform some of his evergreens, furthering the sense of '60s nostalgia.

The breakups of '60s groups had led to a large number of successful solo careers. It wasn't just the ex-Beatles who were prospering. On the *Billboard* album chart for June 17, 1972, five of the top-ten slots were held by former group members: ex–Buffalo Springfield and Crosby, Stills, Nash and Young member Stephen Stills at number four with *Manassas* (Atlantic); ex–Big Brother and the Holding Company singer Janis Joplin at number five with another posthumous release, *Joplin in Concert*; *History of Eric Clapton* at number seven; ex–Buffalo Springfield and CSN&Y member Neil Young's *Harvest* at number nine; and the duo album *Graham Nash/David Crosby* (Atlantic), by former Hollies and CSN&Y member Nash and former Byrds and CSN&Y member Crosby at number ten. In 1972, the best way to be a successful new artist, it seemed, was to be an artist from a defunct group now performing under your own name. For the year, overall sales of recorded music rose 10 percent, closing in on $2 billion.

Meanwhile, the industry was consolidating even as it grew. In this period, the major labels expanded to six entities: CBS Records (which owned the venerable Columbia Records label and its primary subsidiary, Epic Records); RCA Victor Records; EMI (which owned Capitol Records); Warner Records (or WEA, for Warner-Elektra-Atlantic, as it became known in the early 1970s after purchasing both the folk and rock label Elektra and the rock, R&B, and jazz label Atlantic); MCA (which had absorbed Decca along with several smaller labels and even discontinued the Decca imprint in 1973); and PolyGram, the 1972 merger of the Dutch Philips label (which owned Mercury Records among other acquisitions) and the German Siemens company (which owned the renowned classical label Deutsche Grammophon).

Roberta Flack had the year's top single for the second time in a row in 1973 with "Killing Me Softly with His Song," and War had the top album with *The World Is a Ghetto* on United Artists (featuring the number-two single "The Cisco Kid"). But the major artists of the year were Carly Simon and Elton John, each of whom placed both an album and a single among the ten most successful records in that category (Simon's *No Secrets* and "You're So Vain"; John's *Don't Shoot Me, I'm Only the Piano Player* and "Crocodile Rock"), and George Harrison, Paul McCartney and Wings, and the Rolling Stones, each of whom had both a number-one single and a number-one album: Harrison's *Living in the Material World* and "Give Me Love [Give Me Peace on Earth]"; McCartney's *Red Rose Speedway* and "My Love"; and the Stones' *Goats Head Soup* and "Angie."

Another notable artist who succeeded on both the singles and albums charts was Jim Croce, a folk-rock singer-songwriter with a flair for novelty tunes, who became a major star in 1973 just before being killed in an airplane crash. Croce, born in Philadelphia in January 1943, struggled until the release of the tall tale "You Don't Mess Around with Jim," which peaked in the top ten on ABC in September 1972. After a couple of additional Top 40 hits in a more serious style, Croce returned to humorous storytelling with "Bad, Bad Leroy Brown," which hit number one in July 1973. On September 20, Croce's plane crashed in Louisiana, after which his more thoughtful songs, such as "I Got a Name" (a rare number for the artist, because he did not write it himself; it was written by lyricist Norman Gimbel and composer Charles Fox) and "Time in a Bottle," became hits as well.

The album charts of 1973 featured recordings by many rock acts, played on FM radio, that succeeded without generating equally big hit singles (although some of them enjoyed modest ones), among them the Moody Blues, Loggins and Messina (Columbia), the Doobie Brothers (Warner Bros.), and Deep Purple (Warner Bros.), each of whom placed two or (in the case of Deep Purple) even three albums among the forty best-sellers of the year without having a 45 do that well. The greatest example of this, however, was Pink Floyd. The group's breakthrough hit, *The Dark Side of the Moon*, released on Capitol on January 17, placed eleventh for the year, and it became a perennial seller; it was the eleventh-biggest album of 1974, too, and at last count it had sold 15 million copies in the United States.

Kenny Gamble was the year's most successful songwriter on the pop singles chart, his biggest hit coming with the O'Jays' "Love Train"—which he cowrote with the year's second-biggest songwriter, his usual partner Leon Huff—and the Stylistics' "Break Up to Make Up," which Gamble cowrote with Thom Bell and Linda Creed. Stevie Wonder, meanwhile, having wrested creative control from Motown after he turned twenty-one and reintroduced himself to the rock audience by opening shows for the Rolling Stones on their 1972 tour, broke through to mass success with two number-one singles, the propulsive "Superstition" and the lovely ballad "You Are the Sunshine of My Life" (both his own compositions), from *Talking Book*, his first top ten pop album since his debut ten years earlier. Motown also continued to score with hits by Marvin Gaye ("Let's Get It On," co-credited to Gaye and Edward Townshend), former Temptation Eddie Kendricks ("Keep On Truckin' "), and Diana Ross ("Touch Me in the Morning"). For the year, revenues were up about $4^3/_4$ percent, breaking the $2 billion mark, helped by an across-the-board price rise to $5.98 for LPs (a price previously used only for superstar releases).

In retrospect, one of the more significant events of 1973 was the founding of Casablanca Records by record executive Neil Bogart, a veteran of labels like Cameo-Parkway and Buddah. Casablanca would barely make it to the end of the 1970s, being sold to PolyGram in 1980, but before then it was responsible for some of the major musical movements of the rest of the '70s. On Valentine's Day 1974, *Rolling Stone* magazine reported that the start-up label had signed two flamboyant new acts: KISS, a New York–based hard-rock quartet that wore outrageous makeup, and Parliament, a loose congregation of funk musicians (many of whom also recorded for Westbound Records under the name Funkadelic) led by George Clinton. KISS would break through to success in 1975 with their fourth LP, *Alive!*, on the way to a career that, at last count, included twenty-three gold or platinum albums; Parliament would achieve widespread success in 1976 with its platinum album *Mothership Connection* and its single "Tear the Roof Off the Sucker (Give Up the Funk)." But these two seminal artists were not what Casablanca became best known for: it became famous for its roster of disco artists.

Music historian Paul Grein flatly states, in an essay called "From the Sublime to the (Profoundly Ridiculous)," published in the lengthy booklet accompanying the box set *Have a Nice Decade: The '70s Pop Culture Box* (Rhino Records, 1998), that the Hues Corporation's single "Rock the Boat" on RCA, which entered the charts in May 1974 and topped them in July, "launched the disco era." There are those who maintain that the real end of the '60s came with the resignation of President Nixon on August 8, 1974. It might be argued that the music of the '70s wasn't really born until around the same time. "Rock the Boat" led to a series of other simple dance hits in the ensuing months, being followed immediately at number one by George McCrae's "Rock Your Baby" on T.K. Records, Barry White's "Can't Get Enough of Your Love, Babe" on 20th Century Records in September, and Carl Douglas's "Kung Fu Fighting," also on 20th Century, in December. With such songs, discos began to spring up all around the country, and they began to generate their own hits.

Discos were especially popular in New York, but they were an uptown phenomenon. Downtown, something else was happening. On August 16, 1974, one week after Nixon left office, four denim-clad musicians got up on the stage of a bar on the Bowery called CBGB's. They were named the Ramones, after a pseudonym once used by Paul McCartney, but they didn't sound much like the Beatles, unless you think back to the early Beatles in their Hamburg days. The Ramones played punk rock: short, simple, aggressive songs that reveled in their primitivism. Along with disco, punk would come to define '70s music in the second half of the decade.

But all of that was just emerging. At the top of the charts, 1974 was the year of John Denver, who placed two singles, "Sunshine on

My Shoulders" and "Annie's Song," at number one, along with two albums, *John Denver's Greatest Hits* and *Back Home Again*. On his heels was Elton John, who placed three singles in the top five ("Bennie and the Jets" "Don't Let the Sun Go Down on Me," and "The Bitch Is Back") and two albums, *Caribou* and *Greatest Hits*, at number one, as well as having the year's biggest selling album, 1973's *Goodbye Yellow Brick Road*. In soul music, the major performers were Gladys Knight and the Pips on Buddah Records, who had three number-one soul hits ("I've Got to Use My Imagination," "Best Thing That Ever Happened to Me," and "I Feel a Song [In My Heart]") and ranked as the year's top pop singles act, and Stevie Wonder, with two number-one soul hits ("You Haven't Done Nothin'" and "Boogie On Reggae Woman") and the year's biggest soul album, *Fulfillingness' First Finale*, which also topped the pop charts and won the Grammy for Album of the Year.

Buoyed by another price increase for LPs to $6.98, revenues were up 9 percent, even though actual unit sales declined more than 12 percent, from 616 million copies in 1973 to 539.9 million in 1974. (The price rises were part of an overall inflation that continued through the rest of the 1970s. The Consumer Price Index rose 12.4 percent in 1974, the largest increase since 1946.) Keeping in mind the distinction between rising revenues and falling unit sales, this is perhaps a good place to insert another caveat having to do with the statistics used in the record industry, which are cited frequently in this book. Just as all reconstructed chart rankings from before 1940 and all actual ones from after 1940 should be taken with a grain of salt and considered to represent estimates, so should revenue numbers. The revenue figure for 1974, $2.2 billion, is from the RIAA, the music industry association representing the major labels, which also certifies gold and platinum records. In February 1976 *Cash Box* magazine reported that this figure was based on *list prices*, while virtually all records are sold at a discount. If the estimate were based on the prices at which manufacturers sold records to their distributors, the article noted, "the record business appears to be an $850–950 million industry, less than half the $2.2 billion published figure. Which figures are more accurate is hard to determine," the article continued. "The RIAA reflects industry sales at an unrealistic list price level, presumably to make the number larger than it should be. And yet when record retailing and manufacturing, music publishing and domestic revenue from international deals are added in, the overall record industry is a multi-billion dollar industry. But how many multis will remain hard to determine until more accurate sales statistics are made available."

If anything, Elton John and John Denver were even more ubiquitous at the top of the charts in 1975 than they had been in 1974. Elton John had the year's top album, *Greatest Hits*, and with three number one singles (a revival of the 1967 Beatles song "Lucy in the Sky with Diamonds," "Philadelphia Freedom," and "Island Girl") he was the top pop singles artist. His albums *Captain Fantastic and the Brown Dirt Cowboy* and *Rock of the Westies* each entered the *Billboard* chart at number one. No artist had ever had an album enter the charts at number one before, and now John had done it twice within months; in addition to demonstrating his massive popularity, this indicated that record distribution was becoming more uniform around the country. Denver, meanwhile, with two number-one singles ("Thank God I'm a Country Boy" and "I'm Sorry") and one number-one album, *Windsong*, ranked just behind John. In soul music, the big winner was Earth, Wind & Fire, with its number-one single "Shining Star" and album *That's the Way of the World* on Columbia. The continuing success of hard rock/heavy metal in general and of Led Zeppelin in particular was confirmed by a look at the March 29, 1975, issue of *Billboard*, on which the group's new album, *Physical Graffiti* (released on the Swan Song custom label through Atlantic), which had entered the charts two weeks earlier at number three, was now number one, and where all five of their previous albums were back on the chart.

Mainstream rock was also healthy. Bob Dylan, who had made a notable commercial comeback with a national tour and his first number one album, *Planet Waves* (on Asylum Records), in 1974, returned to number one with his critical comeback, *Blood on the Tracks* (on Columbia), in early 1975, then embarked on another tour, the gypsy caravan called the Rolling Thunder Revue, in the fall. Other acts broke through to major success. The Eagles, after struggling for several years, topped the LP charts with their fourth album, *One of These Nights* (Asylum). Bruce Springsteen, after two commercially marginal albums released in 1973, had built up a following for his live show, accompanied by his E Street Band, and with the release of his third album, *Born to Run*, became a sensation, making the covers of *Time* and *Newsweek* on October 27, 1975. And reggae, which had been building in popularity, broke big especially in England, where Bob Marley and the Wailers (Island Records) became stars, and Marley also placed three albums in the U.S. charts during the year.

Disco, meanwhile, continued to grow, with chart-topping hits like Silver Convention's "Fly, Robin, Fly" on Midland International Records and Van McCoy's "The Hustle" on Avco Records. Disco began to attract white rock imitators like Elton John with "Philadelphia Freedom" and, most tellingly, the Bee Gees, the British/Australian trio of brothers Barry, Maurice, and Robin Gibb, who first rose to fame in the 1960s imitating the Beatles, then declined, but launched a comeback by disguising their voices in falsetto and recording "Jive Talkin'" on RSO Records, their first major hit in four years. And in England, where the Ramones had planted the seed, the punk movement took hold; the Sex Pistols played their first, shambling gig on November 6, 1975.

For the year, revenues were up more than $8^1/_2$ percent, although actual sales continued to decline slightly. Meanwhile, following the introduction of Dolby noise-reduction technology, 150 million blank cassette tape cartridges were sold in the United States during the year, an indication that music fans were looking for an alternative to the rising prices of records and pre-recorded tapes.

The musical fragmentation that constituted the 1970s is especially apparent in the year 1976. Whose year was it? That depended on what kind of music fan you were. For mainstream rock fans, 1976 began with the January 16 release of Peter Frampton's double album *Frampton Comes Alive!* on A&M, which topped the charts for ten weeks on its way to sales of 6 million copies, making it the year's most successful LP. Then there was February 24, the day *Eagles/Their*

Greatest Hits 1971–1975 was released, an album that ranks at this writing as the biggest selling album in history, at 27 million copies. All year, sales of the newly reconstituted Fleetwood Mac's self-titled 1975 album on Reprise sold more copies until it hit number one in September. And Paul McCartney's biggest selling post-Beatles album, *Wings at the Speed of Sound*, was goosed by its number-one hit "Silly Love Songs" and his first North American tour since the Beatles quit the road a decade earlier.

If you were a country fan, the important date on the calendar was February 7, when the compilation *Wanted! The Outlaws* (RCA), featuring Willie Nelson and Waylon Jennings, entered the charts, launching the "Outlaw" movement that would transform country music. But February 7 was also the day that Donna Summer's erotic "Love to Love You Baby," a disco smash on Oasis Records, peaked at number two on the Hot 100. It launched Summer—the only real star to emerge from disco—and it helped popularize the extended 12-inch single, developed for use in clubs. So maybe 1976 was the year of disco, with other hits such as Johnnie Taylor's "Disco Lady" on Columbia, Diana Ross's "Love Hangover," KC and the Sunshine Band's "(Shake, Shake, Shake) Shake Your Booty" on T.K., and even parodies like Rick Dees's "Disco Duck" on RSO and Walter Murphy's "A Fifth of Beethoven" on Private Stock Records topping the charts. Or perhaps, with the release of the Ramones' self-titled debut album in the United States on Sire Records and the British appearance of the Sex Pistols' first single, "Anarchy in the U.K.," on EMI in Great Britain, it was the year of punk. In any case, it was another successful year, with revenues up nearly $14^1/_2$ percent and unit sales rebounding.

By the mid-1970s, lengthening sales patterns for albums began to lead to a change in release schedules that became dramatic over the next several years. In the days of 78 rpm singles, artists recorded frequently, issuing new discs every few weeks on average. With the onset of the LP-and-45 era in the 1950s, a more regular pattern emerged, with most major artists releasing two albums and three or four singles per year. This, of course, was at a time when artists were not expected to write—or often even choose—the songs they recorded. Artist contracts followed the release pattern, and even after the start of the 1960s, when performers began to write their own songs as a matter of course, those contracts continued. Records tended to sell at their peak for relatively short periods of time, and artists and record companies feared that a fickle public would forget a performer who had not put out a record recently. The Beatles, for most of their career, maintained the old schedule, even though they were writing most of the songs they recorded and touring as well. By the end of the '60s, however, an album a year was more the norm and, as previously noted, by this time singles usually contained songs also featured on the albums, rather than being separate items. Also, record companies and artists had come up with various ways to fill the pipeline besides releasing studio albums of new material each time out. There were greatest hits albums; live albums on which the artists re-recorded songs from their repertoires; Christmas albums; and albums of cover songs. In the 1970s the time between releases by superstar acts began to stretch out. Pink Floyd, for example, given the long-term success of *The Dark Side of the Moon*, took two and a half years to craft its 1975 follow-up *Wish You Were Here* (Columbia) and was not penalized; the new album topped the charts. After that, the time between albums for many performers continued to get longer and longer, which meant that more was riding on the new album when it did appear.

Nineteen seventy-seven, the year that saw the deaths of Elvis Presley and Bing Crosby, began with another price increase, as Queen's *A Day at the Races* (Elektra) was released at a list price of $7.98, followed quickly by the year's most successful album, Fleetwood Mac's *Rumours*, which arrived on February 19. The year's second-biggest selling album had been released the previous September, Stevie Wonder's sprawling *Songs in the Key of Life*, which went on to win him another Album of the Year Grammy. Released in December 1976 was 1977's third-biggest album, the soundtrack to the critically lambasted, but wildly popular remake of *A Star Is Born* (Columbia) starring Barbra Streisand and Kris Kristofferson. The Eagles' long-awaited *Hotel California*, also issued in December 1976, was the fourth most successful album of the year (its sales have since outdistanced the two albums ahead of it), and fifth was the definitive arena-rock album, Boston's self-titled debut on Epic, which had been released in September 1976. These albums were all massive sellers; four out of five of them eventually sold more than 10 million copies each. And they were typical of a year that redefined the size of entertainment vehicles.

Nineteen seventy-seven was also the year that *Star Wars* opened and quickly became the highest-grossing movie in history. And, inevitably, it was the year that saw the release of *Saturday Night Fever.* Issued in November in advance of the disco-oriented movie for which it served as a double-LP soundtrack, the *Saturday Night Fever* album on RSO topped the charts in 1978 for twenty-four weeks and eventually sold 15 million copies while throwing off numerous hits, including three chart-toppers for the Bee Gees: "How Deep Is Your Love," "Stayin' Alive," and "Night Fever." On March 18, 1978, four of the top five singles on the Hot 100 were written and/or performed by the Bee Gees: "Night Fever," "Stayin' Alive," Samantha Sang's "Emotion" on Private Stock, and youngest Gibb brother Andy Gibb's "Love Is Thicker than Water" (cowritten by Andy and brother Barry) on RSO, a Beatles-like feat.

Coming late in the year, *Saturday Night Fever* was just the icing on the cake for 1977, a year when revenues rose more than $27\frac{1}{2}$ percent, to $3.5 billion, and unit sales rose 18 percent, to nearly 700 million units. With *Saturday Night Fever* dominating the year and being followed into the movie theaters and record stores in the spring by the film adaptation of the Broadway musical *Grease* (also starring John Travolta) and its own multiplatinum double-LP soundtrack on RSO, 1978 was another enormous year for the record business. Revenues topped $4 billion, rising another 18 percent (with another LP price rise, to $8.98, in October), while unit sales were up more than 9 percent. The sky seemed to be the limit.

Then the ceiling fell in. For the year 1979, gross revenues for recorded music declined for the first time since 1960, dropping more than 11 percent, and unit sales were down almost as much. In an industry that depended on growth and spent accordingly, that made for an estimated pretax loss of more than $200 million, not including revenues from overseas. What happened? Well, the *Saturday Night Fever* and *Grease* phenomenon, which briefly looked like a new renaissance in movie musicals and soundtracks, turned out to be a fluke. A movie version of *Sgt. Pepper's Lonely Hearts Club Band*, starring Peter Frampton and the Bee Gees, which had looked like a sure thing before release in the summer of 1978, was a fiasco (the industry joke was that the inevitable RSO soundtrack album shipped platinum and returned double platinum), and other big-budget movies intended to spawn big soundtracks were also busts. Disco had become so pervasive, with more white rock acts like the Rolling Stones ("Miss You") and Rod Stewart ("Do Ya Think I'm Sexy?") taking stabs at it, that it provoked a reaction, notoriously the "Disco Sucks" rally held at Comiskey Park in Chicago on July 12, 1979, which turned into a riot. Meanwhile, the industry's new big guns were late in releasing their big new albums. The Eagles' *The Long Run* and Fleetwood Mac's *Tusk* both appeared in October, too late to bolster the year's figures much, especially since neither was nearly as successful as its predecessor. And punk, or new wave as it was called in the United States, had turned out not to be a big commercial success in America, despite critical hosannas.

But as the 1970s closed on this sour note for the music business, there were positive indications on the horizon. Some involved a new generation of recording artists. On March 22, 1978, A&M Records in England had signed the Police, who reached the Top 40 in the United States and the United Kingdom a year later with "Roxanne," presaging a major career. Blondie had become the first American new wave act to emerge from the downtown New York scene, albeit with a disco-styled hit, "Heart of Glass" on Chrysalis Records, which topped the charts in April 1979. Michael Jackson, on the verge of becoming twenty-one, made a substantial comeback with his album *Off the Wall* (Epic), which spawned four top-ten hits, "Don't Stop 'til You Get Enough," "Rock with You," "Off the Wall," and "She's Out of My Life." Signed to Warner Bros. Records before his twentieth birthday, Prince (Prince Rogers Nelson) scored his first number-one hit on the soul charts and his first Top 40 pop hit with "I Wanna Be Your Lover" in the fall of 1979. On September 1, rock band U2 released its debut recording, a three-song EP called *U2-3*, in Ireland, and the same month, Sugar Hill Records released the Sugarhill Gang's "Rapper's Delight" (music and lyrics by Bernard Edwards and Nile Rodgers), the first rap record, which hit the soul top ten and the pop Top 40.

Other good signs could be found in technological advances. On August 1, 1979, the Sony Walkman was introduced. This portable stereo with headphones, which played cassettes, would stimulate sales and provide a whole new way to listen to music. And by early 1979, Philips had developed a new compact disc system by which a $4\frac{1}{2}$-inch optical disc could be read by a laser beam. These artists, these technological developments, and several others, would have a profound effect on the music business in the decade to come.

MADONNA PAPA DON'T PREACH

Words and Music by **BRIAN ELLIOT**   Additional Lyrics by **Madonna**

Recorded on Sire Records

Exclusive Selling Agent for
the United States and Canada
WARNER BROS. PUBLICATIONS INC.
265 Secaucus Road • Secaucus, N.J. 07094
A Warner Communications Company

US $3.50

9

THE 1980s

THE RISE OF THE MUSIC VIDEO STAR

"The 70's Are So 90's. The 80's Are the Thing Now," read a headline on the front page of *The New York Times*' Arts & Leisure section for Sunday, May 5, 2002. In the article underneath, writer Simon Reynolds detailed the fad for the 1980s, especially its music, in the early years of the twenty-first century. Such a fascination is nothing new; in fact, since the 1970s, people have been gazing back two decades regularly. In the '80s, an affection for '60s music gave new impetus to the careers of the Beatles, among others, and '60s political activism was mirrored in Live Aid and other socially conscious activities. The tacky '70s were celebrated in the '90s with books and CD compilations, not to mention retro fashions. In the early '00s, Blondie and the Go-Go's re-formed, and there were radio stations devoted to the techno-pop sound of the "Big '80s."

Reynolds discerned a combination of causes for this twenty-year renewal. "Two tendencies coalesce in revivals like this," he wrote. "In one, people who were young during the period being celebrated reach middle age and experience pangs for the styles of their youth. In the other, a new generation becomes fascinated by the pop culture that prevailed when the generation was in its infancy. So the 80's revival is driven in part by pure nostalgia and also by the more intriguing notion of nostalgia for something never lived through." Although the revivals seem to turn up like clockwork, and therefore appear to be automatic, one might also suggest that they represent a longing for something different. It is notable that there was no '40s revival in the '60s (though there was something of a '20s boomlet in mid-decade), and that each revival represents an infatuation with times noticeably different from the current one. Perhaps the safe, antiseptic '50s looked good to people of the early '70s in the aftermath of the tumultuous '60s; in the '80s, with the country moving in the conservative direction of President Reagan, some people longed for the progressive times of the '60s; in the complicated, morally confusing '90s, the goofy '70s days of platform shoes and disco sounded like fun; and by the '00s, the '80s stylistic extremes—the big hair of the metal bands, the heavily synthesized music—attracted people in a time of national challenge and reduced expectations.

Of course, the 1980s wasn't just about music and fashion, nor is any decade. It was, depending on your political standpoint, a period in which traditional moral values were being restored or one in which there was, as author Susan Faludi later put it in a book title, a revisionist "backlash" bent on returning to the bad old days of sexism and racism. Such political issues are not our primary focus here, but in discussing a decade that included not only Live Aid, but also the PMRC, they can't be ignored completely.

Meanwhile, however, back in the music business, the 1980s dawned darkly, at least as far as the major labels were concerned. After rising consistently throughout the 1960s and '70s, especially in the booming years of 1977 and 1978, record sales took a big dip in 1979. Actually, the revenues of $3.67 billion were second only to the previous year's $4.13 billion, and the unit sales of 683 million copies were higher than any years except '77 and '78, but the fall-off was more than a psychological speed bump for the industry because it was spending on the assumption that growth would go on forever. For example, as a result of the downturn, EMI Records announced in April 1980 that it had lost £28 million in the second half of 1979.

To explain why sales were down, the record industry blamed the blank cassette tape, claiming that people were taping albums instead of buying them. This was the same rationale that had turned up before in the industry's history, when radio was viewed as a threat to sales, and that would appear again later in the century when the Internet was charged with the same crime. Always quick to look for a scapegoat, the music business failed to acknowledge that such technological advances increased the exposure of music and in so doing promoted the very recordings claimed to be endangered. Instead of addressing the real problems, the industry began lobbying for a share of blank-tape revenue.

Of course, there had always been two infallible predictors of dropping record sales. Whether it was in the late 1920s, the early 1950s, the late 1950s, or the turn of the twenty-first century to come, record sales went down when economic conditions in general declined and when the music itself began to stagnate. By the late 1970s, American consumers seemed to have heard as much formulaic disco as they wanted to, while the major recording artists whose multiplatinum sales provided a big chunk of the industry's income seemed to have tired. In the second half of 1979, Led Zeppelin, the Eagles, and Fleetwood Mac all released new albums, *In Through the Out Door*, *The Long Run*, and *Tusk*, respectively. All three were viewed as disappointments critically and commercially as compared to the groups' previous albums (although, over time, the first two each amassed sales of 7 million copies) and all three marked significant turning points in the groups' careers. Led Zeppelin announced on December 4, 1980, that it was disbanding following the September 25 death of drummer John Bonham; the Eagles also broke up, following a 1980 tour; and Fleetwood Mac, whose members began launching solo careers, would never again scale the commercial heights of 1977's 18-million-selling *Rumours*.

There was one other 1970s behemoth that reached a turning point at the turn of the decade. Pink Floyd released its double-LP concept album *The Wall* late in 1979 and in February 1980 played a series of concerts in New York and Los Angeles to promote it. The album spawned a number-one single in group member Roger Waters's sardonic "Another Brick in the Wall (Part II)" and topped the *Billboard* LP charts for fifteen weeks. *The Wall* became the top album of the year, inspired a movie adaptation, and went on to a platinum certification twenty-three times over and still counting (although, under current RIAA rules, each disc of the set counts, so the certification only registers sales of $11^{1}/_{2}$ million copies of the set). But *The Wall* was Pink Floyd's last great gasp; afterward, the band's sales declined as it underwent internal dissension.

In addition to Pink Floyd, there were three other recording artists who placed in the year-end top ten in both the albums and singles listings, and they suggested the broad outlines of the music business. If Pink Floyd represented album-oriented rock (AOR), Kenny Rogers, who scored with *Kenny* on United Artists and the year's biggest single, "Lady" (music and lyrics by Lionel Richie), represented cross-over country-pop, a style of music that was heard more extensively on the soundtrack to the John Travolta film *Urban Cowboy* (on the Asylum subsidiary of WEA), which featured half a dozen Top 40 hits. "Lady" also marked the ascendance of Lionel Richie, still at this point a member of the Commodores, although his success at writing and singing ballads like "Three Times a Lady" (number one for the Commodores in 1978) inspired talk of a solo career.

Meanwhile, Blondie's late-1979 album *Eat to the Beat* and their early 1980 single "Call Me" were both among the year's big successes, though the single, which was the theme to the movie *American Gigolo*, was not on the LP. Blondie's breakthrough symbolically suggested the commercial potential of punk/new wave, the music that had excited rock critics and a cult of fans in the late '70s, but that never really made it to the American mainstream; that is, not in anything like its original form. Blondie, at least, was from New York's Lower East Side, like many more authentic new wave acts, but the group was actually far more eclectic. "Call Me," for example, cowritten by Euro-disco producer Giorgio Moroder with Blondie lead singer Debbie Harry, was something of a rock-disco hybrid. Nevertheless, new wave was making inroads; in 1980 such performers as the B-52's (Warner Bros.), the Buzzcocks (I.R.S. Records), the Cars (Elektra), the Clash (Epic), Elvis Costello and the Attractions (Columbia), Devo (Warner Bros.), Joe Jackson (A&M), the Jam (Polydor), Madness (Sire, a subsidiary of Warner Bros.), the Pretenders (Sire), the Psychedelic Furs (Columbia), Talking Heads (Sire), and XTC (Virgin) appeared in the American charts.

The fourth act to place in both the LP- and 45-format top rankings for 1980 was the real herald of the decade just born. Michael Jackson might have seemed like a child-star has-been for much of the 1970s, but *Off the Wall* sold 7 million copies after its August 1979 release, spending 169 weeks in the charts. Jackson was attempting a broad pop synthesis of the type that the Beatles had pulled off in the mid-1960s and that Elton John had achieved in the mid-1970s. He could turn out a dancefloor throwdown like his own composition "Don't Stop 'til You Get Enough" and then turn around and sob his way through a ballad like "She's Out of My Life" with equal effectiveness. In 1980 there was no way to tell that this was just the start of his remarkable adult career.

In addition to these major stars, several other performers placed both a single and an album among the forty most successful in each category, indicating widespread appeal. Piano-playing singer-songwriter Billy Joel, who had emerged with his 1977 album *The Stranger* (Columbia) and won the Grammy Award for Album of the Year for its follow-up, *52nd Street*, spent six weeks at number one in 1980 with *Glass Houses*, containing the number-one hit "It's Still Rock & Roll to Me" (somewhat of a sardonic response to the popularity of new wave bands). Dan Fogelberg, another singer-songwriter who first gained recognition in the second half of the 1970s, reached number three with his late-1979 album *Phoenix* (Full Moon Records), propelled by its number-two single "Longer." Bette Midler, whose successful albums of the early 1970s, *The Divine Miss M* and *Bette Midler* (Atlantic), were based on her mixture of nostalgic and contemporary pop styles and her comic persona, but who had faltered in the interim, made a comeback by starring in *The Rose*, a film that was inspired by the doomed career of Janis Joplin. The soundtrack album was a substantial hit, and the title song sung by Midler reached number three. Donna Summer defied the decline of disco by topping the LP charts for the third consecutive time with her late-1979 double-disc compilation *On the Radio—Greatest Hits—Volumes I & II* (Casablanca) and reaching number three with her first single for her new record company, Geffen, with "The Wanderer" (co-credited to Summer and producer Giorgio Moroder). And the ever-reliable Rolling Stones, passing the fifteen-year anniversary of their 1964 American debut, spent seven weeks at number one with their twenty-seventh chart album, *Emotional Rescue*, the title track reaching number three.

With such varied performers, 1980 marked a slight monetary recovery over 1979, although unit sales actually continued to drop, dipping below 650 million copies, with pre-recorded cassettes, for the first time, equaling sales of LPs. So, how could revenues have increased? As Russell Sanjek puts it, in a comment that speaks volumes about the industry and the inflationary environment of the economy at the time, "When the major record companies began to make profits again late in 1980, it was not because of increased volume, but because they had raised prices for the fifth consecutive year." With LPs heading for the $10 mark, no wonder sales of blank tape were brisk.

As is often the case with decades (especially the 1960s and 1970s), the early years of the 1980s were in many respects a holdover of the previous era, with the elements that would give the ten-year period its unique character only gradually emerging. Certainly, that is the impression one gets looking at the most popular music of 1981, a year when unit sales continued to fall, this time below 600 million copies. The year's biggest album was REO Speedwagon's *Hi Infidelity* (Epic), spurred by sales of the number-one single "Keep On Loving You." Also included in the top ten were fellow arena rockers Styx with *Paradise Theatre* (A&M) featuring the number-three single "The Best of Times." Another hard-rock band had a banner year, Australia's AC/DC. Unlike Led Zeppelin, the group lost a primary member in the late '70s, singer Bon Scott, but went on to their greatest success. Released in the summer of 1980, their *Back in Black* (Atlantic), featuring new singer Brian Johnson, not only ranked among the top-selling albums of 1981, but has become one of the biggest selling albums ever, with sales of 19 million copies. *Dirty Deeds Done Dirt Cheap*, recorded with Scott in 1976 but not released in the United States until 1981, was also one of the year's big sellers.

Soft rock continued to have considerable appeal, in the comeback work of ex-Beatle John Lennon and new artist Christopher Cross. The incomprehensible assassination of Lennon on December 8, 1980, shortly after the release of his and wife Yoko Ono's album, *Double Fantasy* (Geffen), added to the sales of what would have been a very popular record anyway, as did lead-off single "(Just

Like) Starting Over," which topped the charts in the last week of 1980, and its follow-up, "Woman," which peaked at number two in March 1981. Cross, armed with a fistful of Grammys, sold millions of copies of his self-titled debut album on Warner Bros., which had been released in January 1980 and already spawned the number-one hit "Sailing" and the number-two hit "Ride like the Wind" (both written by Cross) in 1980, and even added to his awards with the Oscar-winning movie song "Arthur's Theme (Best That You Can Do)" from the film *Arthur*, but his career faded quickly thereafter.

The breakthrough acts of the year were Pat Benatar (Chrysalis), whose 1980 album, *Crimes of Passion*, peaked at number two, with its 1981 follow-up, *Precious Time*, reaching number one; the Police, whose 1980 album *Zenyatta Mondatta* reached number five, with its 1981 follow-up, *Ghost in the Machine*, reaching number two and its single "Every Little Thing She Does Is Magic" reaching number three; and the pop-soul duo of Daryl Hall and John Oates (RCA Victor), with their 1980 album *Voices* and number-one singles "Kiss on My List" and "Private Eyes," who would go on to become the most successful twosome since Simon and Garfunkel.

Bruce Springsteen made one of his periodic returns to the charts, going to number one with *The River*. Springsteen's mainstream rock sound had become hugely influential, spawning a crop of soundalikes including Tom Petty and the Heartbreakers (the Backstreet subsidiary of MCA), John Cougar (né Mellencamp) (the Riva subsidiary of Mercury), and Bob Seger and the Silver Bullet Band (Capitol). The Rolling Stones spent more weeks at number one with their 1981 album *Tattoo You* than they had with any previous LP and added another signature song to their repertoire with the number-two hit "Start Me Up." And Barbra Streisand, who had enjoyed renewed success by teaming with Bee Gee Barry Gibb as writer-producer and sometime duet partner for the number-one album *Guilty* and its chart-topping first single "Woman in Love" (music and lyrics by Barry Gibb and Robin Gibb), continued that success with the number-three single "Guilty" (music and lyrics by Barry, Maurice, and Robin Gibb).

Most of these performers were essentially throwbacks to music of an earlier time. But the 1980s got its first significant look (and *look* is the word) at the future on August 1, 1981, when MTV premiered. The music video channel did not change things overnight, if only because it was not broadcast across the whole country at first; New York and Los Angeles didn't come on line for more than a year after the debut. But it began to change not only the way music was marketed, but also the way it was made, and it influenced all the major changes in the music over the course of the decade.

In the meantime, however, things did not change that much. Nineteen eighty-two was the year when the industry bottomed out. Sales were just above 575 million units, the smallest figure since 1975, although with inflated prices revenues stood at $3.59 billion. But the year's biggest sellers suggested the problem. They included newly formed AOR supergroup Asia's self-titled debut (Geffen), featuring the number-four single "Heat of the Moment"; journeyman blues-rock outfit the J. Geils Band's pop move, *Freeze-Frame* (EMI America), featuring the number-one single "Centerfold" and the number-four title track; arena rockers Journey (*Escape* on Columbia), featuring the number-two single "Open Arms"; Loverboy (*Get Lucky* on Columbia); Foreigner (the 1981 album *4* on Atlantic, still selling due to the inclusion of the top-ten 1981 singles "Urgent" and "Waiting for a Girl like You"); and John Cougar's breakthrough, *American Fool*, featuring the number-one hit "Jack & Diane" and the number-two hit "Hurts So Good." The only really contemporary sounds in the top ten were the Go-Go's' *Beauty and the Beat* (I.R.S.), featuring the number-two single "We Got the Beat," and the Police's *Ghost in the Machine*. And it was all white pop-rock; you had to go to fourteenth place on the album list to find R&B band Kool & the Gang's *Something Special* (De-Lite) and to eighteenth place to find *So Right* (RCA Victor) by Alabama, one of the most successful country acts of the decade and the biggest country group ever.

Among the other more successful recording artists of the year were: Daryl Hall and John Oates, with their top-ten album *Private Eyes* and number-one singles "I Can't Go for That (No Can Do)" and "Maneater"; teen idol and soap opera actor Rick Springfield, with his top-ten albums *Working Class Dog* and *Success Hasn't Spoiled Me Yet* and top-ten single "Don't Talk to Strangers" for RCA Victor; light pop singer Olivia Newton-John, enjoying a career resurgence thanks to the toughened image she achieved in her screen appearance in *Grease* and dance-rock album *Physical*, with her top-ten singles "Make a Move on Me" and "Heart Attack" for MCA; and country veteran Willie Nelson, having long since expanded his Outlaw country following to the pop mainstream, with his top-ten revival of the 1972 song "Always on My Mind" and multimillion-selling albums *Willie Nelson's Greatest Hits (& Some That Will Be)* and *Always on My Mind* for Columbia.

More important than the homogeneity of the most popular music as far as the industry was concerned was its relative unpopularity. The biggest albums of the year sold in the range of 1 to 3 million copies each, a far cry from the salad days of the 1970s.

Interestingly, 1982 also marked an uptick in more traditional forms of popular music that continued throughout the decade. Linda Ronstadt's *What's New* (Asylum), an album of pop standards made with Frank Sinatra's arranger-conductor Nelson Riddle, became a multimillion-seller and spawned two sequels. Trumpeter Wynton Marsalis (Columbia) sold records and won Grammys touting a revisionist view of traditional jazz. And lavish Broadway shows, starting with Andrew Lloyd Webber's *Cats* (Geffen) and including *Les Misérables* (Geffen) and Lloyd Webber's *Phantom of the Opera* (Polydor), achieved long runs and sold millions of cast albums with music that was a throwback to operetta, tricked out with rock bombast. Later in the decade, Barbra Streisand topped the charts by returning to the style of her early-'60s records with *The Broadway Album*, and Tony Bennett enjoyed a career resurgence.

The turning point in the decade in terms of popular music, the period during which the '80s became the '80s we now remember, occurred in the fall of 1982. Three factors were involved. Having premiered in 1981, MTV had a hard time finding space on cable lineups around the country, but by late 1982, the station's "I Want My MTV" ad campaign, featuring major rock stars, was turning the tide. MTV was starting to influence national tastes in a big way, particularly by supporting photogenic performers from overseas who had a leg up in the video game since they had been making short promotional films for the European market already. Nineteen eighty-two saw the U.S. pop singles chart debuts of the Human League (A&M/Virgin), Billy Idol (Chrysalis), Culture Club (Epic/Virgin), and Duran Duran (the Harvest subsidiary of Capitol), the last two premiering with major hits (Culture Club's "Do You Really Want to Hurt Me" and Duran Duran's "Hungry like the Wolf"), all of them visually striking performers with videos that got heavy play on MTV.

The second factor was the compact disc. LPs had ruled the roost in the music business for more than thirty years, but by the start of the '80s that reign was endangered. The invention of the Sony Walkman portable cassette player increased the popularity of cassettes to the point that they began to outsell LPs. (Given this boost, cassettes became the format of choice in automobiles, too, and the 8-track cartridge declined precipitously.) At the same time, record companies cut costs by using inferior vinyl for LPs, which created consumer resentment and gave birth to a healthy specialty market in imported LPs and audophile releases that were "half-speed mastered" and pressed on high-quality vinyl. Meanwhile, Philips and Sony were working on a new digital format, and on October 1, 1982, Sony introduced a commercial CD in Japan.

The major record labels initially opposed CDs, as did retailers. Nobody wanted to undertake the expense of building new factories and retrofitting stores for a new record format. But independents and others began pushing CDs. Classical music fans supported them, and when Japanese- and European-manufactured CDs began to sell in the United States, they gained an ever-increasing foothold. Eventually, of course, the majors recognized that CDs presented a way to jack up prices and resell catalog, and then they got behind them all the way.

The rise of MTV and CDs were important, but the music business is primarily about music, and it was the music that had to change for things to improve meaningfully. On December 1, 1982, a watershed event took place with the release of Michael Jackson's second mature solo album, *Thriller*. It had been preceded by its first single, a ballad duet with Paul McCartney, "The Girl Is Mine," which was a major hit yet did not hint at the depth of the LP as a whole. The second single was "Billie Jean," Jackson's rhythmic denial of an imagined paternity claim, which really broke things wide open. Epic Records, Jackson's label, managed to get a video for the song on MTV, and it hit number one in March 1983, the same spot held by *Thriller* in the album charts.

While today it seems obvious that an artist of Jackson's stature would be played on MTV, the network had come into being thinking of itself as the television equivalent of a teen-oriented rock radio station, and it was programmed accordingly. R&B acts were not featured because the teen-rock format favored white pop stars. No one accused an AOR station of racism (nor an R&B station, for that matter), but at a time when MTV was the only music video channel in the country, people began to think it had a responsibility to play music other than just white pop-rock. Specifically, it was suggested that MTV's policy was racist in that it excluded R&B with the potential to cross over to the white audience. (Nobody seems to have suggested that the channel had any responsibility to play country or jazz.) Michael Jackson (or, it was suggested, Epic parent CBS Records' threat to withhold videos by other acts) managed to overcome MTV's reluctance to play crossover R&B.

Jackson quickly released a third single from *Thriller*, the rock-oriented "Beat It," along with an influential dance-oriented video that recalled the dance sequences of the film version of *West Side Story*. "Beat It" reached number one at the end of April, reversing the usual trend for successive singles from an album. Typically, even successful artists were able to break only one or two hit singles from a given album. They might release more, but radio began to become resistant. Jackson had broken four top-ten singles from *Off the Wall*, but the second two did not do as well as the first two. "Beat It" gave him three consecutive top-five hits from the same album, and counting.

Then, on May 16, 1983, Jackson appeared on the television special *Motown 25*, a celebration of Motown Records' twenty-fifth anniversary featuring its stars past and present. After performing a medley of hits with his brothers, Jackson stayed onstage alone and performed "Billie Jean," gliding backward in a dance move soon to be known as the "moonwalk." The appearance gave Jackson national exposure, and it dominated reviews of the program. Still at number one, *Thriller* began to sell in even bigger numbers. Before the end of the year, three more singles had made the top ten, and early in 1984 the album's seventh single, its title track, accompanied by a lengthy video based on the 1957 film *I Was a Teenage Werewolf*, gave it an unprecedented seven top-ten singles. On October 30, 1984, during the second consecutive year in which it was the most successful album of the year according to *Billboard*, *Thriller* was certified for sales of 20 million copies in the United States, making it the best-selling album in American history. (Sixteen years later, it had tacked on another 6 million copies for a total of 26 million and ranked second to the Eagles' *Eagles/Their Greatest Hits 1971–1975*.)

Like Bing Crosby and Benny Goodman in the 1930s, Glenn Miller and Frank Sinatra in the 1940s, Elvis Presley in the 1950s, the Beatles in the 1960s, and Elton John and the Bee Gees in the 1970s, Michael Jackson in the 1980s redefined the terms of success in the music business, selling more records more quickly than anybody had before. And like those predecessors, he led the way to an expansion in the industry as a whole. Jackson, of course, was not the only success of 1983. The Police, who had been selling better and better in the early '80s with their new wave/reggae sound and lead singer Sting's throaty tenor, broke through to massive success with *Synchronicity*, which was on top of the LP chart for seventeen weeks, with its number-one single "Every Breath You Take" and number-three follow-up "King of Pain" before breaking up. Australia's Men at Work were a slightly more comic Police soundalike, which was fine with fans who put the albums *Business as Usual* and *Cargo* (Columbia) high in the charts, along with the singles "Down Under" and "Overkill." Duran Duran added the number-four hit "Is There Something I Should Know" to the number-three success of "Hungry like the Wolf," along with the top-ten albums *Duran Duran* and *Rio*.

Meanwhile, other R&B artists benefited from Jackson's ascent. Lionel Richie, having left the Commodores, became a massive success among the "adult contemporary" crowd with his fall 1982 debut, *Lionel Richie* (Motown), and singles "All Night Long (All Night)" and "You Are." The disco days were successfully recalled in the soundtrack to the film *Flashdance*, director Adrian Lyne's story of a young female steelworker (Jennifer Beals) who aspires to a dancing career. Although dismissed in some quarters as little more than a series of music videos, it was a box-office hit, and the soundtrack on Casablanca topped the charts and threw off two number-one singles, Irene Cara's "Flashdance … What a Feeling" and Michael Sembello's "Maniac."

Mainstream pop-rock also fared well. Billy Joel found success by aping the past, with his album *An Innocent Man*, in the style of the early 1960s, and its singles "Tell Her About It" and "Uptown Girl." And though it never hit number one due to the logjam created by *Thriller* and *Synchonicity*, British heavy metal band Def Leppard's *Pyromania* (Mercury), which peaked at number two and remained in the charts for 116 weeks, marked the American breakthrough for the group and a resurgence in heavy metal music.

Revenues were up to $3.78 billion in 1983, but it was 1984 that would see new highs for the record business. At the end of 1983, labels had begun to test the $10 barrier, charging $9.98 for superstar releases and $10.98 for high-profile soundtracks. In 1984, as *Thriller* continued to sell, boosted by a summer tour by the Jacksons (including Michael), who scored a top-ten album with *Victory* featuring the number-three single "State of Shock," several other major multiplatinum artists emerged. Bruce Springsteen, of course, had been touted as a major star as early as 1974 and had fulfilled that promise in the late 1970s and early 1980s. But *Born in the U.S.A.*, released in June 1984, outstripped any success he had had before. As he launched a worldwide tour that ran through 1985, Springsteen released "Dancing in the Dark," the first of seven top-ten singles to emerge from the album, which had sold 10 million copies by the end of 1985 and currently stands at 17 million. Prince had emerged as a star in 1983 after several years as a prodigy and critics' darling with his album *1999*. But that didn't prepare anyone for his film debut, *Purple Rain*, and its soundtrack album, which also appeared in June 1984. The album spent nearly six months at number one, spawning the number-one singles "When Doves Cry" and "Let's Go Crazy," and the number-two single "Purple Rain." By the end of the year, it had sold 8 million copies; it currently stands at 13 million. Van Halen had been a force to reckon with in the heavy metal realm since the late 1970s, but in 1984 they took a leap to the top of the charts by turning to a more pop sound with the number-one single "Jump" from the album *1984 (MCMLXXXIV)*, which reached number two.

And 1984 was the year Madonna broke big. Her first, self-titled album was released on Sire in the summer of 1983, but peaked in the top ten in 1984 as its singles, "Holiday," "Borderline," and "Lucky Star," crossed over from the dance clubs to the pop charts and her dance-oriented, fashion-conscious videos got onto MTV. Her success was consolidated by the release of *Like a Virgin*, the album and title single (music and lyrics by Billy Steinberg and Tom Kelly) that confirmed her provocative style. At 10 million copies, the LP is still her biggest seller in a career that remained massively successful twenty years later. Cyndi Lauper was equally successful (at least at first), breaking out with her debut album, *She's So Unusual* (the Portrait subsidiary of Epic Records), and singles that reached number one ("Time after Time"), number two ("Girls Just Want to Have Fun"), and number three ("She Bop").

Holdovers Duran Duran had two top-ten albums, *Seven and the Ragged Tiger* and *Arena*, a number-one single, "The Reflex," and a number-two single, "The Wild Boys." Also extending their winning streaks were Lionel Richie, with his album *Can't Slow Down* and singles "Hello" (number one) and "Stuck on You" (number three), and Daryl Hall and John Oates, whose number-one single for the year was "Out of Touch," while their albums *Rock 'N Soul, Part 1* (a hits set) and *Big Bam Boom* made the top ten. And, as in 1983, there was a dance-oriented film in the theaters that reminded reviewers of MTV and earned similar success through its various-artists soundtrack. *Footloose* (Columbia) topped the charts, as did Kenny Loggins's title song and Deniece Williams's "Let's Hear It for the Boy." With such artists leading the way, 1984 marked a new peak in music industry revenues of $4.37 billion (although sales, which were just below 700 million copies, still lagged behind the totals of the late 1970s).

Nineteen eighty-five could hardly match 1984 for firepower. In some ways, it marked a continuation of trends from the previous year. Bruce Springsteen's *Born in the U.S.A.* continued to sell, as did its singles. So did *Purple Rain*, and Prince released a follow-up album, *Around the World in a Day*, which also topped the charts, while its single, "Raspberry Beret," reached number two. *Like a Virgin* was also a holdover, as Madonna broke another single, the number-two "Material Girl" from it, then returned to number one with "Crazy for You" from the film *Vision Quest*. In music terms, the most significant film of the year was *Beverly Hills Cop*, starring Eddie Murphy. The soundtrack album on MCA, another various-artists collection that included some songs that were not even featured in the film, hit number one, spurred by ex-Eagle Glenn Frey's number-two single "The Heat Is On" and Harold Faltermeyer's number-two single "Axel F." Frey was also the beneficiary of a television soundtrack for the hit series *Miami Vice* (MCA). He enjoyed a second number-two hit from that album with "You Belong to the City," while Jan Hammer, who composed the show's score, hit number one with "Miami Vice Theme."

The British Invasion of the early 1980s continued in 1985, led by two groups. Duos seemed to be the order of the day in the United Kingdom, and Wham!, the team of George Michael and Andrew Ridgeley, had topped the U.S. charts in 1984 with "Wake Me Up Before You Go-Go" (written by Michael) on Columbia. The song came from their album *Make It Big*, which topped the charts in 1985 and threw off two more number-one hits during the year, "Careless Whisper" (co-credited to the duo as songwriters) and "Everything She Wants" (by Michael). Even while this success was occurring, Michael stood out ("Careless Whisper" was even credited to "Wham! Featuring George Michael"), and after one more album with Ridgeley, he went solo. Tears for Fears, the British duo of Roland Orzabal and Curt Smith, was similarly successful in the United States in 1985, hitting number one with the singles "Everybody Wants to Rule the

World" and "Shout," as well as the album *Songs from the Big Chair* on Mercury.

The most successful recording artist of 1985 was also British. Phil Collins, born in London in January 1951, was a child actor (he can be glimpsed as an extra in *A Hard Day's Night*) who became a drummer. In 1970 he joined progressive rock band Genesis, and in 1975, following the departure of lead singer Peter Gabriel, he took over as vocalist in the group, which thereafter pursued a more conventional pop-rock style. His first solo album, *Face Value*, was released on Atlantic in 1981 and sold well, as did its 1982 follow-up, *Hello, I Must Be Going!*, but his career took a quantum leap in 1984, when "Against All Odds (Take a Look at Me Now)," the theme song from the film of the same name, performed in his characteristically intense ballad style, topped the charts. In 1985 he dominated the singles charts, reaching number two in February with "Easy Lover" on Columbia, actually credited to Philip Bailey, lead singer of Earth, Wind & Fire, "(with Phil Collins)," although it was in fact a duet. "One More Night," the first single from Collins's third solo album, *No Jacket Required*, hit number one in March the same week that the album did. "Sussudio" hit number one in July, and Collins closed the year by topping the singles charts for a third time with another movie song, his duet with Marilyn Martin on "Separate Lives," the theme from *White Nights*.

The year's most auspicious debut belonged to Whitney Houston. Born in Newark, New Jersey, in August 1963, Houston was the daughter of singer Cissy Houston, and a cousin of Dionne Warwick. She sang in church as a child and worked as a backup singer in her teens before beginning a career as a model in the early 1980s. But then she was signed by Arista Records, where label head Clive Davis carefully groomed her before releasing her self-titled debut album in the late winter of 1985. The album, and Arista's marketing, attempted to sell Houston across genres from R&B to pop to rock, and the effort succeeded. Before the end of the year, the first single, "You Give Good Love," had peaked at number three and the second, a revised version of the 1977 song "Saving All My Love," at number one, and the album had reached number two. In 1986, "How Will I Know" and a revival of the 1977 song "Greatest Love of All," originally written for the Muhammad Ali film biography *The Greatest*, hit number one, as did the album, which went on to sell 12 million copies.

But 1985 remains best remembered for its benefit recordings and concerts. They began at Christmas 1984, when a group of British musicians dubbed "Band Aid" and led by Bob Geldof of the Boomtown Rats recorded the charity single "Do They Know It's Christmas?" with the proceeds earmarked for famine relief in Ethiopia. A similar recording was mounted by American performers in January 1985 when they cut "We Are the World" (written by Michael Jackson and Lionel Richie) as USA for Africa. Released on Columbia, the single sold 4 million copies and was followed by a *We Are the World* album that sold another 3 million copies. Geldof, meanwhile, organized Live Aid, twin benefit concerts held in stadiums in London and Philadelphia, broadcast live on MTV, that raised more funds. These and other charity projects improved the image of the music business and, incidentally (and perhaps not unintentionally), served the purpose of promoting the careers of many artists.

Maybe it wasn't coincidental that within months of these projects, the industry was under fire in Washington as the Parents Music Resource Center (PMRC), an organization founded by the wives of prominent politicians, pushed through record labeling of supposedly obscene recordings. If anything, however, the PMRC, odious as it was to music fans, turned out to be prescient in forecasting the content of pop music moving forward into the late 1980s. Rap music, which had continued to be made without crossing over significantly in the first half of the decade, broke out in 1986 with the release of Run-D.M.C.'s triple-platinum *Raising Hell* (Profile Records) and its top-five single, a revival of Aerosmith's 1976 song "Walk This Way," coperformed by Aerosmith members (and the song's composers) Joe Perry and Steven Tyler. And heavy metal, which had also continued with modest success but without appealing to a mass audience, made a breakthrough the same year courtesy of "light metal" act Bon Jovi's *Slippery When Wet* (Mercury) and the number-one singles "You Give Love a Bad Name" and "Livin' on a Prayer." Bon Jovi, led by photogenic singer-guitarist Jon Bon Jovi, played in a more melodic style than earlier metal bands, and their good looks and carefully tousled long hair brought them an enormous female audience to go with the young males who traditionally made up the heavy metal fan base. Soon, the record stores and airwaves were awash with "gangsta" rappers and "hair bands," and as time went on some of these performers began expressing points of view previously anathema to prevailing social attitudes. Since the 1960s, there had been a tacit assumption that pop music was on the side of the liberal social trends toward peace and tolerance born in that decade. But some rappers and new metal bands began reflecting violent and intolerant attitudes in their music, forcing the music business to confront issues of free speech and censorship that have not been resolved to this day.

Meanwhile, some people just wanted to entertain, and in the late 1980s, along with rappers like the Beastie Boys (on Def Jam Records) and metal bands like Ratt (Atlantic), Poison (the Enigma subsidary of Capitol), Guns N' Roses (Geffen), and Mötley Crüe (Elektra), the charts were topped by a succession of pop artists who had made the music video connection and combined upbeat songs with heavily choreographed promotional films. Michael Jackson and Madonna continued to score. Janet Jackson, Michael Jackson's younger sister, teamed up with the writing/producing team of James "Jimmy Jam" Harris III and Terry Lewis, and emerged with her first big album, *Control* (A&M), in 1986, which featured six top-twenty singles, the most successful of them being "When I Think of You" and "Let's Wait Awhile." In 1989 she returned with *Janet Jackson's Rhythm Nation 1814*, which had seven top-ten hits extending into 1991, among them the chart-toppers "Miss You Much," "Escapade," "Black Cat," and "Love Will Never Do (Without You)." Paula Abdul, Jackson's former choreographer, spent more weeks at number one with her debut album *Forever Your Girl* (Virgin) than did anyone else who released an LP in 1989, meanwhile hitting number one with the singles "Straight Up," "Forever Your Girl," "Cold Hearted," and "Opposites Attract." And a new wave of teen pop acts—Tiffany (MCA), Debbie Gibson (Atlantic), New Kids on the Block (Columbia)—began to dominate the charts. The logical extreme of this trend came with Milli Vanilli, a European duo who, it turned out, were hired by producer Frank Farian for their looks and dancing ability, and did not actually perform on their album *Girl You Know It's True* (Arista) at all. When the story came out, they had to give back their Best New Artist Grammy.

Mainstream rock, meanwhile, continued to do well, with the likes of Springsteen, Steve Winwood (Virgin), and U2 (Island) topping the charts. Toward the end of the decade, newer rock bands like R.E.M. (I.R.S. and Warner Bros.), which began to reach the top-ten in 1987, were being referred to as "alternative rock," a growing phenomenon. Even singer-songwriter folk-rock, as performed by Tracy Chapman (Elektra), Suzanne Vega (A&M), and others, enjoyed a resurgence. And the CD, which had become the dominant format by the end of the decade, with the once mighty LP banished to near-novelty status, led to increasing catalog sales and the popularity of comprehensive box sets of the works of major artists like Eric Clapton and Bob Dylan. Sales were up, prices were up, and, not surprisingly, the record labels themselves were up for sale. German publisher Bertelsmann purchased RCA Victor Records and Arista, and toward the end of the decade PolyGram acquired Island Records, followed soon after by A&M Records. Such mergers and acquisitions would continue in the 1990s.

During the 1960s and most of the '70s, the music industry had lived the capitalist dream of continual market growth. That dream had soured at the end of the '70s, but the '80s saw several strategies that the industry initially resisted—the promotional power of music videos, the evolution of a new recording format—restoring big profits at least temporarily. The scale of Michael Jackson's success was unprecedented and suggested new goals to which recording artists might aspire. But the elements of that success were not new. Record buyers had hoisted Fred Astaire to the top of the charts fifty years before, after seeing him dance. The triumph of 1980s popular music lay in its packaging as much as its content. Most of the big new stars—Michael and Janet Jackson, Madonna, Prince, former Wham! member George Michael, Whitney Houston—were at least as concerned with their wardrobes and their choreography as they were with their music, if not more so. Even the stars of rap and heavy metal shared this attitude to a great extent, though their taste was different. Not surprisingly, such a preoccupation with form would produce a reaction in the 1990s, but it also became a permanent part of popular music on a mass scale.

Or perhaps we should say it returned to being a part of popular music. The 1960s may have enjoyed a resurgence of interest in the '80s, but just as the dominant politics of the '80s represented a deliberate reversal of the '60s that has yet to be overturned, so the popular music of the '80s marked a denial of the earnestness, authenticity, and naiveté of '60s music. If the music of the '60s often seemed to emerge from a garage, the music of the '80s often seemed to come from a dance studio by way of an expensive clothing store. In this sense, the '80s revival that was witnessed twenty years later made sense, because much of the music of the 2000s had its seeds in the music of the '80s. Indeed, many of the same stars were still popular and still making essentially similar-sounding music. But in between then and now came a decade in which many of the new assumptions about what popular music ought to be would be questioned all over again, resulting in unexpected conflicts and convergences.

ORIGINAL SHEET MUSIC EDITION

...baby one more time

Recorded by

Britney Spears

on Jive Records

Words and Music by
MAX MARTIN

10

THE 1990s

THE DIGITAL REVOLUTION BEGINS

The early 1990s were a long time ago. So it seems even from the vantage point of the early 2000s. They represent a primitive era when people were forced to sit in restaurants and walk down streets without being able to talk on cell phones; when the Internet was still largely the province of college math professors; when Princess Diana was still alive and still married to Prince Charles, and O.J. Simpson was still just a sports commentator and minor movie actor. Many things changed during that decade.

The music business changed too, in ways that often followed old trends familiar to it or new ones that corresponded to developments in business in general. At the turn of the decade, PolyGram, one of the six major record companies, had purchased two of the biggest independents, Island Records and A&M Records. In March 1990, MCA, another of the majors, acquired yet another large independent, Geffen Records. Not surprisingly, in 1990 the majors accounted for 93 percent of the American record market. This, however, was a peak. Although mergers and acquisitions continued, notably the combining of PolyGram and MCA to create Universal, which reduced the number of majors to five by the end of the decade, there really were no more big independents to buy. But there were more and more small independents able, through technological innovations, to operate inexpensively and sell to niche customers, so that, by 1996, the majors controlled only a little over 80 percent of the market—still a lot, but much less.

In terms of the music itself, a similar kind of decentralization of the pop marketplace had been under way for some time, but by 1990 it seemed to have reached an advanced stage. There were still big-selling records, but increasingly they seemed to be selling to one segment of the large market or another, not to pop fans as a whole. Theoretically, rock 'n' roll and its variants remained the country's dominant form of popular music, as it had been since at least the late 1960s. But an examination of the charts and sales statistics in 1990 made that belief hard to justify. The first year of the decade was one that saw the release of a series of top-ten million-selling rock albums in styles ranging from heavy metal to new wave—AC/DC's *The Razors Edge*, the Black Crowes' *Shake Your Money Maker* (Def American), Jon Bon Jovi's *Blaze of Glory/Young Guns II*, Depeche Mode's *Violator* (Sire), Heart's *Brigade* (Capitol), INXS's *X* (Atlantic), Poison's *Flesh & Blood*, and ZZ Top's *Recycler* (Warner Bros.)—but none of these dominated popular music the way you would expect if rock was really the major popular music genre and not just one of many. On the contrary, the major album and singles artists of the year included the rappers, one black and one white, M.C. Hammer and Vanilla Ice (who, between them, occupied the top of the *Billboard* album charts for thirty-seven of the year's fifty-two weeks with *Please Hammer Don't Hurt 'Em* [Capitol] and *To the Extreme* [SBK], respectively); the dance-pop stars Janet Jackson, Madonna, and Paula Abdul; and the adult-contemporary singers Phil Collins, Bonnie Raitt (Capitol), Sinead O'Connor (Ensign), and newcomers Wilson Phillips (SBK). In addition to that trio of offspring of the Beach Boys and the Mamas and the Papas (who would prove a short-lived success), several other performers who would dominate the decade made their first notable impressions in 1990. None of them were rockers, either.

Mariah Carey, the top pop singles artist and second-biggest pop album artist of the 1990s, began her reign with the release of her debut single on Columbia Records, her own composition "Vision of Love," in the spring of 1990. The twenty-year-old daughter of a black Venezuelan father and a white Irish-American mother who was an opera singer, Carey typified what record companies had traditionally looked for in pop artists, and what they still look for today. It wasn't just that, with her mixed background, she could appeal to different races (although, with the increasing globalization of pop, that was, and remains, an important consideration). It was that in her music she also mixed a taste for large-scale romantic pop balladeering (and the pipes to sell it) with an interest in the trendier aspects of black music, particularly the emerging style of hip-hop (an umbrella term embracing rap and recent trends in R&B that gained currency in the 1990s). Unlike Madonna and Janet Jackson, Carey didn't need to learn elaborate dance steps and make heavily choreographed videos to distract attention from her vocal inadequacies; she could sing. In fact, she could, in the style patented by Whitney Houston, wildly oversing, investing with gobs of undifferentiated emotional force lyrics that did not justify all that embellishment. She was Columbia's answer to Houston, and she was younger and lighter-skinned, attributes that, however crass it may be to admit, contributed to her breakthrough and her ability to remain commercially successful throughout the decade.

Another singer representing another kind of cross-genre appeal who made her first appearance in the American charts in 1990 was Canadian Celine Dion. Her Epic Records single "Where Does My Heart Beat Now" entered the adult-contemporary charts in October. Dion's career in the United States would build gradually in the early 1990s until she broke through to massive popularity in 1994, but the singer, already a star in Canada and France, where she had sung in French, gained a foothold at the start of the decade.

A more phlegmatic balladeer who came to the fore at this time was Michael Bolton. He was one of those journeyman performers who try various approaches to reach stardom before finally hitting on one that works. Born Michael Bolotin in February 1953 in New Haven, Connecticut, he was recording for Epic Records as early as 1968. In the mid-'70s, he had a couple of albums under his real name on RCA Victor, then formed the band Blackjack, which recorded for Polydor in the late '70s and early '80s. As Michael Bolton, he was signed to Columbia and released a self-titled album in a hard rock style in 1983. By the late '80s, still on Columbia, he had switched to a ballad approach that emphasized his wheezy voice and had gotten to number eleven in 1988 with a revival of the 1967 song "(Sittin' On) The Dock of the Bay" that was criticized for copying Otis Redding's original. But he really broke through in early 1990, when "How Am I Supposed to Live Without You" (co-credited to Bolton and Doug James) hit number one, and he went on to be one of the biggest pop singers of the first half of the '90s, his flowing locks and emotive singing attracting a legion of female fans while critics held their noses.

Garth Brooks made his first country singles chart appearance with "Much Too Young (To Feel This Damn Old)" (co-credited to Randy Taylor and Brooks) on Capitol on March 25, 1989, and reached number one on the country charts for the first time with the ballad "If Tomorrow Never Comes" (co-credited to Kent Blazy and Brooks) on December 9 of that year, but he was a Nashville secret until his self-titled debut album broke into the pop charts on May 12, 1990, on its way to sales of 9 million copies and counting. In fact, the Garth phenomenon that made him the top pop album artist of the decade didn't really become apparent until 1991, when *Garth Brooks* and its 16-million-selling follow-up, *No Fences*, peaked in the pop charts. That was the year *Billboard* revamped the way its charts were determined, one result of which was to emphasize (or reveal) the mass popularity of country music.

Since it had begun publishing charts on a regular basis at the start of the 1940s, *Billboard* had relied on surveys of selected radio stations to determine airplay and of selected record stores to determine sales. The *Billboard* singles charts, notably the Hot 100 that had been established in 1958, used a mixture of this information to calculate its rankings, while the album charts were based on the sales estimates alone. The system, of course, involved a lot of judgment and outright guesswork, and it was readily subject to manipulation. Flaws in the system were graphically revealed by the payola scandal of the late 1950s and early 1960s and even the late 1980s–early 1990s repeat of the same, when record companies were accused of spending heavily on promotion men who virtually bribed radio station personnel to play particular records. But in 1991 *Billboard* formed a partnership with a company called Sound Scan that used the bar codes printed on album covers to obtain actual piece counts from the overwhelming majority of the nation's record stores, projecting sales from the remaining ones.

By the 1990s, most Americans bought their records from record store chains like Tower Records and department store franchises like Wal-Mart, not from the "mom and pop" independent stores that had once dominated the market. Record companies were able to ship out their records across the country for release on the same day everywhere. The result was that sales patterns for records changed. Heretofore, even the most popular albums had taken several weeks to reach their chart peaks. By the end of the 1960s, for example, it still took the Beatles' *Abbey Road* until its third chart week to reach number one: released on October 1, 1969, it first topped the *Billboard* album chart for the week ending November 1. In 1975 Elton John became the first artist to have an album debut at number one, with both *Captain Fantastic and the Brown Dirt Cowboy* and, later that same year, *Rock of the Westies*. Stevie Wonder did the same thing with *Songs in the Key of Life* in 1976. These feats were achieved largely through the process of pre-ordering, which allowed for early reporting of sales. But this procedure was abandoned after it proved deceptive in the case of albums like the 1978 soundtrack album to the film *Sgt. Pepper's Lonely Hearts Club Band*, which suffered massive returns. The RIAA even extended the time it would wait to certify gold and platinum sales to make sure that the records had actually achieved "sell-through" to the consumer, not just that they had shipped in big numbers. As a result, few artists entered the charts at number one again until after the changeover to Sound Scan; then everybody started doing it. Before the end of 1991, hard rock/heavy metal bands Skid Row (*Slave to the Grind* on Atlantic), Van Halen (*For Unlawful Carnal Knowledge*), Metallica (*Metallica* on Elektra), and Guns N' Roses (*Use Your Illusion II*), as well as Garth Brooks (*Ropin' the Wind*), U2 (*Achtung Baby*), and Michael Jackson (*Dangerous*), had all debuted at number one. A new sales pattern appeared; now, most albums started at their peaks and declined thereafter. Also, long runs at number one became less common. As the 1990s went on, a stay of one, two, or three weeks became the norm, with only the occasional exception.

The new chart, unveiled in May 1991, vastly increased the presence of country music. At the same time, it would have increased the presence of older albums that continued to sell well, had not *Billboard* made the arbitrary decision to strip out all albums more than two years old that had fallen below a certain threshold and banish them to a newly created "catalog" chart, no matter how well they sold. The rise of CDs in the 1980s had led to a large market in reissues of older recordings, as the record companies transferred vintage records to the digital format and induced fans to re-buy them, with the promise of better fidelity. Catalog sales flourished, both for the old albums themselves and for repackagings of various sorts, particularly high-ticket, multidisc boxed set career retrospectives of major artists. At the same time, however, the record companies didn't want Pink Floyd's *The Dark Side of the Moon* taking up a spot on the *Billboard* chart that might be occupied by an album from a new artist, especially since that artist's ability to book tours and get other exposure might be tied to ranking on the chart. However much music fans may treat record charts as sacrosanct registers of actual popularity, to the music industry they constitute a promotional device, and *Billboard* did not hesitate to skew its charts in favor of new and current albums.

While introducing Sound Scan to the album chart, *Billboard* also instituted a computer-derived method of radio monitoring that enabled it to establish what songs were really being played and how often, not what songs radio personnel *said* were being played. The major result of this was an increase in the amount of rap and hip-hop in the singles charts. At the same time, however, a new problem was making the singles charts less reliable. As sales of singles declined, record companies became more reluctant to release them, although they continued to promote individual songs from albums through music videos and to radio stations, who didn't care particularly whether a song they were playing was commercially available as a single. Increasingly during the 1990s, popular songs were not listed on the Hot 100 because they were not released as singles. Finally, *Billboard* began including popular songs on the chart whether or not they were actually for sale as singles.

Back in 1991, the pop singles charts painted a picture of a far more homogenous audience than the pop album charts did. Look at the music of the year's ten top singles acts—from one to ten, they were Mariah Carey, C&C Music Factory, Paula Abdul, Whitney Houston,

Amy Grant, Cathy Dennis, Bryan Adams, Michael Bolton, Gloria Estefan, and Color Me Badd—and you find a lot of light dance-pop and adult-contemporary power balladeering. But consider the music of the artists who hit number one on the album chart—in chronological order, Vanilla Ice, Mariah Carey, R.E.M. (*Out of Time*), Michael Bolton (*Time, Love & Tenderness*), Paula Abdul (*Spellbound*), N.W.A (*EFIL4ZAGGIN* on Ruthless Records), Skid Row, Van Halen, Natalie Cole (*Unforgettable with Love* on Capitol), Metallica, Garth Brooks, Guns N' Roses, U2, and Michael Jackson—and musical taste seems to be all over the place. It's possible to imagine the same person enjoying the music of all the singles artists, but it seems quite unlikely that the same fan would appreciate the adult pop of Cole, singing a macabre duet with her late father Nat "King" Cole on "Unforgettable," and the raw, invective-filled rap of N.W.A. All of these albums may have sold in the millions, but they sold to several different, and largely discrete, audiences.

They also sold to fewer people than had bought records in 1990. For the year, total unit sales of all recorded formats stood at 801 million copies in the United States, according to the RIAA, a drop of more than 6 percent, although revenues increased slightly. The reason for the difference was the shift in formats that went on throughout the decade. The dominant format, by default, was the cassette, because, in the late 1980s, record companies and retailers had dumped the LP, which was selling fewer than 5 million units by 1991, in favor of the CD. CDs sold for much more than cassettes (in 1992 the most common list price for them was about $17, while cassettes were less than $10), but fewer of them were being sold. In 1991 the only format to increase its sales was CDs; cassettes fell precipitously, from 442.2 million copies to 360.1 million. But the rise in the more expensive CDs offset the fall in the less expensive cassettes, resulting in overall revenue growth. By 1992 CDs would overtake cassettes, and by the end of the decade the ratio of CD to cassette sales would be almost ten to one.

We said earlier that rock 'n' roll seemed to have taken a back seat to other genres of popular music as the 1990s began. It might be more accurate to say that, while rock pervaded popular music, old-fashioned, mainstream rock of a kind that had been successful from the late 1960s to the 1980s no longer held sway. Now, increasingly, that was being called "classic rock" as a radio format. But, again, rock offshoots continued to attract masses of fans whether that music was called heavy metal or, in a term that had gained currency in the 1980s, alternative rock. Alternative rock (much of which just sounded like rock to the uninitiated) drew upon the punk/new wave revolution of the late 1970s and early 1980s for some of its attitude and sound, and it tended to be developed by small, independent record companies. Nevertheless, as it became more recognized and successful, the majors came calling with their checkbooks, and by the end of the '80s nominally alternative bands like U2 and R.E.M. were making chart-topping albums for major labels, while other alternative bands like Hüsker Du and the Replacements were signing on with the majors.

One such band was the trio Nirvana from Seattle, which jumped from the tiny, trendy Sub Pop label to DGC in 1991. (DGC stands for "David Geffen Company"; the label was an imprint of Geffen Records, in turn owned by the major label MCA.) Led by singer-songwriter-guitarist Kurt Cobain, Nirvana released its major-label debut, *Nevermind*, in September 1991. In January 1992, buoyed by the top-ten success of the single "Smells Like Teen Spirit," *Nevermind* hit number one, on its way to selling 10 million copies. The group, particularly the fragile, heroin-addicted Cobain, never seem to have recovered from this popular breakthrough. They managed one more album, 1993's 5-million-selling *In Utero*, before Cobain committed suicide in April 1994. It was a tragically appropriate ending for a band that led a '90s cultural and musical trend of middle-class, suburban disaffection, its "Generation X" members referred to as "slackers" and their punk-influenced rock music as "grunge." Seattle quickly became the locus for a rock scene in the way that San Francisco had been in the mid- to late '60s, with bands such as Pearl Jam, whose debut album *Ten* (Epic/Associated), released in late 1991, sold 11 million copies, and Soundgarden (A&M).

The emergence of grunge energized rock in 1992, and helped turn around the music business, which sold nearly 900 million units for revenues over $9 billion. In a sense, each of the major genres of popular music was being redefined. If grunge, and the larger style of alternative rock, was transforming mainstream rock into a music with fresh artists for a new generation of fans, another young set of R&B artists such as female vocal group TLC (LaFace Records) and male vocal group Boyz II Men (Motown) was taking the rhythmic impetus and street sensibility of rap into a contemporary urban style called "new jack swing." And Garth Brooks, who brought a sense of rock staging to his concerts and exhibited enormous business savvy in the marketing of his albums, was forging a new, pop-styled country music that allowed him and Billy Ray Cyrus (Mercury) to dominate the pop charts in 1992. Cyrus's *Some Gave All*, spurred by the hit single "Achy Breaky Heart" (promoted through line-dance clubs), spent seventeen weeks at the top of the charts that year, only one week less than the 1991–92 run of Brooks's *Ropin' the Wind*. Unlike Brooks, however, Cyrus proved to be a fleeting success.

The difference between the singles and album markets in 1992 was profound; none of the year's ten top singles artists also ranked among the ten top album artists. Nineteen ninety-three was another story, and the year's major artists illustrated another important pop trend of the '90s. Janet Jackson, Mariah Carey, and Whitney Houston all placed among the most successful singles and album artists. Jackson, the year's top pop singles artist, who moved from A&M to Virgin Records (by now a subsidiary of EMI) in a record deal thought to be worth between $50 and $70 million, began to justify that expense. She had three major Hot 100 hits, the number ones "That's the Way Love Goes" and "Again," and the number-three "If" (all co-credited to Jackson and her producers James Harris III and Terry Lewis), and her Virgin debut album, *janet.*, spent six weeks at number one and sold 6 million copies. Carey scored the year's most successful chart single with "Dreamlover" (co-credited to Carey and Dave Hall) and a second chart-topper with "Hero" (co-credited to Walter Afanasieff and Carey), both from her album *Music Box*, which was number one for eight weeks and sold 10 million copies. Houston scored with such singles as "I Have Nothing" and a revival of Ashford and Simpson's 1978 song "I'm Every Woman."

Obviously, Jackson, Carey, and Houston had a lot in common. They were female, black (or half-black), and able to appeal across boundaries of musical style (pop, R&B, dance, adult contemporary) and both as ballad and rhythm singers. All three had acting aspirations. Jackson, who had been a TV sitcom star as a child, made her big-screen debut in 1993 in *Poetic Justice*. But Houston really made a splash by way of *The Bodyguard*, which opened in late 1992 and featured not only "I Have Nothing" and "I'm Every Woman," but also her revival of Dolly Parton's 1974 song "I Will Always Love You." The single spent fourteen weeks at number one, the longest run at the top of the singles chart since 1947. It takes nothing away from the record's success to point out that, with radio station playlists becoming ever narrower and fewer major songs being released as singles, songs tended to stay at number one longer in the '90s. Not counting "I Will Always Love You," which first hit number one in 1992, there were only ten number-one hits in 1993, compared to sixteen in 1983, twenty-seven in 1973, and twenty in 1963. (In the 1960s, '70s, and '80s, no single occupied the number-one position on the Hot 100 for more than ten weeks; during the 1990s, ten different singles stayed on top for eleven weeks or more.) All told, Houston, Jackson, or Carey occupied the top spot for twenty-eight weeks out of fifty-two in 1993.

The synergy between movies and pop music was discernible not only in the tendency of pop singers to aim to become movie stars, but also in the presence of movie songs and soundtracks in the charts. The top songs of 1991 (Bryan Adams's "[Everything I Do] I Do It for You," the theme song for *Robin Hood: Prince of Thieves*) and 1992 (Houston's "I Will Always Love You") were associated with movies, as were such number-one hits of the early '90s as Jon Bon Jovi's "Blaze of Glory" from *Young Guns II*; from *Boomerang*; Boyz II Men's "End of the Road" and Peabo Bryson & Regina Belle's "A Whole New World (Aladdin's Theme)," from *Aladdin*. The soundtrack albums for *Ghost* (Varèse Sarabande), *Pretty Woman* (EMI), *New Jack City* (Giant), *Robin Hood: Prince of Thieves* (Morgan Creek), *Aladdin* (Disney), *Boomerang* (LaFace), *The Bodyguard* (Arista), *Mo' Money* (Perspective), *Singles* (Epic), *Wayne's World* (Reprise), *Last Action Hero* (Columbia), and *Sleepless in Seattle* (Epic Soundtrax) all became million-selling top-ten hits in the same period. In most cases, the films were also very successful, but not always. Often, the soundtrack albums consisted of pop songs that were heard only in snatches, if at all, in the films, while the nominal "theme" songs that played under the opening or closing credits usually didn't mention the movie titles, a break from the common practice years earlier. But the films served to expose the music to fans, and the soundtrack albums sold as souvenirs, then, with any luck, on their own after a single caught on. This was not a new phenomenon of the '90s, of course, but soundtracks were more deliberately and successfully marketed in the '90s than they had been before. In 1993 this helped the music business to sales of over $10 billion for the first time.

If Boyz II Men—who scored two of the biggest hits of the decade with "End of the Road" and "I'll Make Love to You," and would go on to pair with Mariah Carey for the top hit of the '90s, "One Sweet Day," in 1995—represented the convergence of traditional R&B with rap/hip-hop, they also represented a coming trend in popular music, one that always had been present to one extent or another, but would gain new ascendance in the second half of the decade. Four personable young men who alternated lead and harmony vocals, they were teenage heartthrobs and precursors of the market impact of a new generation of pop music buyers. New Kids on the Block, themselves a recasting of an earlier teen-pop sensation, New Edition, had flared into popularity in the late '80s and early '90s, but like most such acts, quickly faded. By the mid-1990s, however, a teen and preteen audience was ready to embrace new heroes. The presence of this audience was attested to by the 1994 success of the Swedish pop group Ace of Base, which spent six weeks at number one with "The Sign." But the trend was still a couple of years from breaking out big.

Meanwhile, mainstream rock, having been revitalized by its alternative and grunge tributaries, was spawning successful new performers. In 1994 these included two who would be influential on the rock of the late '90s and early 2000s. Counting Crows, led by singer-songwriter Adam Duritz, were another in a long line of bands that played in a folk-rock style that served as a focus for the angst-ridden lyrics of the frontman. Their *August and Everything*

After (DGC), released in late 1993, would sell 7 million copies and lead to numerous imitators. Green Day was a punk-rock trio led by Billie Joe Armstrong that finally managed to sell the revved-up punk sound of 1976 to the American masses. Their major-label debut *Dookie* (Reprise), released in early 1994, sold 10 million copies, and, with that, record companies began signing up similar performers.

Such emerging artists helped the record industry to another sales surge in 1994, when sales passed 1 billion copies and revenues rose above $12 billion. But the business stagnated in 1995, when sales dropped for the first time in four years. Unlike 1991, there was no bad economy to blame things on; rather, superstar acts seemed to be repeating themselves, while new ones made music that sold without really being compelling. The year's top-selling album, at 7 million copies (of the 16 million it would amass eventually) was *Cracked Rear View*, the debut album by Hootie and the Blowfish, released on Atlantic in mid-1994. The likable quartet from South Carolina boasted a distinctive lead vocalist in Darius Rucker, and its melodic pop-rock sound brought a string of top-ten hits. But as is often the case with artists who succeed massively the first time out, that success was disproportionate and impossible to sustain. Their second album, *Fairweather Johnson*, sold 3 million copies upon release in 1996, their third only a million in 1998.

The second major new artist of the year was former children's TV star Alanis Morissette, a Canadian who crossed over from hard rock to pop on her mature debut *Jagged Little Pill* (Maverick, a custom label of Warner Bros. founded by Madonna), which went on to sell 16 million copies, the first 4.2 of them in 1995, with the next 7.4 making it the best-selling album of 1996. Morissette, born in June 1974 in Ottawa, teamed with veteran songwriter Glen Ballard to write such songs as the vengeful "You Oughta Know." Like Hootie and the Blowfish, she experienced steadily diminishing sales with her follow-up albums in 1998 and 2002.

Arguably the most successful recording artists of 1995 were the three members of TLC, Tionne "T-Boz" Watkins, Lisa "Left Eye" Lopes, and Rozonda "Chilli" Thomas. Based in Atlanta and signed to the LaFace label run by songwriter/producers Kenneth "Babyface" Edmonds and L.A. Reid, the vocal trio had scored a hit with their 1992 debut album, *Ooooooohhh...On the TLC Tip*, then encountered legal problems after Lopez set fire to the house belonging to her boyfriend, NFL player Andre Rison, and was sentenced to five years' probation in 1994. Nevertheless, their 1995 album, *CrazySexyCool*, was an enormous success, selling 4.8 million copies in 1995 and 10 million over time, buoyed by the number-one singles "Creep" and "Waterfalls," which employed a mixture of vocal group harmonies and rap.

The best-selling records of 1996 continued to show a disparate listenership. Just behind Alanis Morissette's still-surging *Jagged Little Pill* was Celine Dion's Album of the Year Grammy-winner *Falling into You*, selling 6 million of its eventual 10 million copies on the strength of the number-one single "Because You Loved Me" and the number-two "It's All Coming Back to Me Now." "Because You Loved Me," the theme from the film *Up Close & Personal*, was a typically passionate and melodic effort from songwriter Diane Warren, who specialized in this style and who, the same year, gave an equally successful one to the top pop singles artist, Toni Braxton (another protégée of LaFace), with "Un-Break My Heart."

Behind Dion in album sales were the Fugees, a rap/R&B trio featuring Wyclef Jean, Pras Michel, and Lauryn Hill with their debut album *The Score* (Ruffhouse, a subsidiary of Columbia), which sold 4.5 million of its eventual 6 million copies largely due to a revival of "Killing Me Softly." The group's success would lead to its demise (or at least a lengthy hiatus) as each member pursued a solo career, most prominently Hill, who went on to sell 7 million copies of her own Album of the Year Grammy-winner *The Miseducation of Lauryn Hill* in 1998.

With sales of 4.4 million copies, *Tragic Kingdom* (Trauma) established the Orange County, California, quartet No Doubt, aficionados of the 1960s Jamaican musical style ska, as a major act after years of struggling. The band's lead singer, Gwen Stefani, would join the ranks of Blondie's Debbie Harry and Madonna as one of rock's major fashion plates, helping to give the group success into the twenty-first century.

The reliable Mariah Carey sold 3 million copies of her fourth album, *Daydream*, in 1996, tying her with the equally reliable, if stylistically opposed, Metallica and *Load*. Also selling 3 million copies, on the way to 9 million, was *All Eyez on Me* (Death Row Records) by rapper 2Pac, whose real name was Tupac Shakur. Born in June 1971 in New York City, Shakur succeeded as both an actor and a rapper, but lived a life of controversy and violence that culminated in Las Vegas on September 13, 1996, when he was shot to death. As is often the case, however, his death had no discernible effect on his record label's ability to release his recordings, and he was still reaching the charts with new albums more than six years later.

Although sales increased very slightly in 1996, the music industry did not return to steady growth, and, indeed, would not for the rest of the decade. Revenues grew in most years due to rising prices, but sales changed only slightly. In 1994, they had been 1,122,700,000; in 1999 they were 1,160,600,000, an increase of only about 3.4 percent over five years. And in two of those five years, sales had actually declined. It seemed clear that, by the mid-1990s, the industry had absorbed the benefit of mature buyers replacing their LP collections with new CD versions, although such buyers remained a little-heralded engine of the industry: in 1997, 40 percent of album sales came from catalog (i.e., albums more than eightteen months old), but by 1999, that number had dropped to a still-hefty one-third, as record companies scrambled to issue second and even third versions of vintage albums on CD, spiffing up the sound and adding bonus tracks to get fans to buy them over and over. Meanwhile, prices continued to edge up; by 1999 some single CDs were selling for a list price of $18.98.

The real, if temporary, savior of the music business in the second half of the 1990s was resurgent teen pop, which first made itself felt in early 1997 with the success of the United Kingdom female vocal quintet the Spice Girls (Virgin). Already a sensation at home, the fashion-conscious group broke through in the United States with "Wannabe," which topped the charts in February, and went on to a year and a half of success in America. *Spice*, their debut album, was

1997's top seller at 5.3 million copies. Also coming by way of Europe, even though they were U.S. citizens, were the Backstreet Boys, a male vocal quintet auditioned and trained by an Orlando, Florida, production company that had first reached the American charts in 1995 but then had focused on Germany before returning in mid-1997 with their first major stateside success, "Quit Playing Games (With My Heart)" on Jive Records.

If frivolous, such performers were a bright spot in a year in which some of the most successful records mourned the deaths of famous people, with Puff Daddy and Faith Evans rewriting the Police's "Every Breath You Take" to create "I'll Be Missing You" on Bad Boy Records for slain rapper the Notorious B.I.G., and Elton John applying new words to his 1973 song "Candle in the Wind" for Princess Diana following her death in an automobile accident while eluding paparazzi in Paris. By the end of the year, Celine Dion was singing about a fictitious drowned lover in "My Heart Will Go On," the theme from the blockbuster film *Titanic*, which not only was the biggest box-office hit of the year but also produced the best-selling album of the year, moving 9.3 million copies of the soundtrack. Dion finished second with a not-shabby 5.9 million copies of *Let's Talk About Love*, which also featured the ubiquitous song.

Nineteen ninety-eight marked the widespread break-out of teen pop, as the Backstreet Boys continued to score, selling 5.7 million copies of their self-titled album, and were joined by 'N Sync (RCA), another male vocal quintet out of the same Florida factory, whose own self-titled release sold 4.4 million copies. Then, at the end of the year, soon-to-turn-seventeen Britney Spears, a former *New Mickey Mouse Club* cast member, groaned her way through the platinum-certified number-one hit "... Baby One More Time" on Jive and put a new twist on the kind of dance-pop still being pursued successfully by Janet Jackson and even Madonna. Indeed, the emergence of the Backstreet Boys, 'N Sync, and a host of other so-called boy bands (a term that ignored the conventional view that bands consisted of people playing instruments), and adolescent girl singers such as Spears, marked a new renaissance in choreographed dancing as these young performers, weaned on the music videos of Michael Jackson and

Madonna, gave work to an industry of dance instructors and dancers for their own videos and stage shows.

The teen-pop phenomenon continued in 1999, as the Backstreet Boys sold 9.4 million copies of their album *Millennium*, besting the 8.4 million of Spears's ... *Baby One More Time* album. Christina Aguilera (RCA) joined the throng, selling 3.7 million copies of her self-titled debut album and providing a bridge to a subgenre of teen pop, Latin-crossover teen pop. Latin stars who made it big in 1999 included Ricky Martin (Columbia), formerly of the Latin boy band Menudo, whose self-titled English-language debut was the year's third-biggest seller, at 6 million copies, and Jennifer Lopez (Epic/Work), who reversed the usual direction of pop singers to movie stars by getting her start as an actress before cutting her first hit record, *On the 6*.

But, although teen pop grabbed most of the headlines, the last year of the century was also one of comebacks, with Cher, who had mounted numerous comebacks since her 1960s days with Sonny and Cher, emerging yet again with her dance hit "Believe" on Warner Bros., and Santana returning to the fore with his guest-filled *Supernatural* album on Arista, achieving multiplatinum sales on the wings of its single "Smooth," featuring singer Rob Thomas of the band Matchbox 20, which spent twelve weeks at number one. Meanwhile, Whitney Houston and Mariah Carey continued to score hits; Shania Twain (Mercury) and the Dixie Chicks (the Monument subsidiary of Epic) demonstrated the continuing appeal of crossover country; Limp Bizkit (Flip) and Kid Rock (Lava) were the new gods of hard rock; and rap continued to be popular and controversial in the hands of stars, one black and one white: Jay-Z (Roc-A-Fella) and Eminem (Aftermath). In a sense, little but the names had changed in ten years.

Another example of "the more things change, the more they stay the same" was the industry's reaction to its flat sales and the emergence of new technology. Across one hundred years, whenever these two factors coincided, the industry denied any fault of its own and blamed the new machines for its woes. When radio came in the 1920s, the record business bemoaned loss of sales, not recognizing the medium's potential for promoting recorded music. When recordable cassettes appeared in the 1960s, the industry again complained of supposed lost revenues, still not acknowledging that the increased availability of music was expanding the business. And so it was at the end of the century, with the arrival of the Internet and computers in every home. The ability of consumers to download music through MP3 technology and services such as Napster led them to hear things they had never heard before (much of it languishing in the vaults of major labels who felt they needed to sell in the millions to justify a reissue or to maintain records in print). But the record business only saw lost sales, assuming that every downloaded file was a CD it would have sold otherwise. And, as before, the industry went to court and to Congress seeking recompense, with surprising success, perhaps in part due to its immense and sophisticated lobbying efforts, which convinced many casual observers of its dubious claims. That the industry had probably matured in the 1980s, with further sales increases artificially inflated due to the new CD technology; that CDs were wildly overpriced; that too many albums were released, glutting the marketplace; and that the industry was hoping for salvation in yet another new format that would allow it to resell the same music for the umpteenth time—these and other considerations were ignored in the cry that Napster was cheating the business out of its money.

If the century had provided any lesson, however, it was that technological development does not stop or even slow down. The minor legal victories of the turn of the twenty-first century that put Napster out of business did nothing to turn the tide. The industry faced new challenges, not only from technology, but from a resurgent group of recording artists criticizing long-term exclusive contracts and questioning the need for the industry as it existed. Probably, the music business of the twenty-first century will not resemble that of the twentieth. But there will always be music, and it will always be recorded and replayed with pleasure.

Bartelt, Chuck, and Barbara Bergeron. Compilers. *Variety Obituaries, 1905–1986* (New York: Garland Publishing, 1989).

Bianco, David. *Heat Wave: The Motown Fact Book* (Ann Arbor, MI: Popular Culture, Ink, 1988).

Billboard Music Guide (CD-ROM). (Portland, OR: Creative Multimedia, 1996).

Billman, Larry. *Fred Astaire: A Bio-Bibliography* (Westport, CT: Greenwood Press, 1997).

Bloom, Ken. *American Song: The Complete Musical Theatre Companion, Second Edition, 1877–1995* (New York: Schirmer Books, 1996).

Bordman, Gerald. *American Musical Theatre: A Chronicle, Third Edition* (New York: Oxford University Press, 2001).

Brown, Tony, Jon Kutner, and Neil Warwick. *The Complete Book of the British Charts, Singles and Albums* (London: Omnibus Press, 2000).

Castleman, Harry, and Walter J. Podrazik. *All Together Now: The First Complete Beatles Discography, 1961–1975* (New York: Ballantine Books, 1975).

Connor, D. Russell. *Benny Goodman: Listen to His Legacy* (Metuchen, NJ: Scarecrow Press, and the Institute of Jazz Studies, 1988).

Editors of Rolling Stone, The. *Rolling Stone Rock Almanac: The Chronicles of Rock & Roll* (New York: Collier Books, 1983).

Epstein, Daniel Mark. *Nat King Cole* (New York: Farrar, Straus and Giroux, 1999).

Ewen, David. *All the Years of American Popular Music* (Englewood Cliffs, NJ: Prentice-Hall, 1977).

Feather, Leonard. *The Encyclopedia of Jazz* (New York: Da Capo, 1960).

Frum, David. *How We Got Here: The 70s* (New York: Basic Books, 2000).

Gardner, Edward Foote. *Popular Songs of the Twentieth Century: A Charted History, Volume I: Chart Detail & Encyclopedia, 1900–1949* (St. Paul, MN: Paragon House, 2000).

Gilbert, Martin. *A History of the Twentieth Century, Volume One: 1900–1933* (New York: Avon Books, 1997).

Goldman, Herbert G. *Jolson: The Legend Comes to Life* (New York: Oxford University Press, 1988).

Gracyk, Tim, with Frank Hoffmann. *Popular American Recording Pioneers, 1895–1925* (Binghamton, NY: Haworth Press, 2000).

Gronow, Pekka, and Ilpo Saunio. Translated by Christopher Moseley. *An International History of the Recording Industry* (London: Cassell, 1998).

Hamm, Charles. *Yesterdays: Popular Song in America* (New York: W.W. Norton & Company, 1979).

Henretta, James A., W. Elliot Brownlee, David Brody, and Susan Ware. *America's History, Volume 2: Since 1865, Second Edition* (New York: Worth Publishers, 1993).

Jasen, David A. *Tin Pan Alley: The Composers, the Songs, the Performers and Their Times* (London: Omnibus Press, 1988).

Kahn, Ashley, Holly George-Warren, and Shawn Dahl. Editors. *Rolling Stone: The '70s* (Boston: Little, Brown and Company, 1998).

Katz, Ephraim. Revised by Fred Klein and Ronald Dean Nole. *The Film Encyclopedia, Fourth Edition* (New York: HarperResource, 2001).

Krogsgaard, Michael. *Positively Bob Dylan: A Thirty-Year Discography, Concert & Recording Session Guide, 1960–1991* (Ann Arbor, MI: Popular Culture, Ink, 1991).

Lax, Roger, and Frederick Smith. *The Great Song Thesaurus, Second Edition, Updated and Expanded* (New York: Oxford University Press, 1989).

Lefcowitz, Eric, *The Rhino History of Rock 'n' Roll: The 70s* (New York: Pocket Books, 1997).

Lissauer, Robert. *Lissauer's Encyclopedia of Popular Music in America: 1888 to the Present* (New York: Paragon House, 1991).

Lowe, Allen. *American Pop: From Minstrel to Mojo: On Record, 1893–1956* (Redwood, NY: Cadence Jazz Books, 1997).

Martland, Peter. *Since Records Began: EMI, the First 100 Years* (London: B.T. Batsford, 1997).

Murrells, Joseph. *Million Selling Records: From the 1900s to the 1980s: An Illustrated Directory* (New York: Arco Publishing, 1984).

Neely, Tim. *Goldmine Price Guide to 45 rpm Records, 3rd Edition* (Iola, WI: Krause Publications, 2001).

—. *Goldmine Record Album Price Guide, 2nd Edition* (Iola, WI: Krause Publications, 2001).

Norton, Richard C. *A Chronology of American Musical Theater* (New York: Oxford University Press, 2002).

Osborne, Jerry. *The Official Price Guide to Movie/TV Soundtracks and Original Cast Albums, Second Edition* (New York: House of Collectibles, 1997).

Osterholm, J. Roger. *Bing Crosby: A Bio-Bibliography* (Westport, CT: Greenwood Press, 1994).

Rust, Brian, with Allen G. Debus. *The Complete Entertainment Discography: From the mid-1890s to 1942* (New Rochelle, NY: Arlington House, 1973).

Sackett, Susan. *Hollywood Sings! An Inside Look at Sixty Years of Academy Award–Nominated Songs* (New York: Billboard Books, 1995).

Sanford, Herb. *Tommy & Jimmy: The Dorsey Years* (New York: Da Capo, 1972).

Sanjek, Russell. Updated by David Sanjek. *Pennies from Heaven: The American Popular Music Business in the Twentieth Century* (New York: Da Capo, 1996).

Shaw, Arnold. *The Jazz Age: Popular Music in the 1920s* (New York: Oxford University Press, 1987).

Spaeth, Sigmund. *A History of Popular Music in America* (New York: Random House, 1948).

Toll, Robert C. *The Entertainment Machine: American Show Business in the Twentieth Century* (New York: Oxford University Press, 1982).

Trager, James. *The People's Chronology* (New York: Henry Holt and Company, 1994).

Waldo, Terry. *This Is Ragtime* (New York: Da Capo, 1991).

Ward, Ed, Geoffrey Stokes, and Ken Tucker. *Billboard Hot 100 Charts—The Sixties* (Menomonee Falls, WI: Record Research, 1990).

—. *Rock of Ages: The Rolling Stone History of Rock & Roll* (New York: Rolling Stone Press/ Summit Books, 1986).

Whitburn, Joel. *Billboard Pop Hits, Singles & Albums: 1940-1954* (Menomonee Falls, WI: Record Research, 2002).

—. *Top Country Singles, 1944 to 2001, Fifth Edition* (Menomonee Falls, WI: Record Research, 2002).

—. *Top Pop Albums, 1955–2001* (Menomonee Falls, WI: Record Research, 2001).

—. *Pop Annual, 1955–1999* (Menomonee Falls, WI: Record Research, 2000).

—. *Top Pop Singles, 1955–1999* (Menomonee Falls, WI: Record Research, 2000).

—. *Top R&B Singles, 1942–1999* (Menomonee Falls, WI: Record Research, 2000).

—. *A Century of Pop Music: Year-by-Year Top 40 Rankings of the Songs & Artists That Shaped a Century* (Menomonee Falls, WI: Record Research, 1999).

—. *Top 10 Album Charts, 1963–1998* (Menomonee Falls, WI: Record Research, 1999).

—. *Top R&B Albums, 1965–1998* (Menomonee Falls, WI: Record Research, 1999).

—. *Country Annual, 1944 to 1997* (Menomonee Falls, WI: Record Research, 1998).

—. *Pop Memories, 1890–1954: The History of American Popular Music* (Menomonee Falls, WI: Record Research, 1986).

—. Compiler. *1999 Music and Video Yearbook* (Menomonee Falls, WI: Record Research, 2000).

—. Compiler. *1998 Music and Video Yearbook* (Menomonee Falls, WI: Record Research Inc., 1999).

—. Compiler. *1996 Music and Video Yearbook* (Menomonee Falls, WI: Record Research, 1997).

—. Compiler. *1995 Music and Video Yearbook* (Menomonee Falls, WI: Record Research, 1996).

—. Compiler. *1991 Music and Video Yearbook* (Menomonee Falls, WI: Record Research, 1992).

Whitcomb, Ian, *After the Ball: Pop Music from Rag to Rock* (New York: Limelight Editions, 1986).

INDEX

217